The virtual suppression of explicit ethical and evaluative discourse by current literary theory can be seen as the momentary triumph of a sceptical post-Enlightenment reflective tradition over others vital to a full account of human and literary worth. In *Ethics, theory and the novel*, David Parker brings together recent developments in moral philosophy and literary theory. He questions many currently influential movements in literary criticism, showing that their silences about ethics are as damaging as the political silences of Leavisism and New Criticism in the 1950s and 1960s. He goes on to examine *Middlemarch, Anna Karenina*, and three novels by D. H. Lawrence, and explores the consequences for major literary works of the suppression of either the Judeo-Christian or the Romantic-expressivist ethical traditions. Where any one tradition becomes a master-narrative, he argues, imaginative literature ceases to have the deepest interest and relevance for us. Overall, this book is an essay in a new evaluative discourse, the implications of which go far beyond the particular works it analyses.

ETHICS, THEORY AND THE NOVEL

ETHICS, THEORY AND THE NOVEL

DAVID PARKER

Australian National University

CAMBRIDGE
UNIVERSITY PRESS

Published by the Press Syndicate of the University of Cambridge
The Pitt Building, Trumpington Street, Cambridge, CB2 1RP
40 West 20th Street, New York, NY 10011-4211, USA
10 Stamford Road, Oakleigh, Melbourne 3166, Australia

First published 1994

Printed in Great Britain at the University Press, Cambridge

A catalogue record for this book is available from the British Library

Library of Congress cataloguing in publication data
Parker, David, 1943–
Ethics, theory, and the novel / David Parker.
p. cm.
Includes bibliographical references and index.
ISBN 0 521 45283 x (hardback)
1. Criticism – Moral and ethical aspects. 2. Literary ethics.
3. Fiction – 19th century – History and criticism.
4. Fiction – 20th century – History and criticism.
1. Title.
PN98.M67P37 1994
174'.98–DC20 93-43929 CIP

ISBN 0 521 45283 x hardback

For Jean, Fabian, and Tim

Contents

Acknowledgements

This book has been shaped in discussion with many friends and colleagues. It owes much to the following: John Barnes, Michael Black, Richard Campbell, John Casey, Axel Clark, Cora Diamond, Frances Dixon, Paul Eggert, Richard Eldridge, John Finnis, Marie Finnis, Richard Freadman, Jennifer Gribble, Robin Grove, Simon Haines, Dirk den Hartog, Michael Holquist, Rob Jackson, Nicholas Jose, Ann Loftus, Kevin Magarey, Michael Meehan, and John Wiltshire.

The research for the book and much of the writing were done while on study leave from the Australian National University, to which I am grateful.

I am grateful too to the Institute for Advanced Study of Indiana University, where as a Visiting Scholar in late 1991 I wrote nearly half the book. The Director, Henry Remak, was an unfailing stimulus during this period and the Assistant Director, Ivona Hedin, was always there when needed. Among the many members of faculty at Indiana University who helped to make my stay there so productive, I wish to thank John Eakin and Albert Wertheim especially.

I am much indebted to the work of the late Sam Goldberg. As a reader and editor he was the most searching of critics as well as a supporter of my work over many years. Chapters 1, 6, 7, 9 and 10, are based on articles published in numbers 31, 26, 27, 30, and 20 respectively of *The Critical Review*. Chapter 8 began as an article published in *Meridian* in 1988.

This book owes a great deal to Jane Adamson, who has been generous as a friend and collaborator over many years. I am also grateful to Iain Wright, who made many fruitful suggestions; and to Fred Langman, who read the whole manuscript at a late stage and gave me invaluable advice and encouragement. Sue Fraser and Christine Carroll helped in important ways at the eleventh hour.

My debt to Helen and our children is all-pervasive.

PART I

The ethical unconscious

As Bernard Williams said about the difficulties of justifying ethics in the modern world, 'there is no route back from reflectiveness'. We can try to forget the new thoughts, either individually or collectively, but in the long run there can be no stopping dissidents raising questions that are now simply 'there to be raised'.[1] Equally, in the past ten or fifteen years post-structuralist theory[2] has so changed what it is possible to think about literature that (even if one wanted it) there is no way back to the relative theoretical innocence of the 1950s or 1960s. The new insights are now simply there to be had, expressed by such words as 'essentialism', 'patriarchy', 'ideology', 'aporia', 'referentiality' or 'hegemony'. This is why counter-attacks that have tried to deny all legitimacy to the new reflections, either by saying that the whole movement is more or less intellectually fraudulent, or philosophically mistaken, or not really new after all,[3] have not commanded widespread respect, for all the cogent arguments their proponents have sometimes made.

Consequently, we have not been forced to attend adequately to the uneasiness underlying intellectual resistance to post-structuralism, felt by many who otherwise accept the new, that some vital continuities with the past are in danger of being occluded. That the uneasiness continues to be expressed is a sign that, in the long run, there is no escape route from certain old thoughts either. My assumption here is that ultimately there is no evading *any* important way of thinking about ourselves deep enough to have made a permanent impress on the culture. There can only be temporary forgettings or suppressions.

The explicit and implicit case represented by this book is that the irresistible expansive moment of post-structuralism in the 1970s and early 1980s has suppressed some discursive possibilities which, constituted as we partly are by various religious and humanistic

3

traditions, we stand in abiding need of, and are poorer without. The possibilities I mean are evaluative, and especially ethical ones. In the past ten years, the virtual absence of explicit ethical interest in contemporary literary discourse[4] has been remarked on with surprise by people outside the field, notably by some eminent moral philosophers such as Martha Nussbaum and Richard Rorty, who have themselves recently started to move into ethical literary criticism as if to fill the vacuum. Perhaps only they have had the intellectual confidence or temerity to do so, since (as I have argued elsewhere) conventional literary humanism seems so largely frozen with self-doubt.[5] The work of these philosophers is a significant marker, however, indicating that a point in the cultural dialectic has been reached in which literary studies can no longer ignore the ethical without yielding up a once central part of its intellectual responsibility and constituency to other disciplines. My point is not that these incursions of moral philosophy into literature necessarily pose a territorial threat, though in the short run they might; it is rather that they indicate a new road which literary studies in the end must take. It will not be, and, partly for reasons already given, cannot be, simply an old road retravelled. The great value of the recent work in literature by moral philosophers is that it offers a variety of new meta-discursive insights and possibilities from which a theoretically self-aware ethical criticism can now move out in dialectical response to post-structuralist theory, re-establishing the evaluative criticism of particular texts as an important part of what literary studies are about. This book attempts to offer an example of what such a new route might look like.

The title of this section, 'The ethical unconscious', of course alludes to Fredric Jameson's influential book, *The Political Unconscious: Narrative as a Socially Symbolic Act*. The point of the allusion is to suggest that post-structuralist theory has been largely unconscious of its of ethical bearings, in much the same way as the older humanist criticism was often unaware of its allegiances to the interests of a particular race, social class, and gender. The suggestion of a looking-glass symmetry here is intended: just as many of the key progressive insights of the last twenty years have been about the significant political silences of the older critical mode (together with the literature it helped to canonise), so the silences of post-structuralist theory in regard to ethics have recently begun to seem ethically significant. In the past two or three years, commentators have begun to tease out the ethical implications of genealogical and deconstructive work such as that of Foucault and de Man, which is avowedly either uninterested in substantive ethics or else altogether hostile to it. But, as political analysts have been fond of pointing out, claims to neutrality are not themselves diagnostically neutral. To adapt a well-known adage of Jameson's, everything is ethical, and our only options are to be conscious or unconscious of the fact.

But I am only mirroring Jameson up to a point. I am not saying, as he says of politics, that everything *in the last analysis* is ethical. Nor am I saying, as he says vice versa, that political discourse is necessarily false consciousness, a mode of mystifying realities that are actually ethical ones. My argument is that there is no last analysis, merely various different sorts of analysis, all of them more or less il- luminating, of which ethical analysis is one and political analysis another. My theme is not, in other words, that ethical criticism should be what Richard Rorty throughout *Contingency, Irony, and Solidarity* calls a 'final vocabulary' – a sort of master-narrative in terms of which all other theories and critical approaches can be definitively described, comprehended, and evaluated. The ethical criticism called Leavisism, though it distrusted theory for good reasons and resisted being called a theory, had this in common with many other theories – that its aspiration to be the master-narrative of our culture seemed often to demand that we see all alternative views as forms of false consciousness. It seems to be in the nature of theories to aspire to such comprehensiveness and rival-swallowing mastery. The so-called jungle law of eat or be eaten applies at the very loftiest theoretical altitudes – perhaps especially there, given the earthly institutional structures that usually support such enterprises.

But then competitive mutual voracity is not the only possible way in which theories can coexist. That great ever-developing, multi- sided conversation so often reified as 'the literary canon' offers much more valuable models of theoretical interaction. The various theories of culture or existence that the best imaginative literature compre- hends tend to be set in dialogical interrelationship with each other, in a searching, mutually revealing exploration in which there is no final vocabulary or master-narrative. In this literature the will-to-master- narrative comes up time and again as an issue to be analysed. It is seen, among other ways, as an ethical issue – often portrayed as a manifestation of a desire to forget or to obliterate some painful or resistant aspect of reality or experience. The will, in other words, to be in possession of 'the last analysis', the final vocabulary, is presented *as a form of unconsciousness*. This is a further implication of my title: imaginative literature has been a good deal preoccupied with various forms of ethical unconsciousness – and among these is a sort to which theory and theorists are especially prone.

It is for this reason, among others, that a reconceived defence of the 'literary canon' (understood as ever-developing and multi-vocal) is still important – despite recent evidence that it remains central in the literary curriculum of English-speaking countries such as the US and Australia.[6] For if this literature can be read as a probing critical commentary on the enterprise of theorising, then the theoretical moves of recent years to unseat the whole notion of canonicity take on a rather different significance. The literature ought to be regarded as theory's resistant Other, having anticipated many of its major moves and implying compelling answers to them. For this reason, arguments in favour of decanonisation need to be scrutinised carefully, both on their own terms as well as genealogically – in terms of their will-to-power. And, above all, the arguments need to be examined without ever losing close concrete touch with literary texts. If this touch is maintained, the anti-canonical case is, as I shall suggest, considerably weakened.

CHAPTER I

Evaluative discourse: the return of the repressed

On many fronts the realisation is beginning to resurface that, as Charles Taylor has expressed it, 'we all as human agents define ourselves against a background of distinctions of worth'. The force of that 'all' should not be overlooked. Some, whom Taylor calls 'naturalists', or who might otherwise be described as positivists or evaluative sceptics, do not acknowledge the point and may even explicitly deny it, but they cannot be exceptions 'just because they do not *recognize* that they are constituted by strongly evaluative self-interpretations'.[1] In his major recent book, *Sources of the Self: The Making of the Modern Identity*, Taylor does more than make the essential point that naturalist denials are everywhere contradicted by their practices. He also shows why the naturalist picture is *inherently* mistaken by showing that identity, our sense of who we are, is a kind of 'orientation in moral space'. To be without any evaluative framework at all would involve a profound psychic disorientation; such a person would not simply be morally shallow or unpredictable, he or she would be frighteningly disturbed, perhaps pathological. For a person of relative normality, the naturalist picture *cannot* obtain, simply on the grounds that such a person must be oriented in terms of the multiple evaluative distinctions needed to answer coherently for herself in everyday life.[2]

Taylor is not the only contemporary philosopher to argue for the inescapability of the ethical dimension, but his formulations are especially helpful in that they indicate the links between ethics and other dimensions of value. The strongly evaluative self-interpretations by which we constitute ourselves include everything in which our selfhood is expressed, including what we feel, think, and say (or do not say) about books. At this level, there is an inevitable continuity between the distinctions of worth by which we define ourselves and those by which we make judgments of value about literature.

Analogously, at the level of intellectual discourse, the arguments used to justify either ethics or scepticism towards the whole enterprise overlap with the arguments for and against the enterprise of literary evaluation. Although these are in principle distinct, and (as the example of Kant shows)[3] there is no reason for any given individual to conflate them, there is a marked parallelism between the two, such that ethical criticism and the literary canon (with which it is in any case interdependent) tend to share a common rise and fall of fortune.

One sign of a recent rise in the fortunes of evaluative discourse is a strengthening focus, in different disciplines, on the relative absence or loss of traditional evaluative concepts. In philosophy, for example, there have been claims that the powerful current of ethical scepticism running from Hume to C. L. Stevenson and J. L. Mackie has produced in our culture a collective loss, as well as a significant impoverishment, of ethical concepts. Two philosophers who have argued something like this are Stanley Cavell, whose book *The Claim of Reason: Wittgenstein, Scepticism, Morality and Tragedy* has a chapter entitled 'An Absence of Morality', and Alasdair MacIntyre, in *After Virtue: A Study in Moral Theory*. As Cora Diamond points out in her illuminating discussion of the two in a recent symposium in *Ethics*, both independently confront what they take to be a 'sort of conceptual amnesia'.[4] This image of a widespread cultural amnesia or suppression has become an extremely significant one in the last ten years. Charles Taylor, who, as we have seen, is preoccupied with naturalist denials of the ethical discriminations we all make, including naturalists themselves, talks of the need to 'fight uphill to rediscover the obvious, to counteract the layers of suppression of modern moral consciousness'.[5] Both Taylor and MacIntyre give genealogies of this modern suppression that go back to the Enlightenment, where strongly valued goods, such as freedom and disengaged reason, gained such authority that they have paradoxically become invisible *as* goods. And this is true, according to Taylor and MacIntyre, not simply of the sceptical tradition. Even Kantianism and utilitarianism, which emerge in this century as the dominant modes of moral philosophy, constrict the field to what Taylor calls 'procedural reason', which claims to be able to direct moral choice by purely rational algorithms that are themselves substantively value-neutral. These are the so-called 'foundational' or 'theoretical' modes of moral philosophy that are being rejected in many quarters today by the 'anti-theorists' or 'anti-foundationalists' who are so important to my argument here.

In the literary field, the widespread move to theory is much more recent, and, although there are few obvious surface affinities between Kantianism or utilitarianism and post-structuralism (quite the reverse), there are some less obvious parallels that are instructive to notice. The relationship between the rise of literary theory and the fall of ethical criticism has already been well documented by Wayne C. Booth in *The Company We Keep: An Ethics of Fiction*. Particularly striking are the continuities between the 'suppression' Taylor talks of and Booth's account of ethical criticism as a partly 'Banned Discipline', yet one in which those who would ban it none the less necessarily participate.[6] The metaphor of banning is what many might expect of Booth, given a well-known view of him as defensive lineman for ethical criticism. But it is a different matter when Barbara Herrnstein Smith, who is herself quite sceptical about evaluation, recently reminds us that not merely has the study of literary evaluation been neglected by literary theory, 'the entire problematic of value and evaluation has been evaded and explicitly exiled by the literary academy'.[7] The terms 'ban' and 'exile' reveal quite a lot about the regal authority exercised by the collective enterprise of theory, though this is not especially new. More interesting is Smith's word 'evaded', which suggests an uncomfortable reaction to something theory would rather not know about.

The idea that evaluative discourse is something that literary theory has systematically evaded is supported by the strange 'absence of the ethical' in literary theory pointed out by Martha Nussbaum in *Love's Knowledge: Essays on Philosophy and Literature*. Nussbaum notes that amidst literary theory's indebtedness to such areas of philosophy as ontology, semantics, and epistemology, and despite its multitudinous references to such figures as Nietzsche and Heidegger, the work of contemporary leading moral philosophers such as John Rawls, Bernard Williams, and Thomas Nagel is hardly noticed at all. This is especially hard to understand, she says, as it is a time of great ferment in moral philosophy: 'One cannot find for generations – since the time of John Stuart Mill, if not earlier – an era in which there has been so much excellent, adventurous, and varied work on the central ethical and political questions of human life.' Nussbaum goes on to suggest that, in view of the importance of this work, literary theory's apparent uninterest in it is itself significant:

But in the midst of all this busy concern with other types of philosophy, the absence of moral philosophy seems a significant sign. And in fact it signals a further striking absence: the absence, from literary theory, of the organizing questions of moral philosophy, and of moral philosophy's sense of urgency about these questions. The sense that we are social beings puzzling out, in times of great moral difficulty, what might be, for us, the best way to live – this sense of practical importance, which animates contemporary ethical theory and has always animated much of great literature, is absent from the writings of many of our leading literary theorists.[8]

The value that Nussbaum places on 'practical' immediacy and relevance is itself an important feature of the new developments in ethics she mentions – of which her own new work is a further notable example. Beside this, the contrastingly disengaged nature of much literary theorising, its very lack of practical 'urgency', its lack of any sense that moral practice much matters, seems to Nussbaum to be a significant sign. It is a sign, in fact, that the naturalist 'suppression' of value reaches well beyond post-Enlightenment philosophy into contemporary post-structuralist theory.

A further indication that an important dialectical moment has been reached is the sudden prevalence across several discourses of a form of argument variously known as the 'self-refuting', 'self-referential' or '*ad hominem*' argument, in which the sceptic's suppressed evaluative assumptions are used to subvert his own case. The legal philosopher John Finnis, for example, argues that 'reasonableness ... requires us to reject radical [ethical] scepticism as both unjustified and literally self-refuting ... ' He develops this view at length in his argument against J. L. Mackie's book *Ethics: Inventing Right and Wrong*:

when we observe that the picture or model to which Mackie implicitly appealed cannot accommodate even the simplest facts about intention, meaning and truth – facts instantiated by every one of his assertions – we are entitled to conclude that his talk about queerness and special faculties in relation to our judgments about the good and the bad, the right and the wrong, fails to give any reason for doubt about the objectivity or truth of such judgments.[9]

With his belief in 'facts' about intention, meaning, and truth and the 'objectivity' of judgments, Finnis is very far from the more modish perpectivalism of Richard Rorty, and yet his case against Mackie is characteristic of the sort of argument used so often against evaluative scepticism in the 1980s. It is in one respect a kind of deconstruction:

Finnis is pointing to the destabilising absence or *aporia* in Mackie's argument, his repressed assumptions about intention, meaning, and truth, which ultimately undo the logic of his position. The interesting thing is that this sort of deconstruction is performed by philosophers who otherwise have no surface affinities with post-structuralism: the argument is now suddenly 'there' to be made. Bernard Williams himself deconstructs the ethical assumptions presupposed both by sceptics and by moral foundationalists such as Kant: 'We are interested in the idea that ethical considerations are presupposed by rational freedom, and this will have to mean a freedom to which the moral skeptic, among others, is *already* committed.'[10] That emphasis on 'already' might have come from Paul de Man or Barbara Johnson.

The fact that such arguments can be called deconstructive suggests that this is a dialectical movement and not simply a rather broadly based reactionary counter-attack: inherent logical fissures within naturalist post-Enlightenment philosophy and literary theory now seem wide open to analysis. Similar arguments are 'there' to be made within literary theory against both positivist and post-Saussurean forms of evaluative scepticism. A much discussed case of the former is that of John Carey's commentary in the *TLS* of 22 February 1980, entitled 'An end to evaluation'. Carey argues that the age of literary value-judgments has passed, that judgments were once thought to be objective and values part of the nature of things, but are now seen by the enlightened as merely subjective: the judgments we make merely tell us about ourselves and not about the world. The 'modern' cosmology on which this account of value depends is given to us explicitly by Carey:

But how can such values retain their credibility in the godless universe which most people now inhabit? Modern man is quite used to the idea that we are the temporary occupants of a cooling solar system; that human life is an accident of chemistry; that all the ages, from the first dawn on earth to its extinction, will amount to no more than a brief parenthesis in the endless night of space; that good and evil and other such ephemera were created by the human mind in its attempt to impose some significance on the amoral flux which constitutes reality.[11]

Wayne Booth and Raymond Tallis have both made the point that Carey's theory here is undermined by his own critical practice elsewhere, which (necessarily) embodies both explicit and implicit evaluations, about the importance of the very authors, Shakespeare and Donne, he has spent much of his scholarly life expounding.[12] They might have gone on to note, as I have myself elsewhere,[13] the allied fact that Carey himself is making value judgments, even in 'An End to Evaluation'. For example, he implies that it is good that literary evaluation is at an end and that modern scientific thought is non-evaluative. He also implies that scientific, non-evaluative discourse is better than, specifically more truthful than, the medieval discourse it replaced. But if these are value judgments, it can be asked why he seems to believe in their truth. Suppressed assumptions of value underlie Carey's discourse in much the same way as they do Mackie's, and they expose him to the same sort of deconstructive analysis. *Both* elements of the binary opposition evaluative/non-evaluative are always already present in such discourse. As we shall see, it is one of the *aporias* implicit in deconstruction itself that moral and literary evaluation are inescapable, even in the most rigorously linguistic analysis.

Carey's article embodies a rather old-fashioned scientific positivism which is still reasonably widespread in the literary academy. In the correspondence that followed his article, Carey was not short of defenders. Moreover, he suggests the philosophical roots of his position when he says that 'good and evil and other such ephemera were created by the human mind in its attempt to impose some significance on the amoral flux which constitutes reality'. This is redolent partly of Enlightenment rationalism and partly of Nietzsche, and it helps to suggest why Charles Taylor's phrase 'layers of suppression of the modern moral consciousness' might apply as well to the moral scepticism that post-structuralism derives largely from Nietzsche as it does to the tradition that runs from the Enlightenment to J. L. Mackie. These are not entirely distinct traditions; either might have been responsible for a book with Mackie's subtitle: 'Inventing right and wrong'.

Neo-Nietzscheanism has been no more proof against evaluative deconstruction than Carey's positivism. There is a clear overlap between the arguments that have been used against both. Peter Dews, for example, in his recent influential book *Logics of Disintegration: Post-structuralist Thought and the Claims of Critical Theory* points to the inherent logical instabilities of perspectivalism as part of a broader argument that sees the whole neo-Nietzschean enterprise as well advanced in the process of self-destruction. In a section of his book called 'The return to truth', Dews notes the shifts in views of the main French exponents, Derrida, Lacan, Foucault, and Lyotard, from the 1970s to the 1980s when some of them begin to shift ground as the self-contradictions of their beliefs, particularly on truth, become unavoidable. All, according to Dews, faced what he calls 'the reflexive problem':

There is one obvious difficulty which theories such as those of Foucault and Lyotard, which espouse a perspectivalist account of truth, and – furthermore – attempt to ground a conception of political practice in this account, must confront: the problem of their own status and validity as theories.[14]

The reflexive problem is Mackie's and Carey's problem at a further remove. If truth itself is merely one of those ephemeral values which has been created by the human mind to impose some significance on the amoral flux which constitutes reality, then that raises the problem of how any perspectival statement is any more worthy of attention than its negation. Kate Soper, in *Humanism and Antihumanism*, puts the point well: 'In the concluding pages of *The Archaeology of Knowledge*, Foucault allows his "humanist" critics to place him in the following dilemma: either he must admit that his methods are no better than any others, or he must claim that they are correct. If the latter, then he is allowing his own discourse to constitute an exception to the rules of discourse for which it argues.'[15] The perspectivalist has no option but to concede that his views are in some sense 'correct' (as Foucault later did), and that the value of truth is something to which any act of communication, as Jurgen Habermas points out, is always already committed. There is an inevitable 'cryptonormativism', in other words, at the root of all avowedly value-neutral genealogies and deconstructions.[16]

Recent critiques of deconstruction have also found other assumptions crucial to ethics implied, although explicitly denied, in deconstructive discourse itself. In another influential book of the past few years, *French Philosophy of the Sixties: An Essay on Antihumanism*, Luc Ferry and Alain Renaut argue that in Derrida's writing 'subjectivity stubbornly resists its own disappearance'; he is constantly asking us to think 'the unthinkable', which means that, after all, consciousness, even the Cartesian *cogito*, is at the heart of Derrida's approach.[17] However right or wrong Ferry and Renaut may be here, there is no mistaking the turning of Derrida against Derrida, or the implication that Deconstruction focused reflexively on itself yields suppressed humanistic assumptions. When the point is put plainly, it is hard to see how one could ever have thought otherwise. As Bernard Williams says, 'radical structuralist descriptions of society, whatever they may say, suppose there to be individuals who acquire certain dispositions and aims and express them in action'.[18] Related points are made by critics of anglophone Deconstruction. In an important article in 1983 Murray Krieger points to what he terms 'The thematic underside of recent theory'. His claim is that as hard as post-structuralist theory tries to purify itself of all humanist concerns, it cannot help privileging certain unspoken ethical and ideological meanings, such as the subliminal existentialist themes in Paul de Man's avowedly anti-thematic criticism.[19] Krieger's point (and that of Tobin Siebers, whose important book *The Ethics of Criticism* is also focused on such questions) is that the project of remaining purely descriptive and semiotic is impossible; any critical discourse has an underside of thematic meaning that will always imply the valuation of one conception of the ethical life over another. Krieger shows this by performing deconstructions of certain essays of Paul de Man and Hillis Miller, noting all the camouflaged bridges between semiotics and thematics. He reads these essays against the grain and demystifies their pretension of being purely acts of linguistic attention.

All of these critics of post-structuralism can be seen to be rescuing ethical distinctions from what Charles Taylor has called 'a kind of [naturalist] bewitchment'.[20] Like psychoanalysis (and deconstruction itself), this involves working against the grain of unconscious textual 'resistance', which can only be undertaken with prior philosophical assurance that the repressed 'must' be there. In the case of the evaluative or ethical unconscious, that assurance has been provided by a shift in moral philosophy which has taken place more or less in the past ten years.

The best way to come at this shift is to return to the arguments against evaluation considered so far. These can be represented syllogistically as: (i) All evaluation is subjective. (ii) The subjective realm is ephemeral. (iii) Therefore evaluation is ephemeral. There are at least two versions of this argument. The first is John Carey's (by now) old-fashioned positivist version, which asserts that only 'objective' or 'non-evaluative', scientific discourse addresses reality and is capable of significant truth. The second is the still-fashionable post-structuralist version which says that subjectivity is of no abiding significance because, like so-called 'objective' reality, it is culturally constructed.[21] Both therefore reject the enterprise of literary judgment, either as vapid or as ideologically compromised. However, neither of them looks nearly as tenable as it might have ten or fifteen years ago.

The positivist version of the argument has been answered very persuasively in two or three different ways in recent years. First, Richard Rorty has (not uncontroversially) argued that the all-important positivist distinction between evaluative and so-called objective, truth-telling discourses is illusory. Like the post-structuralist, he asserts that there is no such thing as objective 'truth' as it is usually understood – because there is no such thing as a 'transcendental signified' which takes us beyond all contingency and convention *to* truth. For him, this means that there is no 'first-rate truth-by-correspondence-to-reality' as distinct from 'second-rate truth-as-what-it-is-good-to-believe'.[22] Both sorts of truth depend circularly on socially agreed choices and conventions about what shall count as true. Pragmatism differs from some sorts of post-structuralism in that its levelling is the occasion, not for nihilism, but for the reinstatement of evaluative discourse. If all truth is a matter of pay-off, of usefulness, *for us*, both as individuals and as a society, then scientific discoveries and literary judgments are both equally assessible in terms of their utility in helping us achieve various ends. In its own sphere, each has a claim on our attention.

Second, is the answer Thomas Nagel implies in *Mortal Questions* when he argues that the subjective realm is an ineradicable side of reality. We doubt this, he says, mainly because of the voracious objectivising appetite that has gone along with the prestige of the natural sciences in our culture. In a famous chapter, 'What is it like to be a bat?' he argues very persuasively that there is *something* which it is like to be a bat, though it is no more conceivable to us than what it is like to be us would be conceivable to an extra-terrestrial intelligence. The difficulty of giving an account from the outside, as it were, of our subjectivity is not then an argument for ruling out its reality. For Nagel, there are phenomenological facts just as there are objective ones. These facts are susceptible to 'intersubjective agreement', which confers on them a quasi-objectivity. In a later book, Nagel describes objectivity as a 'centerless view', a view from nowhere. Here he argues that because such a view of the world enables a convergence of viewpoints between different viewers, then objectivity and intersubjective agreement are closely connected.[23] If this is so, then Nagel is headed in a direction that, in this respect, is not so different from the one taken so much further by Rorty when he says that truth is truth *for us*. In their different ways, then, both of them suggest paths around the positivist argument.[24]

A third way of resisting the positivist fact/value distinction is offered by Alasdair MacIntyre, who, as we have seen, rejects the whole post-Enlightenment philosophical tradition. This tradition, he says, has needlessly consigned value to the emotional-volitional side of human experience while giving undue prestige to the rational. Once we accept this split, we are condemned to accept some version of what he calls an 'emotivist' justification of value and morality. Hence there is little fundamental difference between utilitarians, Kantians, Nietzscheans, Sartreans and outright ethical sceptics like Stevenson and Mackie: all implicitly accept the rationalist way of dividing the psyche. In a move that has become increasingly common in the last ten years, MacIntyre argues that the only escape from these terms is to return to ancient philosophy and specifically to an Aristotelian notion of 'practices'.

The refusal of many contemporary moral philosophers to accept the Kantian or utilitarian foundationalist alternatives to ethical scepticism has very often gone hand in hand with positive accounts of value that centre on such classical notions as 'practices', 'the virtues', and 'tradition'. MacIntyre bases his argument on all three. By a 'practice' MacIntyre means 'any coherent and complex form of socially established cooperative human activity through which goods internal to that activity are realised in the course of trying to achieve those standards of excellence which are appropriate to, and partially definitive of, that form of activity, with the result that human powers to achieve excellence, and human conceptions of the ends and goods involved, are systematically extended'.[25] From this definition it is clear that within a given practice an evaluation may be partly factual. To use his own example, if a certain farmer gets a better yield for his crop than any other farmer in his district then it is a fact that he is a good farmer. The reason is that 'farmer' is a functional role defined in terms of the purpose or function which a farmer is expected to serve.

This revival of the notion of practices has turned out to be very useful, for to some extent our lives are made up of roles such as family member, citizen, employee, membership of a trade or profession in which it is possible more or less to specify the teleological purposes served by the practices involved. In this way, we isolate the goods, internal to those practices, by which performance within them can be assessed. For a whole range of agreed and well-defined practices, especially where public performance and responsibility are involved, evaluation is no longer simply a matter of what I happen to like or prefer. Practices do not cover the whole spectrum of moral life, where there are not always defined and agreed roles, or where roles inevitably conflict. And practices are dependent to a large extent on communal consensus about their purpose – a consensus which, since the Renaissance at least, has always been under strain from political dissent and rapid historical change. MacIntyre's account of practices, like Rorty's notion of 'solidarity' and Nagel's 'intersubjective agreement', aims for a measure of objectivity in the sphere of value that will inevitably be fragile in the modern world.

MacIntyre anticipates this criticism to some extent by arguing for the importance of the 'moral tradition'. According to him the problem he is addressing lies deeper than any consensus that might be found among individuals – that is, among individuals conceived as such prior to, and apart from, the communities from which they have derived their individual selfhood in the first place. Such ancient notions as practices, roles, and the virtues have a modern inflection in MacIntyre's account, where individual identity is seen as socially constituted and narratively constructed:

I am never able to seek for the good or exercise the virtues only *qua* individual... I inherit from the past of my family, my city, my tribe, my nation, a variety of debts, inheritances, rightful expectations and obligations. These contribute the given of my life, my moral starting point... For the story of my life is always embedded in the story of those communities from which I derive my identity. I am born with a past; and to try to cut myself off from that past, in the individualist mode, is to deform my present relationships.[26]

This is full of important insights that are the part-truths moderns are most likely to overlook. Our individual identity is embedded in communal stories, which helps us to see why the so-called literary canon, in so far as it has contributed to the shaping of Western culture, is so important for us. The narratives it contains are not simply external to us, imposed on us by authoritative others; they are part of who we are. The moral traditions these stories partly inherit and partly create are therefore important to us, not as things to seek to revive artificially, but to recognise as in some sense *already* within ourselves. But this is only a part-truth because MacIntyre sees modern individuality as set in opposition to the moral tradition, rather than as a more recent part of it. His project therefore does involve an attempt to find a route back from modern reflectiveness. As Bernard Williams has persuasively argued, this is a dead end: we no longer live in the sort of 'hypertraditional society' (that is, one 'maximally homogeneous and minimally given to general reflection')[27] which MacIntyre's version of 'the moral tradition' would need in order to command widespread assent.

Williams is more sceptically inclined than any of the moral thinkers considered so far, and possibly for that reason his rather more astringent contributions to the re-establishment of ethical discourse seem to have met with more respect. One of his best-known contributions has been the notion of 'thick' evaluative concepts, a term derived originally from Gilbert Ryle via Clifford Geertz. Geertz famously argued that too much ethnographic work consisted of 'thin' and relatively detached phenomenological descriptions of behaviour which remain determinedly external to the culture being observed; what were needed were 'thicker' descriptions which interpret behaviour in terms of its cultural 'import' – that is, in terms that are *internal* to the codes of signification and evaluation that operate within that culture itself.[28] According to Bernard Williams, much of our traditional ethical terminology consists of thick concepts like 'coward', 'lie', 'brutality', 'gratitude', and so on. Our use of such terms, he argues, is not just (as a thorough-going sceptic might say) 'action-guiding'; it is also crucially 'world-guided'. Purely thin external description of such concept-use would see only the former; but then that sort of description would leave out a crucial element of meaning. On the other hand, the observer concerned can only fully understand a given concept, that is, anticipate when it would be appropriate to use one, when he or she can 'grasp imaginatively its evaluative point. He cannot stand quite outside the evaluative interests of the community he is observing, and pick up the concept simply as a device for dividing up in a rather strange way certain neutral features of the world.'[29] This has turned out to be an extremely fruitful point; without necessarily implying any denigration of thin description, Williams shows that there are certain areas of experience and discourse that can only be fully understood anthropocentrically, which has important implications that go well beyond ethics to the so-called human sciences and to some forms of literary theory. However, Williams' theme is ethics, which he sums up by returning at the end of *Ethics and the Limits of Philosophy* to thick concepts:

One thing that will make a difference is the extent to which ethical life can still rely on what I have called thick ethical concepts. They are indeed open to being unseated by reflection, but to the extent that they survive it, a practice that uses them is more stable in the face of the general, structural reflections about the truth of ethical judgments than a practice that does not use them. The judgments made with these concepts can straightforwardly be true, and, for the people who have those concepts, the claim involved in assenting to them can correspondingly be honored.[30]

This stringent reminder that thick ethical concepts, together with the practices, virtues, and traditions which go with them, may all be unseated by reflection is still a very far cry from saying, as John Carey did, that evaluative judgments are nothing but the irrational imposition of preference on the amoral flux of reality. Williams' carefully qualified conclusion that ethical judgments made with thick concepts and within defined practices may be true or false represents in a nutshell some of the central ground gained by one promising strand of moral philosophy in the last ten years. It is this ground that gives Carey's article, published only in 1980, its already dated air.

Williams' memorable formulation, that ethical concepts and practices may be unseated by reflection, points straight to what is insecure about MacIntyre's large constructive enterprise: it is embattled (as Williams' work is not) against some of the characteristic reflections of modernity. For example, MacIntyre reminds us that, for Aristotle, 'the human being' is also a functional concept. To return to an earlier example, farmer stands in relation to farming well as the human being stands in relation to living well:

according to [the classical] tradition to be a man is to fill a set of roles each of which has its own point and purpose: member of a family, citizen, soldier, philosopher, servant of God. It is only when man is thought of as an individual prior to and apart from all roles that 'man' ceases to be a functional concept.[31]

This teleological account of 'man' is well and good so long as he is content to be nothing but these roles, but what if he feels, as he is bound to at some time or other in our post-Romantic culture, that these simply do not allow him to be *himself*? In other words, how can he avoid considering himself an individual prior to, and apart from, all the social roles he plays? I might accept, for example, that Farmer Jones, according to the goods internal to that practice, is a good farmer, but why should that stop me believing that (say) he is wasting *himself* by staying on his father's farm, out of a fear of the unknown?

One way of putting this objection to MacIntyre's project is to say that he is trying to rule out of account one whole historical strand of which the modern self is constituted, what Charles Taylor calls the 'expressivist' demand for self-realisation that was born in the Romantic movement. Taylor's monumental and compelling historical account of the making of the modern identity argues that we are made up of at least three mutually conflicting strands in which are intertwined all the important Western formative threads from classical antiquity to the present day. The three are: an other-regarding Kantian-moral one that derives ultimately from the Judeo-Christian religious tradition; one that privileges disengaged rationality, autonomy, freedom, human equality, and universality, which comes from the Enlightenment; and the Romantic one which emphasises the demands of nature, human fulfilment, and expressive integrity. The strands cross in so many ways that any attempt to separate them will have an element of artificiality about it; and the separation could be done in different ways. But neither of these objections ultimately affects the strength of Taylor's thesis, which is that it embraces the whole range of historical sources of modern selfhood and shows how each is essential to who we are now. It is a thesis with enormous explanatory implications, not least of which is that it helps us to see where any particular account of ethics, such as MacIntyre's, or for that matter, Kant's or Sartre's or Nietzsche's or Rorty's or Nagel's, is in some sense only partial and leaves some essential demand of the ethical life out of account. Taylor's point is not that anything needs to be revived, favoured, or suppressed; what is needed is that we come 'to acknowledge the full range of goods we live by'.[32] In a Hegelian spirit Taylor argues that no conception of the good once important to the Western psyche ever entirely loses its importance for us. This importance can merely be temporarily forgotten or suppressed: even those 'who flaunt the most radical denials and repudiations of selective facets of the modern identity generally go on living by variants of what they deny.'[33] What also follows from this is a point of much consequence: goods that remain essential to us are sometimes dismissed because they have historically been taken to excess. The danger lies in what Taylor calls 'one-sided views', which lose from sight the 'genuine dilemmas' implicit in a comprehensive understanding of any given historical situation: 'following one good to the end may be catastrophic, not because it isn't a good, but because there are others which can't be sacrificed without evil'.[34] One-sided views of literature, literary discourse, or the ethical life, views that occlude goods essential to us, are the ones I have in my sights throughout this book.

If the recent work of Rorty, Nagel, MacIntyre, Williams, and Taylor helps us to move beyond positivist dismissals of evaluation, it also helps to set in context more up-to-date forms of evaluative scepticism, ones potentially even more damaging to the 'humanist' enterprise of ethical and evaluative criticism. This broad line of attack focuses on the valuations implied in the existence of the traditional literary canon. Once again, there are two main arguments. The first says that the case for the canon is inevitably based on circularities. Humanist arguments, it is said, are mostly of the following form. The great texts are great because they exemplify certain important and timeless human values. How do we know that they are important and timeless human values? Because they are exemplified in the great texts. That is, the canon and the values it is supposed to illustrate are defined circularly in terms of each other. There can be no doubt that this has been true of humanist thinking. Arnold and Leavis at various times both argue in this way, and at first glance it certainly seems to confirm their generally low repute at the moment to have this circularity pointed out.

At this point, the humanist will often turn to what seems to be more solid ground, the so-called test of time: the great texts are great because they have endured. It is the endurance of Homer, Shakespeare, Mozart, and Leonardo da Vinci over the centuries which shows that their work exemplifies important and timeless values. After all, if they did not keep on offering us something important, why would we keep on going back to them? In the most significant book to be published on literary evaluation for many years, Barbara Herrnstein Smith gives this argument impressively searching scrutiny, tracing the ways in which, for example, unpalatable aspects of canonical works are successively reinterpreted by humanists and either allegorised or formalised out of harm's way. But her most telling points are made against those 'for whom the value of canonical works consists precisely in their "embodying" and "preserving"'...

"traditional values"'. Once the work survives initially, she says, no matter how accidentally, it will increase its own prospects for canonical status:

Second...it will also begin to perform certain characteristic cultural functions by virtue of the very fact that it *has* endured – that is, the functions of a canonical work as such – and be valued and preserved accordingly: as a witness to lost innocence, former glory, and/or apparently persistent communal interests and 'values' and thus a banner of communal identity; as a reservoir of images, archetypes, and topoi – characters and episodes, passages and verbal tags – repeatedly invoked and recurrently applied to new situations and circumstances... In these ways, the canonical work begins increasingly not merely to *survive within* but to *shape and create* the culture in which its value is produced and transmitted and, for that very reason, to perpetuate the conditions of its own flourishing. Nothing endures like endurance.[35]

In the light of Charles Taylor's work, we can recognise this as an extremely important point. The canon does not just passively 'preserve' and 'embody' 'traditional values' (Smith's examples of the relevant humanist terminology), it actively shapes and creates the very values by which it is itself valued. So if a Western reader finds a deeply congenial and satisfying moral sense in Homer, Shakespeare, and so on, it is small wonder: it is precisely these works, among others, which have informed that moral sense. Therefore there is an even more profound circularity in the humanist case: the canonical works embody important values because they themselves have given importance to those very values. It is this which explains, according to Smith, the culture-relativity of what seem to us universal human values – the fact that Africans, for instance, have trouble finding the works of our supposedly universal geniuses so unquestionably universal. We only believe them so because we are constituted by their particular, historically contingent version of human excellence.

Smith makes this point with characteristic clarity, precision, and rigour, and she is essentially right: canons are culturally constructed and probably to some extent culturally relative. However this argument will only corrode belief in the worth of canons if that belief is predicated on essentialist and universalist assumptions about human nature. And presumably she has in mind the holders of such assumptions when she uses the phrase *contingencies of value* as the title of her book; her opponents, it is implied, are those who would argue for *necessities* of value. These would presumably be those who hold a position analogous to Kantianism in ethics, which founds moral duty on the universally applicable constraints imposed by metaphysically conceived first principles. Accede to the first principles and necessities of value follow. Smith leaves us in no doubt that literary evaluations based on metaphysically conceived universalisms are hard to believe in these days – though I would want to add that most of us still tend to believe in them when the human rights of non-Western societies are in question. But what Smith's argument does not weaken is a belief in the importance of literary canons that concedes her point about their deep cultural embeddedness.

This is the sort of account of canonical importance that I propose to offer in what follows. Following the lead of recent anti-foundationalist or anti-theoretical moral philosophers such as those discussed thus far, who 'regard local moral practices [as opposed to universal principles] as primary in moral reasoning',[36] I shall defend a view of the canon that accepts its partial and circular shaping of the values by which we value it. As Richard Rorty frequently says, there are no non-circular justifications to offer, which would include the values Smith implicitly speaks from when she implies that there ought to be – that is, if 'values' (and her inverted commas in the above passage convey a great deal about her own valuations) are not going to be merely 'contingent' or arbitrarily 'privileged'. (Both of these terms really do merit inverted commas, as in this context they invoke the dubious alternatives Smith is often working with.) Smith's clear, thinly descriptive and, in its way, rigorously reasoned work is a very significant example of what Taylor has called 'the cramped postures of suppression' characteristic of much contemporary theorising.

To be fair to Smith, it is important to notice how far she is from John Carey's sort of evaluative scepticism. And perhaps nobody has thought harder than she about the difficulties of coming to terms with both the variabilities and the constancies of literary judgments about particular works; her formulations are incisive, crisp, and illuminating:

The moral of the parable of Shakespeare's sonnets was that, with respect to value, everything is always in motion with respect to everything else. If there *are* constancies of literary value, they will be found *in those very motions*: that is, in the relations among the variables. For, like all value, literary value is not the property of an object *or* of a subject but, rather, *the product of the dynamics of a system*. As readers and critics of literature, we are within that system; and, because we are neither omniscient nor immortal and do have particular interests, we will, at any given moment, be viewing it from *some* perspective. It is from such a perspective that we experience the value of the work and also from such a perspective that we estimate its probable value for others. There is nothing illusory in the experience, however, or necessarily inaccurate in the estimate. From that real (if limited) perspective, at that real (if transient) moment, our experience of the work *is* its value. Or, in the terms I should prefer: our experience of 'the value of the work' is equivalent to *our experience of the work in relation to the total economy of our existence*. And the reason our estimates of its probable value for other people may be quite accurate is that the total economy of *their* existence may, in fact, be quite similar to our own.[37]

What is strong about this account is partly its grasp of the dynamic variability and interactive nature of evaluations of any literary work, and partly the centrality it gives to the experience of valuing, an experience which is neither 'illusory' nor 'necessarily inaccurate'. This seems to be conceding a good deal and it certainly takes us far beyond Carey. Similarly, Smith's formulation about literary value seems to go well beyond the crude positivism which would characterise it as purely subjective: that value is not the property of an object or of a subject but '*the product of a system*'. Smith has the air of standing back from the old battleground and offering a detached, even-handed synthesis of the whole dynamic 'system' that equally transcends both naive objectivism and dismissive scepticism.

But that air of detachment and transcendence of partiality is more apparent than real, for Smith is conceding much less to one side than to the other. Granted that the naive thesis is untenable, that value is not simply the 'property' of an object in the way that being lighter than air is a property of hydrogen within a certain range of pressures and temperatures, does this rule out *any* account of the object that might include, *inter alia*, the location *in it* of some constraints to evaluation?

This is an important question because, having rightly dispatched naive objectivism, Smith implies by her further silences and under-emphases concerning the object itself that no other kind is possible. As we shall see, this is an unwarranted conclusion, but it is supported everywhere in Smith's prose by subtle semantic pressures and twists which end up in retreat from even the highly qualified quasi-objectivism she had seemed to proffer. To say, for instance, that our *experience* of value may not be 'illusory', or that our *perspective* is 'real', appears to be conceding a realism that turns out to be highly equivocal. The experience of hallucination and the perspective of the fanatic are equally real, but how much weight do we put on them? So to say that 'our experience of the value of the work *is* the value' is to put almost the whole weight back onto the subjective side of the interaction and to make value, once again, close to ephemeral. And there are further subtle retreats in the same direction: what reads 'our experience of the value of the work' in one sentence becomes in the next (Smith's 'preferred formulation') 'our experience of "the value of the work"', the inverted commas refining the value even further out of existence. By contrast what follows has all the importance of italics: '*our experience of the work in relation to the total economy of our existence*', which introduces even further qualifications to the significance that any given evaluation might have for us, for it will be further 'contingent' on our mood, our current 'interests', and any other number of factors relevant to any given subject. These factors are undeniable and Smith does us a service to remind us of them. But along the way, almost the whole weight of Smith's account falls on the subjective side of the interaction, which implies, though it does not state, that all these factors have a good deal more to do with literary judgment than does the object itself. These factors are among other things specified, while the object in her account lacks similar illustrative specificity. The whole effect is of a curious over-determination in Smith's argument, as if its deepest (perhaps unconscious) commitment is to avoid any implication that literary texts themselves might be to some degree and in some fashion responsible for the ways in which we value them. In the end, *Contingencies of Value* does not get very far from the thought that it is we who impose value on the qualitatively neutral flux of literary experience.

It is significant that Smith, after an opening seven or eight pages on Shakespeare's sonnets, leaves the literary 'work' itself empty of specificity and particularity for almost two hundred pages. To use Smith's own terms, it might be said that the level of generality at which she conducts her discussion is itself a particular 'perspective' that is not altogether without partisan 'interest' in the matters before her. Once again, it is necessary to look closely at a lengthy passage:

what may be spoken of as the 'properties' of a work – its 'structure,' 'features,' 'qualities,' and of course its 'meanings' – are not fixed, given, or inherent in the work 'itself' but are at every point the variable products of particular *subjects'* interactions with it. Thus it is never 'the *same* Homer'.

This is not to deny that some aspect, or perhaps many aspects, of a work may be constituted in similar ways by numerous different subjects, *among whom we may include the author*: to the extent that this duplication occurs, however, it will be because the subjects who do the constituting are themselves similar, not only or simply in being human creatures (and thereby, as it is commonly supposed, 'sharing an underlying humanity' and so on) but in occupying a particular universe that may be, for them, in many respects recurrent or relatively continuous and stable, and/or in inheriting from one another, through mechanisms of cultural transmission, certain ways of interacting with texts and 'works of literature.'[38]

Here again the value of Smith's astringency emerges strongly in its clear foregrounding of the woolliness of the old untheorised humanist thinking – objectivist woolliness about inherent 'meanings' and the essentialist error about 'sharing an underlying humanity'. And here too her deployment of inverted commas for 'properties' of the work 'itself' and italics for various *subjects'* interactions with it embodies the new theoretical insight: these emphases and de-emphases system-atically reflect contemporary theoretical re-positionings of the ontological status of the literary work and its meanings *vis à vis* the interpreting community – with which I broadly agree.

But here again it is Smith's style itself, and the evaluative choices seemingly *already* inscribed in it, to which attention needs to be drawn. For example, it might be asked why it is that in Smith's account hermeneutic and evaluative agreement is made to sound as adventitious as disagreement. This goes with Smith's displacement (one could fairly say marginalisation) of constraints within the work 'itself' as relevant factors to talk about in such agreement where it occurs. But here too Smith goes as far as stylistically possible to avoid that sort of account by talking of 'duplication' among 'subjects' who are 'similar' enough to constitute the work in 'similar' ways. My objection is not to the substantive points that readers constitute works (though not *in vacuo*) and that readers in the same community will in all likelihood do it similarly. It is rather that Smith's discourse leaves out something that is essential to the experience of valuing works of literature within an interpreting and evaluative community. Note, for instance, the word 'subjects', with its link to 'subjectivity' and its overtones of dualistic separateness both from other subjects and, perhaps significantly, from the world; in this context it must be about the most disengaged, least anthropocentric way of thinking about ourselves and our fellow readers of literature. The word is redolent of a certain sort of analytical rigour, though why that precise term (with its Cartesian overtones) was the right one for Smith's purpose is not easy to say. It is clear, however, that Smith's is an example of what Clifford Geertz and Bernard Williams call 'thin' description.

In order to focus on what is missing in Smith's 'thin' discourse about value it is instructive to return to the moral philosophers who have been wrestling with an analogous sense of discursive loss or absence for much longer and who are farther down the track in transcending it. Charles Taylor, for example, asks the question why we should consider a 'thin' account in ethics the 'best account' we can give. Taylor spends some time on this question, outlining what he calls the 'B. A. [best account] Principle' and asking 'what ought to trump the language in which I actually live my life?' He makes the crucial point that the virtue of this lived language is that it expresses our moral intuitions in a way that the 'thin' language does not. His point is that any language that does not allow us to express these is language about something else, which is subtly constraining us to talk about another subject (to use Donald Davidson's interesting formulation):

But if our moral ontology springs from the best account of the human domain we can arrive at, and if this account must be in anthropocentric terms, terms which relate to the meanings things have for us, then the demand to start outside of all such meanings, not to rely on our moral intuitions or on what we find morally moving, is in fact a proposal to change the subject. How then does practical reasoning proceed?[39]

There are useful analogies here between moral intuitions, the moral 'meanings things have for us' that Taylor is concerned to defend from 'the demand to start outside of all such meanings', and our hermeneutical, evaluative, and ethical intuitions about literature. Similar questions about practical evaluative reasoning are also raised.

To explore these it is necessary to give some specificity to the literary work 'itself'. Here is a short passage from chapter 20 of *Middlemarch*, chosen, as will be evident, not entirely at random:

'Should you like to go to the Farnesina, Dorothea? It contains celebrated frescoes designed or painted by Raphael, which most persons think it worth while to visit.'

'But do you care about them?' was always Dorothea's question.[40]

When I ponder the questions of meaning and value as they are thrown up to me by this passage, I can reflect in Smith's 'thin' terms that the passage is being constituted by me, and that, if George Eliot herself and some of my professional colleagues more or less agreed with me about its meaning and value, that would not *simply* be because of inherent 'properties' of the passage nor *simply* because we are all 'sharing an underlying humanity', but in part because of broad cultural continuities between us (not least our post-Romantic prejudice in favour of 'caring' for things) that help to explain why we all might agree intersubjectively in the way we constitute the passage and so judge its value in similar ways. But all that, true as it is, does not constitute the best account I could give of the meaning and value of the passage *itself*. It simply does not answer to my responsive intuitions about the meaning and value the passage has 'for us'; it is rather an implied response to the demand that 'I start outside of all such meanings.' The 'thin' account, roughly right as it seems to me (I must stress), none the less belongs to another subject altogether, which is, in a word, *theory*.

But what sort of account would answer to my intuitions of meaning and value in this passage? This would have to be, first, a form of *practical* reasoning, which, whatever my ontological sophistication, treats the literary text as what *in practice* it most seems to be, a presence beyond myself, more or less similar to the 'same' text as read by many others. Just as Bernard Williams talks of the use of 'thick' ethical concepts as being partly 'world-guided', so the 'thick' evaluative terms internal to the practice of literary criticism – words such as 'powerful', 'moving', 'impressive', 'shallow', or 'sentimental' – may be spoken of as partly *text-guided*. Odd as it might seem to have to state such a premise, the practical reasoning about novels offered throughout this book will assume the validity of an element of text-guidedness in my readings and qualitative discriminations. In the present case, for example, I would proffer the 'thick' observation that the *Middlemarch* passage itself, in its manipulating of our sympathies, turns out to be more artful, complex and morally consequential (in a Kantian way) than might at first glance seem likely – a view I shall argue at some length in chapter 6. Secondly, this 'thick' form of practical reasoning which answered to my evaluative intuitions about George Eliot's text would not be divorced from what I find 'morally moving' in it, to return to Taylor's phrase. This would reflect my intuitive tendency to side with Dorothea (and

I have little doubt, George Eliot) in her little exchange with her over-precise, under-responsive husband. In other words, such reasoning would not be afraid to risk itself in the emotional engagement of qualitative judgment about texts; it would keep in focus the issue of whether or not we ought to *care for them*, and if so, how much and in what ways. Thirdly, it would be reasoning that was provisional in the sense that it would be open to correction from later readings and significantly from the readings of others. It would be dialogic, in other words, or co-ductive, to take over a useful term. As is already evident, my best account would not be radically unlike the accounts of practical reasoning given in *The Company We Keep* and *Love's Knowledge*. I shall return to these in chapter 2 when I discuss the new turn to ethical criticism in the 1980s.

The passage from *Middlemarch* also focuses an insight for us in the case of Edward Casaubon, which is that disengaged reason is not in all cases and in all ways the best mode in which to come to terms either with life or with works of art. It can be a way of holding them at bay, a way of protecting oneself against their power to disturb. As I shall be arguing throughout, theoretical rationality has as much power to conceal as to reveal, and work such as Barbara Herrnstein Smith's, insightful though it is, still manages to conceal (perhaps from itself) its marked allegiances to a particular view of value. It is probably the dominant view since the rise of theory, one that leaves the reader unconstrained by any substantive account of text-guidedness in literary judgment and so apparently very much in control of her own valuations.

At a certain point contemporary arguments against the canon and those against ethical criticism meet and become one: both ethics and the traditional canon, it is claimed, depend on the misrepresentation of historically contingent and culturally relative values as timeless and universal ones. The various different forms of this argument are too familiar to require extensive examples. Its essence is that the canon is politically loaded in favour of dead, white, bourgeois, heterosexual males, and much the same is said against the ethical criticism that finds its assumptions supposedly affirmed by the same body of work.

In the past fifteen years, the post-structuralists, Marxists, feminists and race-theorists who have made these criticisms have changed the consciousness of most of us, irreversibly, on a whole range of matters,

including our views of which authors and works matter most and
which ethical questions are most worthy of our attention. In other
words, whatever account of canonicity or of ethical criticism we now
might give will be affected by this recent work. Largely because of it
essentialist justifications of value no longer seem to stand up to serious
scrutiny.

At the same time, one of the limitations of a certain recent strand
of politically oriented post-structuralism is its reductive view of
ethics, its tendency to believe that, rather than reformulate ethics, we
need to jettison it altogether. As we have seen, this is impossible, but
the anti-ethical impulse has deep roots in modern experience and
represents one of those major aspects of the modern identity we have
inherited from the Enlightenment. The impulse is reflected, for
example, in common speech in the range of negative associations that
have gathered particularly around the word 'morality'. Very often
when this word is used, it tends to imply a code of merely repressive,
coercive, power-seeking, life-denying and conventional values – a
view which is only too easy to substantiate in the contemporary
world. If this is all morality can be, preferences for freedom from it,
opposition to it, or political demystification of it, are not hard to
understand.

At a more theoretical level, this same wish to be clear of ethics
altogether comes out in Fredric Jameson's *The Political Unconscious*.
For Jameson, ethics occupies the position that metaphysics holds in
the Derridean demonology: it is not, he says, 'metaphysics but ethics
[which] is the informing ideology of the binary opposition; and we
have forgotten the thrust of Nietzsche's thought … if we cannot
understand how it is ethics itself which is the ideological vehicle and
the legitimation of concrete structures of power and domination'.[41]
This is the essential thrust of Jameson's case against ethics: it
legitimates by universalising into a system of binary moral oppositions
the characteristics of one group or class versus another, so that 'evil'
inevitably denotes imagined characteristics of those who are Other to
the hegemonic group. Thus ethics is an ideological mask of the will-
to-power of the dominant class, (or race or gender):

Briefly, we can suggest that, as Nietzsche taught us, the judgmental habit of
ethical thinking, of ranging everything in the antagonistic categories of good
and evil (or their binary equivalents), is not merely an error but is
objectively rooted in the inevitable and inescapable centeredness of every
individual consciousness or individual subject: what is good is what belongs

to me, what is bad is what belongs to the Other (or any dialectical variation on this nondialectical opposition: for example, Nietzsche showed that Christian charity – what is good is what is associated with the Other – is a simple structural variant of the first opposition).[42]

This passage illustrates several points that are crucial to my later argument. The first is that moral thinking is categorical: it consists in 'ranging everything' into pre-existing 'categories'. This is a widely pervasive way of conceiving of ethics. Julia Kristeva, for instance, begins her essay 'The ethics of linguistics' by saying that ethics before Marx, Nietzsche, and Freud 'used to be a coercive, customary manner of ensuring the cohesiveness of a particular group through the repetition of a code'.[43] In this account, the traditional categories are systematised into a pre-existing 'code', on the analogy, presumably, with the Code Napoleon. On this view, ethics is modelled on law, especially French law.

A second point is that these categories are organised in patterns of binary difference, even when they are inverted, as in the Nietzschean account of Christian charity. A third is that moral thinking is essentially 'judgmental', always – apart from the Christian inversion – on the pattern of I am good and the Other is bad. When this becomes a code, it is the means by which my class suppresses difference and heterogeneity – groups that do not fit my self-centred and self-interested conception of good are judged as evil. A fourth is that, because the point of ethics is to confirm hegemonic power, no transcendence of this rigid pattern is conceivable within it. Only political change can achieve that. Ethics so conceived is nothing else but a means of resisting change; it is essentially reactionary.

Jameson's is unquestionably a formidable case, largely resting as it does on Nietzsche's critique of Judeo-Christian morality, a critique which has become part of who we moderns are. But only part. As we see from the strong return to ethics in Anglo-American philosophy, the ethical is an ineradicable part of European identity. The programme of expunging it is as doomed to failure as the search for a route back from Nietzschean reflectiveness.

CHAPTER 2

A new turn toward the ethical

Despite the powerful challenge to ethical criticism by neo-Nietz-schean literary theory, there has been recently what Martha Nussbaum has called 'a marked turn toward the ethical'. The 'turn' has been evident even at the centre of deconstruction in the work of Derrida himself – for example, his address to the American Philo-sophical Association in 1988 on the topic of Aristotle's theory of friendship. Nussbaum also adduces Barbara Johnson's *A World of Difference*, which argues for the ethical and social relevance of Deconstruction. She might have added J. Hillis Miller's *The Ethics of Reading*, though Miller's conception of the ethical is much thinner and less satisfactory than Johnson's, being confined to the act of reading itself. Nussbaum concludes: 'No doubt part of this change can be traced to the scandal over the political career of Paul de Man, which has made theorists anxious to demonstrate that Deconstruction does not imply a neglect of ethical and social considerations.'[1]

There may be more than a grain of truth in this observation, but it would be a pity if it were accepted as the whole explanation of a change that has wider and deeper implications. For this recent 'turn toward the ethical' reaches across a much more varied body of work than Nussbaum suggests. If we exclude those who have laboured fruitfully, but unfashionably, in this particular area for many years, notably the distinguished Australian critic S. L. Goldberg (to whom I am indebted), there has been a profusion of work, especially in the United States, that looks very much like the beginnings of a significant resurgence in ethical criticism. That includes the im-portant work of Martha Nussbaum herself, of Cora Diamond, Wayne C. Booth, Tobin Siebers, Charles Altieri, Richard Eldridge, Paul Seabright, Frederick A. Olafson, and Murray Krieger, many of whom took part in important symposia on ethics and literature published in the journals *Ethics* and *New Literary History* in 1983 and

1988. The resurgence also includes Richard Rorty, Stanley Cavell, and Alasdair MacIntyre, who have all published important books and papers on ethics and literature in the recent past.[2]

Most of these people are philosophers by profession rather than literary critics. In other words, the 'turn toward the ethical' within literary studies is closely connected to a turn towards the literary within ethics. Unlike previous resurgences of ethical criticism that are associated with literary figures such as Dr Johnson, Matthew Arnold, F. R. Leavis, and Lionel Trilling, this movement (though by no means discontinuous with earlier ones) seems to be fuelled primarily by something going on within philosophy, which we have already touched on. According to Rorty this is nothing less than a major paradigm-shift that has taken place in our own time in which the culture of positivism has been replaced by the culture of pragmatism:

Pragmatism, by contrast, does not erect Science as an idol to fill the place once held by God. It views science as one genre of literature – or, put the other way around, literature and the arts as inquiries, on the same footing as scientific inquiries. Thus it sees ethics as neither more 'relative' or 'subjective' than scientific theory, nor as needing to be made 'scientific'. Physics is a way of trying to cope with various bits of the universe; ethics is a matter of trying to cope with other bits. Mathematics helps physics do its job; literature and the arts help ethics do its.[3]

If Rorty is right about this recent cultural shift towards what he calls a 'post-Philosophical' paradigm (in which philosophy is no longer concerned with the foundational questions of metaphysics, ontology, or epistemology), then there are at least two profound consequences for ethical criticism. The first, as we have seen, is that ethics ceases to be what it was in the positivist paradigm, a second-class discourse which dealt only with the 'subjective' or 'ephemeral' side of experience, as opposed to science, which alone addressed 'objective' reality. If, however, as Rorty argues, there is no 'transcendental signified', no 'truth-by-correspondence-to-reality', then ethics and science are simply different discourses dealing with different areas of inquiry, and so the need disappears to secure for ethics the sort of philosophical foundations that would make questions of moral duty as 'objectively' determinable as those of physics. Ethics is thereby released from what Richard Bernstein has aptly termed the 'Cartesian Anxiety' that has dogged it for centuries; it is the anxiety of 'the grand Either/Or' – either there is some basic foundational constraint or we are confronted with 'intellectual and moral chaos'.[4]

At another level, the Cartesian Anxiety drives us to an analogous choice of philosophical positions: either towards a Kantian *Grounding for a Metaphysics of Morals* or else towards the tradition of ethical scepticism leading from Hume to Charles Stevenson and John Mackie in which ethics is at very best a second-class discourse.

Rorty's reading of the present age not only reinstates ethics as a subject of serious inquiry, it also portrays literature as an integral part of that same inquiry. Literature becomes for ethics what mathematics is for physics, a sort of necessary handmaiden. If Rorty is right, this too has profound consequences for ethical criticism. And there is reason to think that Rorty may be right in a broad sense in his reading of our contemporary philosophical culture. While many contemporary philosophers would not share his specifically big 'p' Pragmatist scepticism about the usefulness of the concept of 'truth'[5] – as something 'out there' beyond our attempts to formulate it – quite a number seem to be drawn towards similarly anti-foundationalist reinstatements of ethics which see that enterprise as intimately bound up with close attention to literature, especially to drama and the novel. These would include Stanley Cavell, Cora Diamond, Alasdair MacIntyre, and Martha Nussbaum. The last two trace their philosophical allegiances back to a specifically Aristotelian conception of practical reasoning, which proceeds without any appeal to ultimate foundations, apparently feeling no need for them. In this more general sense, the neo-Aristotelians share with Rorty a small 'p' pragmatist orientation which finds its ethical interests inevitably bound up, as they were for Aristotle, in the analysis of imaginative literature.

Martha Nussbaum goes further than Rorty in treating literature not merely as a sort of servant of ethics ('helping' it do its job), but *as itself* moral philosophy. This is partly an extension of the Aristotelian belief that tragedy is more philosophical than history, and partly a fulfilment of what is in any case implied in Rorty's own characterisation of the age as post-Philosophical. There is a close relationship, in other words, between seeing the literariness of philosophy and seeing anew the philosophical nature of literature. But the claim that literature can *be* moral philosophy is no mere empty gesture of turning Derrida on his head. It is a theme running through all of Nussbaum's work, from *The Fragility of Goodness: Luck and Ethics in Greek Tragedy and Philosophy* onwards. Part of the strong interest of her study of the Greeks is the implicit suggestion that the age of the birth of philosophy speaks with special relevance to the age that is witnessing its death. For the Greeks, there were simply 'human lives' and 'problems', and tragedy and philosophy were simply different moments in a continuous process of reflection on them. Moreover, tragic poetry had an irreplaceably distinctive contribution to make to ethical inquiry, bringing home to the audience, in a way that systematic philosophy could not, the painfully complex, indeterminate, intractable nature of ethical deliberation to human beings caught up in the midst of it. But Nussbaum's insistence that the creative thinking that shapes Sophoclean tragedy and Jamesian novels is moral philosophy[6] goes further than saying that such thinking is, *vis à vis* systematic philosophy, distinctive. It also involves the claim that certain views of life which are candidates for serious consideration can only be adequately conveyed by means of imaginative literature. Such views tend to stress either the mutually antagonistic nature of important values, or the ethical importance of contingency or the passions, or the priority of particulars over generalities – all of which tend to resist systematic theoretical statement of the kind attempted in the available styles of conventional philosophy.

It is important to notice that Nussbaum's view is taken seriously, not merely by those who accept it (such as Cora Diamond and – very guardedly – D. D. Raphael), but also by those who reject it (such as Richard Wollheim, Arthur Danto, and Hilary Putnam.) Hilary Putnam, for instance, in agreeing with Wollheim that 'commentary' on literature can be philosophy while the literature cannot, none the less sees Nussbaum's claim as part of the profound contemporary destabilisation of the whole philosophical enterprise. In making this connection, Putnam admits that 'the great pretensions of philosophy have collapsed',[7] and, while this admission specifically denies any comfort to Derrida or Rorty, it is very much in touch with the intellectual pressures driving some moral philosophers away from Kant and towards Aristotle and imaginative literature.

While literary critics may not be much bothered by the question of whether imaginative literature can be specifically a form of *philosophy*, the important thing for them to observe is that for philosophers that question is largely about the degree of seriousness literature should be accorded as *a mode of ethical reflection* – or what Sam Goldberg some years ago called 'moral thinking'.[8] Literary studies can learn from the fact that a rather diverse group of moral philosophers, none of them conservative *as philosophers*, is treating literature as the mode *par excellence* of a certain kind of kind of moral thinking – at a time when literary theory is still largely uninterested in the whole ethical domain or else hostile towards it.

But among these developments in anti-foundational ethics, it is the return to Aristotle, or rather to certain of his characteristic ways of formulating the organising questions of ethics, that seems to offer some of the most promising starting-points for a renewed ethical criticism. Here I am largely persuaded by Nussbaum, whose argument runs as follows. No starting-point in ethics can be neutral, but Aristotle's is broad and inclusive enough not to foreclose any foreseeably important issue by making an a priori demarcation between areas that are relevant to morality and those that are irrelevant. For Aristotle, the organising question for ethics is some variant of 'How should a human being live?' or 'What does it mean to live well – or to flourish?'

It is perhaps as well to focus on what is non-neutral about these seemingly bland and innocuous questions. Thomas Nagel, for instance, in *The View from Nowhere*,[9] situates Aristotle's basic position among those of Plato, Kant, Nietzsche, and the utilitarians. Aristotle's view he characterises, reasonably enough, as *the moral life is defined in terms of the good life*. This is roughly to say that morality is inextricably linked to the notion of living well, or flourishing. Nagel rejects this position in the following terms:

Position (1) is wrong, in my view, because moral requirements have their source in the claims of other persons, and the moral force of those claims cannot be strictly limited by their capacity to be accommodated within a good individual life.[10]

This rejection of Aristotle, however, nicely illustrates why one might be drawn to him: Nagel's own conception of 'moral requirements' locates their source in the claims of *other* persons. This contains what is to my mind a crippling a priori delimitation of ethics to other-regarding considerations, consigning to the non-ethical realm all those moral requirements that have their source in oneself – in one's own responsibility, if possible, to flourish. The advantage of the Aristotelian approach over Nagel's is that it does nothing to pre-judge either way that clash between Judeo-Christian-Kantian and Romantic-expressivist-Nietzschean moralities which has been a major site of ethical conflict, and a master-theme of Western culture, for two hundred years. To return to Charles Taylor's way of making the point, *both* of these are strands of the modern identity; we cannot deny either without narrowing our understanding of the full range of goods we actually live by. Nor does Aristotelian 'living well' predetermine anything on the question of which faculties should be considered morally central and which peripheral. Kantian ethics, for instance, in placing such weight on a conception of a transcendent rational conscience, has found itself especially vulnerable in this century to psychological insights into the multiple social and individual contingencies in which anyone's sense of right and wrong is initially constituted. Kantians cannot easily accommodate the claim, which is commonplace enough in modern imaginative literature, that subconscious impulses are a large and important part of the ethical life. Nor does Aristotelian ethics organise ethical inquiry around questions of either duty or utility, as Kant and the utilitarians respectively do – which, once again, suppress in advance a good many other considerations that are relevant to the broad and flexible question, 'How to live well?' As Iris Murdoch points out in *The Sovereignty of Good*, the tendency of post-Kantian moral philosophy to focus exclusively on isolated moments of explicit choice loses sight of the fact that moral life is a continuous process which goes on before and after there is any question of conscious volition, expressing itself, for example, in the way in which I characteristically attend, or do not attend, to people. In this account the moral life begins in the world of value I build up in the first place out of my imagination, and ultimately includes everything about me – my whole being, character, and vision of things.[11] This is very much of a piece with the more global ethical understanding of the ancient world. As Aristotle reminds us, I am as responsible for my characteristic dispositions and way of seeing things as I am for my choices and actions.[12]

A second Aristotelian theme with much to offer to a reconstructed ethical criticism is an insistence on the *practical* nature of ethics and ethical reflection, its *raison d'être* being its *relevance* to the deeply problematic business of living well. According to Aristotle, in ethics 'we are not concerned to know what goodness essentially is, but how we are to become good men, for this alone gives the study its practical value.'[13] In this sense, the Aristotelian emphasis falls on the fact that ethics is neither a science nor a theory, but a form of practical reasoning leading, at best, to practical wisdom or *phronesis*. Richard Bernstein glosses this latter term as 'ethical know-how', which nicely distinguishes it from theoretical grasp or clarity, but underplays the element of fine discrimination in regard to ends.[14] *Phronesis* is *not* a matter simply of the application of pre-known moral principles or categories, but is, among other things, the more difficult enterprise of discernment of the morally salient features amongst the multiple particulars in which one is vitally engaged. Nussbaum stresses the anti-systematic nature of *phronesis*, which is part of the Aristotelian insistence on 'the need for fine-tuned *concreteness* in ethical attention and judgment'.[15]

It is perhaps here, in his practical stress on 'fine-tuned *concreteness*' in 'attention and judgment', that Aristotle has most to say to contemporary literary critics, for this sort of *practical* wisdom is one thing that distinguishes the literary imagination in its wrestling with ethical questions. It is found in canonical literary narratives, not, as often implied, in their direct enfleshment of preconceived commit-ments of moral belief, principle, or ideology, but (at best) in their setting-up of exploratory interlocution between *conflicting* ethical claims. The fine-tuning, the attention, and the judgment of such ethical reflection, all lie in a practical discernment that is at once mediation between such claims (which entail principles) and a concern with the particulars in which they have their meaning.

The ethical interest of imaginative literature is not then, as often implied, in ethical propositions that can be gleaned from it. It lies in the spirit, the *ethos* or character of a literary work's creative thinking, which involves both the sense of life that is expressed by the work as a whole[16] and, implicit in that, the practical discernment which mediates between, and explores, the clashes of moral value it embodies. The canonical works are interesting, in other words, not as embodiments of paraphrasable truth or wisdom about human nature, but as expressions of certain modes of intelligence, thought, and feeling. That is, as an Aristotelian would say, the ethical significance of a creative work lies in the sense of human flourishing, of living well (or otherwise), made manifest to us, not simply by its 'themes', but by the work as a whole.

One important outcome of this conception of ethics is that several critics have begun to turn back on criticism itself, especially post-structuralism, asking the question, what character, ethos, sense of life, does this work manifest? The reason for asking this question about post-structuralism may be obvious enough. It is the feeling well expressed by Rorty when he says that the 'serious objections to textualism [that is, post-structuralism] ... are not epistemological but moral'.[17] In his pragmatist fondness for metaphors of financial pay-off, Rorty says that the private intellectual stimulus achieved by figures like Nietzsche, Nabokov, Bloom, and Foucault in their strong misreadings or 'inhumanism' 'is purchased at the price of... separation from [their] fellow-humans'.[18] This is one way of putting the issue, though it does not take into account the answer that most of these figures would give – that they have gone beyond the old, coercive view of morality that Rorty's statement implies. Some would say that they have gone beyond ethics altogether – seeing any morality (for reasons given above) as ideologically compromised. Foucault, for instance, repeatedly denied, not wholly convincingly, that his work implied a positive commitment to an ethic of liberation, given that it everywhere pointed to the subtle enslavements of people by power.[19]

As we have seen, critics have started to scrutinise such denials and to read, against the grain of the insistence that the human has been replaced by the linguistic, the human ethos that genealogy or deconstruction none the less imply. Tobin Siebers, for example, in his strong ethical misreading of Foucault, discovers that Foucault's displacement of the self implies a stoical view of human character which privileges ascetical self-mastery.[20] This is very close to the privileged 'negative vision of existence' found by Murray Krieger in his deconstructions of the work of de Man and Hillis Miller.[21] Both Krieger and Siebers come to the conclusion that it is impossible to remain purely on the level of the linguistic or the semiotic. Claims of ethical neutrality, like those of political neutrality, are simply self-delusive. As Siebers says: 'Whether we assert a theory of the self or deny it, we remain within the sphere of ethics.'[22] It seems that the arguments of philosophers such as Charles Taylor that the ethical sphere is inescapable are beginning to work their way into literary discourse.

Once it is granted that the sphere of ethics is inescapable, a quite new picture of post-structuralism begins to open up. According to Siebers, the ethos of Foucault, de Man, and Hillis Miller is ultimately Romantic. The aspiration to be purely formal, semiotic, and linguistic amounts to a wish to be innocent of the entanglements of everyday reality. At the same time, Siebers notes in Foucault, Derrida, and de Man an attempt to secure a specious innocence by identifying with victims and outcasts, which depends on a

Rousseauistic belief that the marginal – as opposed to those of us who are duped by belonging – have privileged insight. Siebers finds something similar in the notorious linguistic difficulty of this criticism, which shrouds itself in an esoteric vocabulary to evade the difficulties of actual choices in the real world.[23] The burden of Siebers' argument (like Krieger's) is that, by reading this criticism against the grain of its own assumptions, we reveal its suppressed ethical implications, in short its ethical unconscious.

In another recent book, *Canons and Consequences: Reflections on the Ethical Force of Imaginative Ideals*, Charles Altieri takes this project further by examining the ethical implications of pedagogies based on deconstruction and New Historicism. He points out not only the impoverished evaluative vocabularies that these offer, but suggests that a pedagogy centred on the demystification of the canon (such as that defended by Robert Scholes in *Textual Power: Literary Theory and the Teaching of English*,) encourages an unearned sense of superiority in those who arraign the literature of the past for its ideological blindnesses. These, I believe, are extremely important points. Altieri then proceeds pragmatically to accept the inevitable circularity of canon-formation and, wasting no time chasing after mythical non-circular arguments, moves to the all-important issue of practical consequences. When any sense of the ethical arguments for the canon are lost, Altieri says, one important pay-off is that we lose what he calls the 'contrastive grammar' these works present to our own ethos and sense of human flourishing. The lack of such a grammar leaves the door open to an attenuated sense of what is humanly possible, and so to a narrow, narcissistic circle of values. Against the neo-Marxist claim that the canon tends to reflect the self-interest of a certain class, Altieri points out aptly that such a notion of interest is charac-teristically narrow, and that what is in our self-interest in the widest sense is precisely that ethos provided by the canonical works. There are things in *Canons and Consequences* to disagree with, such as Altieri's idea that we need to revere texts *as opposed* to demystifying them. As I shall argue, we need constantly to be doing both. Despite this, his pragmatist reading of the consequences of literary theories centred on demystification throws up significant insights.

For my purposes, the crucial point is that the erosion of the canon, or its retention simply as grist for the mill of demystification, has serious ethical consequences. One is that we close off any sense of being in what Hans-Georg Gadamer calls a 'conversation' with a text within our tradition, such that the (tradition-constituted) preconceptions with which we address it are answered by its assertion of 'its own truth' against those preconceptions.[24] Understanding of literary works is necessarily dialogic: they have the power *to read us* as we perform our various moves in reading them. Losing any sense of that is tantamount to encouraging self-unseeingness (to bend a phrase of Thomas Hardy's), or certain forms of what I am here calling 'the ethical unconscious'. What needs to be added to Altieri's argument is the notion that these works have got there before us by anticipating, so to speak, the consequences of being unconscious of precisely the ethical reflectiveness they themselves offer us. These consequences are, among other things, represented in the canonical works, as well as being contrastively present in their own ethos as works.

As an example, we could do worse than return to Mr Casaubon of *Middlemarch*, whose great unwritten work, the 'Key to All Mythologies', makes all the myths of all the past civilisations grist for its demythologising mill. He is a study of the ethical implications of what I have earlier called 'the will-to-master-narrative'. For George Eliot, one important question is, what sort of human flourishing (or lack of it) is implied in Casaubon's aspiration for theoretical mastery of all the narratives of the past? What sort of character theorises as he does?

But Mr Casaubon's theory of the elements which made the seed of all tradition was not likely to bruise itself unawares against discoveries: it floated among flexible conjectures no more solid than those etymologies which seemed strong because of likeness in sound, until it was shown that likeness in sound made them impossible: it was a method of interpretation which was not tested by the necessity of forming anything which had sharper collisions than an elaborate notion of Gog and Magog: it was as free from interruption as a plan for threading the stars together. (p. 520)

Clearly George Eliot knew a thing or two about the possible excesses of theory. '[F]loated among flexible conjectures', 'not tested by the necessity of anything which had sharper collisions', 'free from interruption as a plan for threading the stars together' – these are not formulations that will be lost on anyone who has read widely in the literary theory of the last twenty years. The novel is also very much alert to, not merely these inclinations of a certain sort of theorising mind, but what such a mind *signifies* ethically. Specifically in this case Edward Casaubon's decidedly monological hermeneutics comes from an at once proud and fearful state of mind: his narcissism is of the infantile sort that is terrified of 'collisions' with actuality because it might discover that he does not possess the Key to All Mythologies, that he is not the centre of the universe. In short, Casaubon's way of theorising, his will-to-master-narrative, is part of what the novel analyses (not wholly satisfactorily) as his 'egoism'. I am not suggesting that this sort of theorising is *only* or *always* (or even often) a product of 'egoism'. I am suggesting firstly that imaginative literature has meditated much and extraordinarily shrewdly on that activity of reading and thinking *about it* we call literary theory; and secondly that any tendency to play down the importance of *its* meditations will rob us of important insights about the often obscured ethical significance of theory (and a great deal else). Theory, in short, needs imaginative literature, at the very least as much as literature needs theory, and any tendency for one to bury the other should be viewed with great suspicion. As the case of Casaubon shows, theory sometimes has good reason not to want to know about its moral clay feet.

On the other hand, to be fair to literary theory, one has to say that the best of it has long been aware of the point I am making. Barbara Johnson, for example, in introducing a book ten years ago, said that theory 'is here often the straight man whose precarious rectitude and hidden risibility, passion and pathos are precisely what literature has somehow already foreseen'.[25] Theory as risible straight man whose 'passion and pathos' are 'hidden' until literature points them up – all that gets very close to the heart of the matter. The comic and the straight man need each other, they are a double act. But unfortunately other theorists have not been quite so sensible of this point as Barbara Johnson, which is why a defence of the continuing importance of the literary canon as theory's necessary Other is continually being called for. Plainly, a great deal of theory does not want to be a double act; it seems to want the limelight all to itself.

CHAPTER 3

The judgmental unconscious

As the case of Edward Casaubon reminds us, imaginative literature has been much preoccupied with forms of ethical unconsciousness: Casaubon is not conscious of his narcissism in the way in which the novel makes us aware of it. Specifically he is never aware of how common it is, according to the novel, to imagine that we are uniquely important in the universe. In this, Casaubon is not 'different' as he imagines, but a certain *kind* of person, with much in common, for instance, with Lydgate, Bulstrode, and, at first, Dorothea Brooke. All of these have in common the fact that they imagine themselves morally better, each in his or her unique way, than the rest of humanity. According to the novel, they are never more *like* the rest of humanity than in their tendency to judge other people's moral shortcomings more or less censoriously. The ordinary Middlemarchers are not slow to respond in the same measure, for example, judgmentally calling Bulstrode a 'Pharisee' – thus mirroring the very judgmentalism they reject in him. But, according to George Eliot, judgmentalism is almost ubiquitous; we face it at every turn in the moral life. As she says, so inimitably, 'for the majority of us scarcely see the faultiness of our own conduct more than the faultiness of our own arguments, or the dullness of our own jokes' (p. 217). If Bulstrode is a so-called 'Pharisee', then so, allegedly, are the majority of us. This tendency to be blind to the signs in ourselves of the very failings we see in others I am calling the 'judgmental unconscious'.

The term 'Pharisee' should remind us that one classic source of thought about the judgmental unconscious is the New Testament, which is never far from the moral thinking of such novels as *Middlemarch*, *Anna Karenina*, and *Lady Chatterley's Lover*. Most relevant of all to these novels is the story of the woman taken in adultery.

43

1. Jesus went unto the mount of Olives.
2. And early in the morning he came again into the temple, and all the people came unto him; and he sat down, and taught them.
3. And the scribes and Pharisees brought unto him a woman taken in adultery; and when they had set her in the midst,
4. They say unto him, Master, this woman was taken in adultery, in the very act.
5. Now Moses in the law commanded us, that such should be stoned: but what sayest thou?
6. This they said, tempting him, that they might have to accuse him. But Jesus stooped down, and with his finger wrote on the ground, as though he heard them not.
7. So when they continued asking him, he lifted up himself, and said unto them, He that is without sin among you, let him first cast a stone at her.
8. And again he stooped down, and wrote on the ground.
9. And they which heard it, being convicted by their own conscience, went out one by one, beginning at the eldest, even unto the last: and Jesus was left alone, and the woman standing in the midst.
10. When Jesus had lifted up himself, and saw none but the woman, he said unto her, Woman, where are those thine accusers? hath no man condemned thee?
11. She said, No man, Lord. And Jesus said unto her, Neither do I condemn thee: go, and sin no more. (John 8, 1–11)[1]

I do not think most of us can read that story any more without feeling the pull of a long and painful history that, one way or another, threatens to draw any reading into its own lines of force. The theological and ecclesiological designs of the Pharisees as they are represented in the text are matched by the theological and ecclesiological designs of the writer who represented them in that particular way. They are ever trapped in the text in their attempted entrapments, condemned in their condemnations, indicted as they indict. As one pole against which the writer is defining his faith, the Pharisees specifically are not portrayed as identified with the traditions of God's love, mercy and forgiveness inscribed in the Old Testament and on which Jesus is continually drawing. There is a plausible argument to be made that Jesus' writing on the ground is a means of reminding them of these very traditions of anti-judgmentalism and anti-legalism within Judaism itself.[2] But representative and historical figures the New Testament Pharisees certainly are not.

None the less, as many nineteenth-century novels show, the story of the woman taken in adultery remains an important part of the Judeo-Christian ethical tradition, and as much a part of the literary canon of the West as most of the ancient classics. It is as ethical and literary text that I wish to consider it, and specifically as the *locus classicus* of judgmentalism.

This is represented, first of all, in the moralistic, reproving, and self-righteous nature of the Pharisees' attitude to the woman. The Pharisee of the story, it might be noted, is in fact the very image of the moralist as he or she is usually conceived in the popular imagination (and not just there). It might also be noted that the Pharisees' judgmentalism is a rigid adherence to a pre-existing legally derived moral code, a system of clear-cut categories: adultery is wrong, the woman is a sinner. They, by implication, are in the right; they are the righteous, the Law-followers. Which means that this code is one of simple and rigid binary differences: good versus evil, right versus wrong. They are within the Law, she is outside, Other, forfeiting her claim to membership of the tribe. Her humanity can therefore be cancelled. In the strongest possible way she is being marginalised, while they affirm their centeredness, their subjectivity, their claim to be the meaning of the moral text. They are also, according to the narrative, power-seeking; they belong to a kind of theocratic New Right trying to trap this revolutionary into open rejection of the Law. In this sense, they are effectively reactionaries, attempting to enforce Judaic solidarity.

I have drawn out these particular features of judgmentalism because the biblical scribes and Pharisees do not only embody the popular caricature, they also fully enflesh Fredric Jameson's conception of ethics (and that of many literary theorists). *Everything Jameson says on the subject is a description of judgmentalism.* Any stress on moral 'difference' (between my goodness and the Other's badness) which swallows up a sense of commonness or continuity between us is not ethics *per se*, it is *judgmental* ethics.

The core of the biblical narrative is this: Jesus' reply forces the woman's accusers to look into their consciences and to admit that they are not simply 'different' from her; they look within themselves and find an element of *similarity* to her, which convinces them that they do not belong to another moral universe at all. This point needs underlining, because Jesus is not simply objecting to 'difference' *per se*; the woman is still guilty of this serious sin, which presumably the Pharisees are not. Nor, *a fortiori*, is Jesus totally transvaluing these differences, such that she, the sinner, is justified, while the Pharisees are condemned. (This, if it is Nietzsche's suggestion, is not happening here.) Jesus is implicitly objecting, once again, to an ethic of difference that obliterates any sense of common humanity. It is this element of commonness, the fact that they are sinners too, that the Pharisees, in the grip of their rigid binary code, appear to have forgotten. Jesus' reply forces them to look within and to recollect two things. First, those traditions within Judaism itself saying that God alone should judge. And secondly the fact that the binary opposition, as the Deconstructionist would say, already exists within themselves: their righteousness already differs from itself.

Judgmental morality, in short, is a form of moral obliviousness. Carl Jung would go further and argue that the Pharisees in this scene are externalising their psychic 'shadow' – that is, the darker side of themselves that resists the moral Law by which they try to live. Jung's point is that they can only silence the accusations of the shadow within by projecting them onto some scapegoat beyond themselves. This process accounts for the often highly 'emotional' and 'obsessive' 'bewailing and cursing a faithless world' so characteristic of the judgmental unconscious in its attempts to hold its distorted vision of things in place.[3] In many cases, according to Jung, the condition is strongly resistant to treatment; as he says in a relevant passage: 'the Pharisee in us will never allow himself to be caught talking to publicans and whores'.[4] The therapeutic aim implied here is to bring the patient to embrace all that he or she is, which must include *both* the binary terms in question, the good and the evil, whatever they are. Along the way Jung makes the very incisive point that intense commitment to any good is fraught with psychic danger: 'In the last resort there is no good that cannot produce evil and no evil that cannot produce good.'[5] This is full of implications for my later argument, because if it is true that, as Charles Taylor says, we define our identities in the 'strong qualitative discriminations' we make,[6] then those identities may be founded on the repression of all that we strongly disvalue in ourselves. (For the novelist, this is the sort of fixed moral identity he or she must be able to set aside in the process of imagining.)[7]

The biblical text does not give a detailed psychological account of what happens within the consciences of the Pharisees. If we were to judge the story by the standards of psychological realism (as we should not), it would have to be said that these Pharisees come around to Jesus' point with remarkably little resistance. What they do show, however, is that the route beyond judgmentalism is by way of fuller self-recognition: by the end of the story they seem to have come to a new sort of awareness. We can call this new awareness empathy or 'vicarious introspection' or, as I think Thomas Nagel might put it, we can say that Jesus' reply opens up an ethical space which is 'intersubjective'. That is, there is a way of recollecting our own subjective lives which is also, by implication, a way of understanding someone else – not simply as an Other, a 'she', but as another subjectivity not altogether discontinuous from our own. Moral philosophers such as Thomas Nagel (and George Eliot) give accounts of moral self-transcendence of an other-regarding kind which seem hardly conceivable if, like Jameson, you focus too narrowly on the 'inevitable and inescapable centeredness of every individual subject'. Inescapable centeredness does not necessarily involve a prison-house of self-centeredness.

On the other hand, Jameson is certainly right if he is implying that any ethical belief will tend to structure the world into hierarchies of binary difference. But then, as Jung's point about good and evil implied, that is true for any sort of belief system, be it ethical, religious, or political. It is as true of Marxism or feminism as it is of any theological creed: all can degenerate into dividing the world rigidly into sheep and goats. And all can prosecute the business of searching out the goats, and all the secret ideological hiding-places of goatism, with puritanical self-righteousness. As we see so often, what begins as a just project for the proper political recognition of difference can easily tip over into a zealous intolerance of it. What otherwise is the meaning of the phrase 'ideologically correct'? And so I would argue that the biblical narrative remains ethically il-luminating here and now. After all the airing it has had, which perhaps ought to have bleached it utterly, it still has the power to read us. Well, anyway, let him or her who is entirely without judgmentalism make the first denial.

One point needs to be underlined: the element of 'commonality' or 'continuity' between the Pharisees and the woman, and, by implication between them and us as we are similarly convicted by our consciences, is not based on any essentialist or universalist notion of

'conscience' or of human nature. Nor are any of these logically
entailed in my account. This is a crucial point for the reinstatement
of ethical criticism, because all too often these are the grounds on
which it is dismissed. Rorty's account of Trilling and Abrams is
characteristic:

> Implicit in this remark is the moral outlook which Abrams shares with
> Trilling: the view that, in the end, when all the intellectuals have done all
> their tricks, morality remains widely shared and available to reflection –
> something capable of being discovered rather than created, because already
> implicit in the common consciousness of everyone. It is this Kantian
> conviction ... [8]

The gospel story certainly depends on *some sort* of 'common
consciousness' between Jesus and the awakened Pharisees and, by
extension, between them and us. But it does not depend either on the
common consciousness *of everyone*, nor, unless some strange time-warp
is involved, does the biblical narrative depend on Kant.[9] All that
needs to be said is *that this sort of common consciousness is possessed by some
who belong to an ethical tradition of which this biblical narrative is a significant
part*. The biblical story does not, in other words, imply some
transhistorical authentic self for which a metaphysical argument is
entailed. It is perfectly compatible, as is my argument, with the
possibility that the common consciousness of Jesus, the awakened
Pharisees, and us is constituted by the ethical tradition itself of which
we are all in some sense part. As I have said, my argument assumes
the cultural construction of such a consciousness.

   Nor does my argument about the continuing ethical relevance of
the biblical narrative, and the common consciousness we share with
the gospel writer and the represented Pharisees, depend on an
ahistorical notion of timeless moral wisdom which suppresses the vast
historical differences between the Pharisees and us.[10] Plainly, there is
an enormous gulf between the metaphorical kind of stone-casting we
in present-day Western societies are more characteristically inclined
to and the Pharisees' literal sort. Even so, it is worth noting that this
literal sort is not unknown in some contemporary societies, and that
most of us, here and now, find it morally repugnant. And that
repugnance in turn reminds us precisely why the idea of a
transhistorical and transcultural human conscience is so implausible.
Something significant has happened between the ancient world and
ourselves – and between ourselves and the values that prevail today
elsewhere in the world.

I would argue that one significant part of that 'something' is the ethical tradition containing *the biblical story itself*. That is, one reason why Western societies have on the whole tended to move away from capital punishment is a deep suspicion of precisely the attitude of judgmental self-righteousness and hypocritical superiority it seems to involve. As is often pointed out, while the specifically religious grip of Judeo-Christianity weakens, its secularised ethical beliefs come to express themselves ever more powerfully as forms of liberal and radical conscience.[11] Which is another way of explaining why biblical passages such as this one retain their force. As Barbara Herrnstein Smith would say, if we find this canonical story ethically illuminating it is because we are in part constituted by it. This story, and others like it, have deeply informed European culture in incalculably pervasive ways. Which might explain why we are susceptible to it in ways in which other cultures may not be – why, for instance, we might not expect Jesus' sort of success were we to repeat his words in similar circumstances in some parts of the contemporary world, or even much closer to home.

But, if this is so, if our culture is in part constituted by this and other biblical narratives, is there not some circularity involved in praising its power to illuminate the moral life – as if there were some objective feature *in it* to which this power is being attributed? Is not the 'power' simply the confirmation of a deep prejudice in favour of our own tradition, and is not this, as Barabara Herrnstein Smith says, 'self-privileging'? That is, the story subtly confirms our 'centered-ness' as we sit in judgment with an even more refined judgmental binary superiority on the Pharisees of the past and on the Islamic world of today. In short, is not any ethical valuing of the gospel narrative on my part simply a reflex of my European cultural ethnocentricity, an ideological product of my unconscious 'white-manism'? And so, is not my defence of this canonical story ultimately of a piece with European imperialism, which has been so constant and disastrous a theme of our culture in its contacts with Africa, the Middle East, and Indo-China?

This is a plausible argument, but there are some telling answers to it. For a start, it can be pointed out that, as Richard Rorty says, no non-circular justification of our values and practices is possible; we cannot get out of the circle of making 'one feature of our culture look good by citing still another, or comparing our culture invidiously with others by reference to our own standards'.[12] That is, there is no real force in pointing out that something we value is 'self-privileging'. The mistake of those who use this term is to imply that there is no alternative between a metaphysically grounded value and pure arbitrary preference – which means that they are still shackled to the alternatives Kant posited. There is no discourse, scientific, ethical, religious, political or 'purely semiotic', that does not 'privilege' some value or other. The only question for the pragmatist is, how valuable is the value *vis à vis* all the alternatives in which we might invest?

The alternatives in this case are whether we should accept the political valuations of many contemporary literary theorists and either throw out the canonical narrative as ideologically treacherous or keep it as an example of the operation of conservative ideology. Or else we keep the story for its ethical value.

This is precisely where it is important to have the actual story before us, because whatever dangers there might be in valuing the insight this story contains, and thus becoming more and more subtly judgmental oneself *vis à vis* other cultures, two important things can be said. The first is that the story remains *a permanent criticism* of this tendency, no matter how subtle and inward is the temptation to divide the world into judgmental binary oppositions. The second is that it contains *a permanent injunction to deconstruct these very oppositions*, to find them *both* already operant within oneself, and so to find common ground with those who would otherwise appear to us simply as Other. In other words, the tendency of this narrative is to work against 'our inevitable centeredness' and so against our inevitable ethnocentricity.

And this, to my mind, is the crucial point of the cost-benefit analysis: which is to see that the ethnocentricity which is our culture's starting-point has, for all its dangers, considerable countervailing strengths – not the least significant of which is a long ethical tradition of self-reflection precisely on the tendency to self-righteous su-periority. As Rorty says, ours is the 'we' of those 'who have been brought up to distrust ethnocentrism'.[13] It is a measure of the strength of this very distrust, that we rightly wish to demystify everywhere the subtle underpinnings of ethnocentrism, and to extirpate anything complacent, self-congratulatory, or remotely judgmental in our attitudes towards any other *ethnos*. Which is paradoxically a crucial point in favour of our own *ethnos* – the one that ambiguously produced not only slavery and imperialism, but also anti-slavery movements, anti-racism, Marxism, feminism, de-construction and New Historicism.

But then none of these emerged, any more than European imperialism itself did, *ex nihilo*. As Michael Walzer shows in his persuasive *Exodus and Revolution*, biblical narratives have long served as models and sources of revolutionary inspiration. That is, radical political consciousness is as much culturally and historically consti-tuted as conservatism – and it has its roots too in the canonical stories, *including this one*. It is more plausible to see this as a radical story, standing in permanent opposition to reactionary legalism and puritanical superiority, than it is to see its religious and ethical focus as a production of conservative ideology. Its thrust, especially as it was taken up in the nineteenth century, was to unmask the subtle hypocrisies underlying the individualistic *laissez-faire* ideology of men like Bulstrode, Murdstone, and Bounderby, who were encouraged to believe that their devotion to the ethic of self-help elevated them spiritually (as well as materially) above other men. The nineteenth-century 'Pharisee' was almost inevitably a capitalist.

Why should we persist in seeing the canon simply as the repository of conservative values – as if this is all 'traditional values' could be? We only assume otherwise because we are blinkered by arguments such as this by Barbara Herrnstein Smith:

since those with cultural power tend to be members of socially, economically, and politically established classes (or to serve them and identify their own interests with theirs), the texts that survive will tend to be those that appear to reflect and reinforce establishment ideologies. However much canonical works may be seen to 'question' secular vanities such as wealth, social position, and political power, 'remind' their readers of more elevated values and virtues, and oblige them to 'confront' such hard truths and harsh realities as their own mortality and the hidden grief of obscure people, they would not be found to please long and well if they were seen *radically* to undercut establishment interests or *effectively* to subvert the ideologies that support them.[14]

This sort of argument has been repeated so often in the 1980s that it has come to seem persuasive, until we notice the dubious premises it depends on. Why, for example, would the ideological subversiveness of canonical texts need to be so overt as to be 'seen' as such, when it is allowed that ruling-class ideology operates quite unseen? Why not radical ideology too? The reason this possibility is not entertained is the assumption that the politically powerful classes *could not* have allowed it simply because it opposed their interests. This has come to have the force of an axiom these days, but it assumes several dubious and unargued propositions, such as that these interests are simple and unambiguous, and that people always judge and act in accordance with this narrow conception of interest. Once you question these assumptions, the notion that the canon is *necessarily and unambiguously conservative* shows itself for what it is, a piece of untested belief. Why should we not assume that the radical tradition has its roots in the canon too?

There would be great loss then, not least to radical political criticism if, *per impossibile* (given its religious status), this little biblical narrative were either to disappear or to become mere fodder for ideological demystification. And this would be a loss, not because the story gives us ethical propositions to live by, or models or ideals to imitate, but because it creatively presents and probes a certain very common form of moral constrictedness. In Aristotelian terms, the story portrays judgmentalism as a severely limited answer to the question 'How to live well?'.

CHAPTER 4

The libidinal unconscious

If judgmentalism is a mode of consciousness that suppresses awareness of commonality, then there is another form of ethical unconsciousness that so stresses commonality as to suppress difference. Where the first is intent on seeing the world entirely in terms of sheep and goats, the other so universalises moral discourse as to lose sight of the dictum of Blake's Hell that 'One Law for the lion & Ox is Oppression.' The writer who made us most distinctly aware of this oppression was Nietzsche, who portrays Christianity as the conspiracy of the oxen to subdue the lions. For him, the attempt of Christianity and Kant to yoke us all to 'One Law' (as if our commonness were more fundamental than our differences) is the work of ox-like resentment. The 'Nietzschean' side of Blake's metaphor is that if the lion submits to the 'One Law' he will be violating his own nature, which is not to bear the yoke.[1] Nietzsche's injunction to the lion is to live as a lion needs to live, and not to be troubled that this differs from the lives of the oxen.

One reason for the current appeal of Aristotle's way of organising ethics around the question 'How to live well?' is that this question is broad enough to include much more than the 'One Law' of Kant and of traditional Christian morality. Significantly, it can include within ethics the Romantic-expressivist self-responsibility in Nietzsche's implied injunction to the lion to live as a lion needs to live. As is well known since Freud, the problem with this injunction is that the voice of the 'One Law' has entered individual consciousness early as a harsh super-ego, which makes it seem dangerous for us to follow the law of our own individual need or desire. It is therefore often safer to forget difference, need and desire altogether. This particular form of forgetting, as it is so closely associated in our minds with Freud, might as well be termed 'the libidinal unconscious'.

The libidinal unconscious is a form of *ethical* unconsciousness

because, like judgmentalism, it involves a constricted mode of being
alive. Since the Romantics, one important answer to the question
'How should one live?' has been characteristically expressed in
organic metaphors: courageously foster the unique unfolding of your
own being. Which also implies the price to be paid for the failure to
do so: dying in the bud, withering on the vine. As the mountain
climber George Mallory says, in a passage quoted by Cora Diamond:
'To refuse the adventure is to run the risk of drying up like a pea in
its shell. Mountaineers, then, take opportunities to climb mountains
because they offer adventure necessary to them.'[2] The risk of
individuals refusing the adventure necessary to them and of drying
up therefore like a pea in its shell is a great imaginative focus of the
post-Romantic period.

It is a central preoccupation for Lawrence; and (perhaps less
obviously) just as important for the Tolstoy of *Anna Karenina*. While
no reader is likely to miss the force of 'Vengeance is mine and I will
repay' in the working out of Anna's destruction, remarkably few
seem to notice the careful counterpointing which gives that terrible
process its tragic, rather than judgmental, significance. For instance,
set against Anna is Levin's older half-brother, Koznyshev, an
intellectual who is full of good will and public spirit, but is one of
those (so Levin finds) who 'were not led by an impulse of the
heart to care for the public good, but had reasoned out in their
minds that it was the right thing to take interest in public affairs,
and consequently took interest in them.'[3] Levin's own antipathy
towards all public affairs is a bias we are alerted to, yet there can
be no doubt that Koznyshev's purely rational kind of 'interest'
in political causes is portrayed as over-mentalised. It is the
symptom of some deeper 'lack' – 'not a lack of kindly honesty and
noble desires and tastes but a lack of the vital force, of what is called
heart, of the impulse which drives a man to choose some one out of
all the innumerable paths of life and to care for that one only'
(p. 259).

Subsequent events work out what it means to be kind, noble, and
unimpeachably moral in the Kantian sense, but to lack that 'vital
force' which drives characters like Anna, Kitty, and Levin to choose
the paths that they individually must choose and to care for those
only. The novel makes it clear that Koznyshev's individual path
opens up before him in the wood on Levin's estate when he and
Varenka are brought together over the mushrooms:

Now or never was the moment for his declaration – Koznyshev felt that, too. Everything about Varenka, her expression, the flushed cheeks and downcast eyes, betrayed painful suspense. He saw it and felt sorry for her. He even felt that to keep silent now would be to wrong her. He quickly ran over in his mind all the arguments in support of his decision. He even repeated to himself the words in which he had intended to put his offer, but instead of those words some perverse reflection caused him to ask:

'What is the difference between a white boletus and a birch mushroom?'

Varenka's lips trembled with agitation as she replied:

'There's hardly any difference in the top part, but the stalks are different.'

And as soon as these words were out of her mouth, both he and she understood that it was over, that what was to have been said would not be said; and their excitation, having reached its climax, began to subside.

'The stalk of a birch mushroom makes one think of a beard on a dark man's face who has not shaved for a couple of days,' Koznyshev remarked, speaking quite calmly now.

'Yes, that's true,' answered Varenka with a smile, and instinctively they changed their course and began walking towards the children. Varenka felt sore and ashamed, but at the same time was conscious of a sense of relief.

When Koznyshev got home and reviewed all his arguments, he found that his first decision had been a mistaken one. He could not be untrue to the memory of Marie. (pp. 594–5)

This painful tragi-comic scene already begins to suggest a consequent waste of human possibilities (their 'changed' course takes them 'towards the children'). The novel makes clear all they each want and admire in the other, which has been quite adequately represented in their previous thoughts and reasonings. And yet when it comes to the decisive moment for Koznyshev to make his offer, 'some perverse reflection' intervenes and deflects him irreversibly away from his intended words. Koznyshev's unconscious is terrified of the risks involved and speaks for him, which more or less echoes the sentence that escapes from Varenka a little earlier, 'against her will, and as if by accident.' Yet for all the seeming accidentalness and slippage of these crucial sentences, the scene leaves us in no doubt that theirs is a subtly interactive evasion of responsibility, in which the whole overmentalised tenor of these two 'noble' lives has disposed them to flee from the risks even of a desirable marriage to the childlike safety of singleness. That this has been an evasion for both of them is made clear firstly in 'the sense of relief' yet the troubling shame Varenka feels afterwards, and above all in Koznyshev's belated discovery that 'he could not be untrue to the memory' of his 'tragic' first love, Marie.

Not only is Koznyshev's return to the memory of Marie a rationalisation of his sense of failure, it also might remind us of Freud's point about the narcissistic origins of 'compassion'. In most respects, there is not much that Tolstoy could have learned from Freud – or from D. H. Lawrence, who insisted (often reductively) that passionate public altruism or idealism was usually a mask for a private sense of defeat. The silence and scorn that later greet Koznyshev's ambitious *magnum opus Sketch of a Survey of the Principles and Forms of Government in Europe and Russia* reinforce something the novel explores time and again: work which is rationalisation or compensation for a private sense of defeat often comes to nothing, however much conscious energy, ability, and good will are thrown into it. But Koznyshev soon seems to recover from his literary disappointment too, giving himself just as generously to the Pan-Slavic movement, convincing himself 'that it was a cause destined to assume vast dimensions and mark an epoch in the history of Russia'. The inflated rhetoric tells us that this too is compensation: 'He threw himself heart and soul into the service of this great cause, and forgot to think about his book' (p. 806). In *Anna Karenina*, anyone compelled to forget some important unrealised need or desire will be living a circumscribed form of life.

CHAPTER 5

Dynamic interrelatedness: or, the novel walking away with the nail

In their need to forget what they cannot, without some degree of psychic distortion, forget, Anna Karenina and Koznyshev are unexpectedly alike. It is this which links the seemingly unlinkable scene of Anna's death (7,31) with the one narrating Koznyshev's literary failure, which immediately follows it (8,1). On the other hand, what they are struggling to forget is so different as hardly to bear comparison. In Anna's case, it is her son, her husband, and that social, spiritual, and moral life which have become impossible in her life with Vronsky. The tragic core of Anna's case is that, in following the path that she individually had to follow, she had to violate the 'One Law' of Judeo-Christianity which demands that we treat all others as morally equivalent to, and continuous with, ourselves. Had that law held sway for her, she could not have left Karenin. Koznyshev, as I have argued, fails before the moral imperative Anna does follow. Anna and Koznyshev might be taken schematically to illustrate failure before two different sorts of moral demands that, as the novel suggests, are incommensurable and only sometimes reconcilable.

On another level, these two different sorts of moral demand have their counterparts in the ethical beliefs, values, and languages of novelists themselves. As Charles Taylor argues, there is a *necessary* tension between the two sorts: 'we are and cannot but be on both sides of the great intramural moral disputes' of our culture.[1] This means that the novelist only apparently resolves the tension by attempting to suppress one sort of moral claim in the interests of the other. The drive to resolve all conflicts in this way is nothing else but a will-to-master-narrative, and where this arises novelists themselves fall into one or other form of unconsciousness outlined here as the judgmental and the libidinal unconscious. The art becomes schematic, shallow, sentimental, evasive, insistent, or non-exploratory.

These traditional 'thick' terms of negative judgment are responses to one or other form of unconsciousness in the writing itself. On the other hand, where the art gives fullest recognition to the *necessity* of both sorts of moral demand, we will intuitively find it deep, balanced, and impersonal.

In saying this I find myself in broad agreement with those moral philosophers who have recently come to imaginative literature, especially the novel, partly because it exemplifies the heterogeneity and the non-commensurability of the basic human goods and values. Here again Martha Nussbaum's work on Aristotle, Greek tragedy, and Henry James has been of great importance. Nussbaum has argued that whereas conventional philosophical and theoretical discourse has generally tended to work towards single self-consistent accounts of values as ultimately commensurable, literature, working from concretely imagined, context-embedded situations, tends to work by the exploratory interrelating of conflicting moral perspectives.[2] As Nussbaum says, it is Aristotle's distinction to reject the metric of the single overarching Good, which makes him preferable not only to Plato, but to Kant and the Utilitarians, whose preference for the single metric lends itself to algorithms of decision-making. (Indeed, as Charles Taylor argues, there are grounds for thinking that, in the case of utilitarianism, it was chiefly the possibility of algorithmic validation that made the ethic appealing in the first place.[3]) At the same time, it is, as Nussbaum argues, only possible to have tragedy when the important goods can be in mutual conflict. We can only come to terms with Sophocles, Shakespeare or Tolstoy if we understand that qualitatively different fundamental commitments of ours can be incompatible, and that forgoing one or the other may bring irredeemable loss.

Richard Rorty, in the introduction to *Contingency, Irony, and Solidarity*, comes near my theme when he talks about the impossibility of giving a unified account, at the level of theory, of the various ethical languages, beliefs, and values that command our allegiance:

If we could bring ourselves to accept the fact that no theory about the nature of Man or Society or Rationality, or anything else, is going to synthesize Nietzsche with Marx or Heidegger with Habermas, we could begin to think of the relation between writers on autonomy and writers on justice as being like the relations between two kinds of tools – as little in need of synthesis as are paintbrushes and crowbars. One sort of writer lets us realize that the social virtues are not the only virtues, that some people have actually succeeded in re-creating themselves. We thereby become aware of our own half-articulate need to become a new person, one whom we as yet lack words to describe. The other sort reminds us of the failure of our institutions and practices to live up to the convictions to which we are already committed by the public, shared vocabulary we use in daily life. The one tells us that we need not speak only the language of the tribe, that we may find our own words, that we may have a responsibility to ourselves to find them. The other tells us that that responsibility is not the only one we have. Both are right, but there is no way to make both speak a single language.

This book tries to show how things look if we drop the demand for a theory which unifies the public and the private, and are content to treat the demands of self-creation and of human solidarity as equally valid, yet forever incommensurable.[4]

There are things here with which I differ. Rorty gives no hint, for example, that these different sorts of demands might also conflict on certain occasions, and so turn out not merely to be incommensurable, but also mutually antagonistic and even incompatible. And, like S. L. Goldberg, I see response to an ethical demand as much more than a matter of adopting and living out the implications of an ethical 'vocabulary', however deeply such vocabularies may be implicated in the process.[5] Moreover the terms 'public' and 'private' conceptualise the problems in an unhelpful way, I believe, as both of Rorty's binary terms can have either public or private dimensions. But where he talks of two forever incommensurable responsibilities, one to our own self-creation and the other to human solidarity, he is charting a conceptual course similar to the one on which I am presently embarking. It is similar also in that Rorty sees literary criticism as paradigmatic for post-Philosophical moral inquiry, not because it can offer a unified theory of the moral life or a univocal canon from which we can deduce moral universals, but precisely because it foregrounds the impossibility of these projects. In placing books in the contexts of other books, we are 'thus in a better position not to get trapped in the vocabulary of any single book'. The important thing is the process of working towards ever-greater dialectical inclusiveness, such that we 'are able to admire both Blake and Arnold, both Nietzsche and Mill, both Marx and Baudelaire, both Trotsky and Eliot, both Nabokov and Orwell'.[6] While I would not myself have chosen these examples, I find Rorty's terms here aptly describe the exploratory dialectic on which I am setting out with George Eliot, Tolstoy and Lawrence, who pose the big and hard ethical questions in such disparate terms.

The major problem with Rorty's project is that his term 'irony' implies too sketchy and open-ended a view of what literary criticism might be in search of, especially within the internal dialectic of any one given work or author. His model of endless eclectic grazing among authors, improvement though it is on the search for a single 'final vocabulary', hardly gives us a vocabulary in which to account for the power of a Shakespeare or a Tolstoy, who may each have more capacity to help us *keep revising* our moral identities than any suitably disparate list of antithetically disposed lesser figures such as Orwell or Nabokov. While Rorty is right in his liberal instinct to emphasise what is *not* wanted, 'irony' is less helpful a way of gesturing towards what *is* than some well-known passages from the 'canonical' authors themselves. John Keats, for example:

several things dovetailed in my mind, & at once it struck me, what quality went to form a Man of Achievement especially in Literature & which Shakespeare posessed so enormously – I mean *Negative Capability*, that is when man is capable of being in uncertainties, Mysteries, doubts, without any irritable reaching after fact & reason – Coleridge, for instance, would let go by a fine isolated verisimilitude caught from the Penetralium of mystery, from being incapable of remaining content with half knowledge.[7]

This passage helps to remind us that, for all that is distinctive about Shakespeare, his achievement does not finally lie in giving us what Keats calls 'fact', 'reason', and 'knowledge', and we might want to call insights or affirmations. His greatness, his 'impersonality' (to use a still meaningful Romantic term) in his best plays, lies in the fact that, whatever univocal insights or affirmations may be expressed within any work, they are thoroughly *dramatised* – that is, set within a complex interlocutory process such that they are never the 'final vocabulary' of individual works nor, *a fortiori*, of his work as a whole. This is not because such insights and affirmations are 'under erasure' in a post-modernist sense, but because they are always being brought into a searching dialogic interrelationship with other dramatised insights and affirmations.

The critic who has written best about the inter-relational basis of the 'uncertainties, Mysteries, doubts' in great works of imaginative literature is D. H. Lawrence. In his essay 'Morality and the novel' he points to the great *moral* value of the novel in destabilising the fixed sorts of insights that tend to be inscribed in discursive modes such as philosophy, religion, and science:

And morality is that delicate, for ever trembling and changing *balance* between me and my circumambient universe, which precedes and accompanies a true relatedness.

Now here we see the beauty and the great value of the novel. Philosophy, religion, science, they are all of them busy nailing things down, to get a stable equilibrium. Religion, with its nailed-down One God, who says *Thou shalt, Thou shan't*, and hammers home every time; philosophy, with its fixed ideas; science with its 'laws': they, all of them, all the time, want to nail us onto some tree or other.

But the novel, no. The novel is the highest example of subtle interrelatedness that man has discovered. Everything is true in its own time, place, circumstance, and untrue outside of its own place, time, circumstance. If you try to nail anything down, in the novel, either it kills the novel, or the novel gets up and walks away with the nail.

Morality in the novel is the trembling instability of the balance. When the novelist puts his thumb in the scale, to pull down the balance to his own predilection, that is immorality.[8]

According to Lawrence, the reason there are no final truths to be grasped from great works of literature is that in them everything is only true in its own particular context. And, the key point, *that context is ever-dynamically interrelational*. Much of this is familiar enough, while some of it bears new attention. The familiar part is that novelistically (or dramatically) realised truths in a canonical work exist only in a system of interrelations with other such truths, from which they cannot be simply extracted like ideas from a treatise. The less familiar part is Lawrence's insistence on the irreducibly *dynamic* nature of such systems: living works are in some sense ever in the process of reweighing, reassessing, rediscovering, which means ever repositioning, the interrelations between one thing and another. For my purposes, this especially means constantly redefining the relations between one sort of moral obligation and another.

The important implication here is that the only morality that finally matters for a work of art is this rigorous, restlessly dynamic attempt to weigh and to balance the truths, values, senses of obligation and so on realised in the creative process. Conversely the only immorality is the artist's conscious or unconscious will to distort the dynamic balance, or the attempt to make a static one. This is nothing else but the will-to-master-narrative, or the will to fix insights in some final vocabulary. The beauty of Lawrence's account is his insistence that there is a countervailing force or will or imperative in the work of art itself (that is, the impersonal 'tale' rather than the 'teller' – see chapter 10), which, if it is strong enough, is able to get up and walk away with the artist's nail. And, once again, the dynamic implications of getting up and walking away are essential.

There are numerous formulations of this imperative of the tale itself in Lawrence's discursive writings. In one place he will talk about the need for writers to be faithful not to their 'theory of being and knowing', but to their 'living sense of being'. In another place, he will compare artistic creation to the action of drawing a fiddle-bow over a tray of sand, which will create lines that run in directions unplanned and, above all, 'unknown'. This is a central intuition of his: however conscious artists may be of their metaphysical and ethical bearings when they start a work, these 'must always subserve the artistic purpose beyond the artist's conscious aim'.[9] There is a desirable sort of ethical unconsciousness in writing, then, whereby the work itself seems to take over, following the directions it itself must take. Fidelity to this sort of unconsciousness, preparedness to pursue the tides of artistic purpose and 'sympathetic consciousness' into 'places unknown', constitutes the supreme moral imperative for the creator of any literary text.

Nobody has had a firmer grasp on these matters than Lawrence. There is point in affirming this because in recent years some similar and similar-sounding things have become the commonplaces of deconstruction. J. Hillis Miller, for example, in his promisingly entitled book, *The Ethics of Reading: Kant, de Man, Eliot, Trollope, James, and Benjamin*, talks about Henry James' 'anticipation' of what Paul de Man says about reading: 'Reading is an argument… because it has to go against the grain of what one would want to happen in the name of what has to happen.'[10] He goes on to relate this to writing as well, in order to outline the ethical importance of criticism:

'Some latent and gathered force': it is subjection to this power, as to an implacable law, that determines both the ethics of writing and then the ethics of reading that writing. Reading is not of the text as such but of the thing that is latent and gathered within it as a force to determine in me a re-vision of what has been the latent law of the text I read. Re-seeing which is also a re-writing, that form of writing we call criticism or teaching. This re-writing, however, is not mis-reading in the sense of a wanton deviation from the text freely imposed by my subjectivity or by private ideology or by the ideology of the community of readers to which I belong. My subjectivity, those ideologies, are more functions of the text, already inscribed within it, than anything coming from the outside. Criticism as re-writing is truly ethical and affirmative, life-giving, productive, inaugural.[11]

There are continuities between this account of the ethics of reading and writing imaginative literature and the conceptions of impersonality in Keats and Lawrence, which are perhaps hardly surprising in view of the importance of the Romantics and the Victorians for such figures as de Man and Hillis Miller. To this extent, I find myself dialectically drawn to deconstruction, not simply in its lately discovered humanistic face (as in the Miller passage above), but as a critical practice that has insistently resisted the reductiveness of some politicised approaches in recent years by reminding us of the literariness of literature and indeed of all discourse. Deconstruction has significantly kept alive a view of the importance of literature as *subversive* of ideology, meta-narrative, and the seeming solidities of everyday life. As Barbara Johnson, ever the most sane and judicious of such practitioners, says: 'Literature ... is the discourse most preoccupied with the unknown ... What literature often seems to tell us is the consequences of the way in which what is not known is not seen as unknown. It is not, in the final analysis, what you don't know that can or cannot hurt you. It is what you don't *know* you don't know that spins out and entangles "that perpetual error we call life".'[12] A related point is made by Jonathan Culler when he says that, according to de Man, canonical literary texts continue to have a great importance: they are often 'the most powerful demystifiers of the ideologies they have been said to promote'.[13]

Nothing could come closer to my argument here than the notion that the novels I am discussing deserve great respect in so far as they demystify the ideologies, or subvert the ethical binary oppositions, that they are most commonly taken to be advancing. And the obverse is also true: in so far as these novels remain trapped within such ideologies or systems of simple binary opposition, they fail to command our deepest respect and interest. In as much as deconstruction implies similar valuations, I find myself in accord with it.

However, an ethics which confines itself to *reading*, extensive as this may be, does not go far enough, and soon demonstrates its hostility to, or inability to grasp, more substantive ethical interests and responsibilities. As we have seen, Tobin Siebers has made a powerful case against the vein of ethical quietism in deconstruction. In view of the recent de Man revelations, it is one that hardly needs emphasis.

But, in any case, dialectical *rapprochement* between a humanist ethical criticism and deconstruction must be limited while there are such fundamental differences about the status of such things as subjectivity, personhood, agency, and the role of language. While a theoretically self-aware humanism insists, as it ought, that our lives are partly constituted by 'the various languages which articulate for us a background of distinctions of worth',[14] deconstruction has typically portrayed such distinctions as rhetorical figures which, 'lacking a solid base in any *logos*', can only undo themselves before our eyes.[15]

This is why de Man's various pronouncements about ethics, which might seem so closely connected to my argument here, turn out to be so evanescent. Take his famous remarks, for instance, in *Allegories of Reading*:

Allegories are always ethical, the term ethical designating the structural interference of two distinct value systems. In this sense, ethics has nothing to do with the will (thwarted or free) of a subject, nor *a fortiori*, with a relationship between subjects. The ethical category is imperative (i.e., a category rather than a value) to the extent that it is linguistic and not subjective. Morality is a version of the same language aporia that gave rise to such concepts as 'man' or 'love' or 'self', and not the cause or the consequence of such concepts. The passage to an ethical tonality does not result from a transcendental imperative but is the referential (and therefore unreliable) version of a linguistic confusion. Ethics (or, one should say, ethicity) is a discursive mode among others.[16]

Up to a point, the drift of this is reasonable. If by 'allegory' de Man means the text's own implied commentary on the contingency of any one of the value-systems embodied within it, then his definition of the 'ethical' is not so far from what Lawrence calls the 'morality' of a novel. In which case, the 'ethical' dimension of a text will equate to 'the structural interference of two distinct value systems' within it. On the other hand, where de Man distinguishes the 'ethical' radically from the 'moral', the one 'linguistic' the other 'subjective' and interpersonal, he falls (as all deconstruction tends to) into the philosophical trap referred to by Richard Bernstein as the 'grand Either/Or'.[17] The fallacy here consists in accepting a set of false alternatives: in this case, either subjectivity is a transcendental signified or it is just an effect of language; either morality is grounded in such metaphysical and essentialist concepts as 'man', 'love', or 'self' or it is nothing but a 'language aporia'. And in the end, this amounts to saying that either morality is as conceived by Kant or it is nothing substantive at all.[18] This is a profound compliment to Kant, but there are alternatives which it neglects, or which it did not conceive of, such as that new (or revived) pragmatic, anti-foundational strand in moral philosophy which has gained such momentum since de Man's death. His binary oppositions have been bypassed as unprofitable, which is something of a pity since there is much to be said for the 'ethical' as de Man defines it – so long as that is not allowed to refine substantive interpersonal 'morality' out of existence.

The modes of ethical impersonality both represented in, and expressed by, the writing of George Eliot, Tolstoy, and Lawrence, are far in spirit from de Man's and Hillis Miller's work. None is conceivable without working concepts of subjectivity, personhood and moral agency – concepts which (as Charles Taylor argues) it only makes sense to abandon if we accept the 'wildly extreme' caricature of them put forward by some post-structuralist theory.[19] Fortunately, the most interesting Anglo-American moral philosophy of the last twenty years finds itself still compelled to make use of such concepts.

George Eliot's notion of impartiality (chapter 6), for instance, can usefully be compared with an evolving strand of thought that runs through the work of Thomas Nagel from *The Possibility of Altruism* to *The View from Nowhere*. Tolstoy's work (chapter 7) implies both a Christian-Kantian view from nowhere as well as a more Romantic-expressivist conception of impersonality closer to Keats' negative capability. This latter involves a profound psychic disorientation that ends in the casting off of the surface personality with its habitual beliefs and predilections and entry into a world in which everything seems to be unfamiliar and repositioned. Lawrence's best work (chapters 8, 9 and 10) manifests a dialectical 'working through' of the resistances of the surface personality issuing in a dimension I call 'the ideological unknown'. The work of all three, in significant ways, runs away with the nail of authorial will-to-vision.

PART II

Social beings and innocents

The current revival in ethical criticism assumes that living well partly depends on the richness, intelligence, and practical wisdom of the stories we tell ourselves, both individually and as a culture. My inquiry begins from the suggestive fact that some of the richest stories in European culture over the past 150 years or so, many of those most widely regarded as 'canonical', have been about adulterous and/or triangular relationships. This includes novels such as *Wuthering Heights*, *Madame Bovary*, and *Portrait of A Lady*, as well as *Middlemarch*, *Anna Karenina*, and *Women in Love* – to name only a few. Why should this be so? Very few critics have addressed this question of why some particular *sort* of story should so fascinate a culture that it needs to go on retelling it.

Michael Black in *The Literature of Fidelity* implies some answers, but only Tony Tanner in *Adultery and the Novel* explicitly proffers some. For Tanner (who offers a very long list of examples), what distinguishes the treatment of adulterous and triangular relationships in 'the great bourgeois novel', as opposed to the presentation of them in Homer, Shakespeare, and the eighteenth century, is the conflict between two originally biblical perspectives. On the one hand, there is the Law, which upholds marriage as the very cornerstone of bourgeois society and therefore condemns transgression, while on the other there is Sympathy, one of the major cornerstones of Christianity, which teaches understanding and forgiveness. Tanner, who also discusses the woman taken in adultery, sees the essential conflict as that between the Old and New Testaments. His comments on *Anna Karenina* (which he strangely does not discuss at length) are apropos:

What I have called the Old Testament and New Testament methods of confronting adultery may both be found operating within the same book, as I suggest they are in *Anna Karenina*. Indeed it is arguable that it is just such a tension between law and sympathy that holds the great bourgeois novel together, and a severe imbalance in either direction must destroy the form.[1]

There is something in what Tanner says here, but it ignores some important things. First, what he says about the Old and New Testaments is a distortion of the Old especially (unless we adhere to the narrow and partisan view of traditional Christian apologetics). Both the binaries of Law and Sympathy are present in both Testaments. The more accurate distinctions (also found in both Testaments) are those between judgmentalism and awareness of a moral continuum between all lives in a given culture. Secondly, a close study of *Anna Karenina* will show that, while judgmentalism (that is, rigid binary and legalistic condemnation of Anna especially) is represented in the attitudes of certain *characters* in the novel, the novel itself is critical of it and marvellously implies elements of commonality between her and many other characters who are not socially condemned. Thirdly, my point about the recognition of a moral continuum underlines the need for an ethical terminology that is much more precise conceptually than such (admittedly unavoidable) words as 'sympathy', which can mean many different things, including a subtle condescension.

The real conflict in *Anna Karenina* is between a Judeo-Christian moral perspective that centres on the recognition of human continuities, and a Romantic-expressivist one that centres on the ethical demands flowing from the recognition of human uniqueness and difference. Remaining faithful might have been the right course had Anna's husband been Vronsky, but not, according to this perspective, if it is Karenin. As I have already argued, it is the realisation of the incommensurability and mutual antagonism of these two *necessary* perspectives that underlies our judgment that this retelling of the story about adultery has the profoundest moral interest and relevance for us. My whole argument turns on this pivotal point – that both the Judeo-Christian and the Romantic-expressivist perspectives are essential ones for modern selves constituted by these very traditions. Neither can be abandoned or subsumed by the other in an imaginative work, except at the price of the art itself either becoming perceptibly judgmental or evasive, failing to recognise the ethical legitimacy of certain unavoidable human needs and desires.

All five novels I consider in detail in this study (and others besides) are preoccupied with a moral dilemma that is even more precisely defined than the terms 'adultery' and 'triangular' would suggest. It is a dilemma which is thrown up for the first time by the Romantic demand for self-realisation – and which, as Charles Taylor argues, remains one for us because the terms have not changed fundamentally since the Victorian period. (One of his chapters in *Sources of the Self* is called 'Our Victorian Contemporaries'.) In these novels it is the dilemma of a woman,[2] always a woman of some sexual vitality, married to a figure D. H. Lawrence called a 'social being'. In his essay on John Galsworthy, Lawrence outlines a set of binaries he calls 'the abiding antitheses' between two sorts of human beings: on the one hand there is the natural person who 'innocently feels himself altogether within the great living continuum of the universe.' On the other, there is the 'social being':

But if a man loses his mysterious naive assurance, which is his innocence; if he gives *too* much importance to the external objective reality and so collapses in his natural innocent pride, then he becomes obsessed with the idea of objectives or material assurance ... The impulse rests on fear.[3]

The fearful 'social being' to whom the woman in these novels is married usually belongs to the hegemonic class; he has the 'assurance' of respectability, law, power, on his side; one of his 'objectives' at some point will be to use this power in order to try to persuade or coerce the woman into empty conformity with his, and society's, will. His position, in Kantian and in purely conventional moral terms, is usually impeccable. Yet he is also vitally deficient in some important expressivist way that has to do with his reliance on society. He tends to be both emotionally repressed and narcissistic, regulating his behaviour not by spontaneous desire, but by social expectation; having collapsed in 'his natural innocent pride', he anxiously needs to find favourable images of himself mirrored in the eyes of others, including his wife. This means that he is curiously both domineering towards his wife and yet dependent on her too, which makes his domineering impotent, petulant, and wilful. He is often, underneath all this, a boy of tears, full of thwarted regressive longings directed towards his wife. He tends to be jealously possessive and, when traduced, capable of cold violence towards her – which society on the whole supports.

All of this comes out because the woman meets another sort of man altogether. He is usually an outsider in some sense, either a foreigner or socially unrespectable, but capable of passionate

spontaneity, vital, independent, 'single', not narcissistically dependent on the woman in the same sense as the 'social being'. This
man Lawrence called an 'innocent': he is in some sense at one both
with his own darker nature and with 'the great living continuum of
the universe'. It is when she falls in love with this man, and his love
calls her to a self-realisation she has not known before, to fulfil the
demands of her own nature, that she begins to come into sharp
conflict with her husband.

The 'social being' and the 'innocent' are what Alasdair Mac-
Intyre would call 'characters', that is, representative figures of
various moral philosophies who also tend to define possibilities of plot
and action of the works to which they belong. In this sense, the 'social
being' and the 'innocent' are not only 'the masks worn' by
Romantic-expressivism, they also help to explain why the basic story
of all five novels I discuss in detail has a Romantic-expressivist
trajectory built into it that cannot fail to come into conflict both with
conventional 'bourgeois' morality and, at a deeper level, the Judeo-
Christian-Kantian demand that we treat the needs of others as
morally equivalent with our own. The reason novelists (and our
culture generally) may have been so drawn to this dilemma is
because it affords no single sustainable answer to the question 'What
is it right for the woman to do?' In other words, this story is a
stumbling-block, perhaps *the* stumbling-block, for *both* sorts of ethical
demand. Which is not to say that novelists have always recognised
that this is what is at the heart of the situation to which their
imagination has led them.

Middlemarch, for example, is an interesting case because George
Eliot did not, or would not fully let herself, realise what was inherent
in the relationships between Dorothea, Casaubon, and Will Ladislaw. She is so consciously committed to a sub-Kantian moral vision,
and to portraying Dorothea as the great exemplar of that vision, that
she attempts to keep the lid on the expressivist impulses of the story;
she blurs the significance of Dorothea's feelings for Will and the
longings thwarted by Casaubon such that her dilemma is at crucial
moments imaginatively suppressed. George Eliot in this way does
not face the implications of what her imagining none the less
presents, that Kantian conceptions of the good cannot, on their own,
answer in certain key human situations. The novel imaginatively
discovers that such conceptions, in the absence of any satisfactory
understanding of the needs of expressive integrity, buckle under the

pressure of concretely imagined situations, and the novelist who clings to them in isolation can only do so by subtle evasions, sentimentalities, and falsities. As Lawrence said, such moral commitments end up either killing the novel or forcing it to resist and to subvert them.

Lawrence himself, on the other hand, is characteristically drawn to believe that the dilemma can be answered – simply by the woman following out the Romantic demands of self-realisation. Where this does happen, the figure of the traduced husband presents a moral problem, which can only be suppressed by some judgmental rationalisation that appropriates him to the evils of society. This happens in the final version of *Lady Chatterley's Lover*, a highly unsatisfactory and morally evasive solution, which does not compare well with the first version of the novel, where Sir Clifford is a more ambiguously human figure – one whose claim to ethical consideration cannot be simply dismissed. Because it allows into play all the realities that tend to resist the Romantic 'solution', *The First Lady Chatterley* is a much richer book.

Where either sort of ethical demand prevails as the final vocabulary within a work then its imagined world will inevitably be polarised into a more or less rigid set of binary oppositions – rather as Fredric Jameson suggested. In the one case, the dominant oppositions will be along the lines of egoism/altruism; in the other, the oppositions will be social being/innocence. Where these remain as rigid binaries, the imagining ceases to be deeply interesting and illuminating to us. But where these binaries break down, undo themselves, such that one term reveals its *dynamic* interrelations with the other, the novel will have the very profoundest ethical interest for us. This is the possibility that the political criticism of the past fifteen years characteristically has not entertained – that our culture's richest stories transcend any ideologies from which they may begin.

I have said that the ethical dilemmas in the novels I am about to discuss are ours too – the terms have not changed essentially since the Victorian period. Of course it is also true that, in countless important ways, the worlds of George Eliot, Tolstoy and Lawrence are not ours. It might be said that the historical and cultural gulfs between these authors are large enough; but when their respective historical situations are set against ours in the 1990s, the discontinuities are simply vast. In what sense then are we, with our liberal divorce laws, contraceptive pill, and women's movements (to mention only the super-obvious), still 'contemporaries' of Dorothea Casaubon, Anna Karenina, or even Connie Chatterley?

This challenge, if it is allowed, might seem to have seriously corrosive consequences for an anti-foundationalist ethics that claims to be based on the cultural embeddedness and historical constituted-ness of moral intuitions, demands, and practices – as opposed to universal moral principles. Does ethical criticism depend on an ahistorical essentialism after all?

Certainly a very much more assiduously historicised approach than mine is possible, one, for example, which sees each work as culturally produced within a dense contemporary intertextual framework. A study along those lines would be in a strong position to show how, at different historical moments and in different national cultures (in the case of *Anna Karenina*), similar moral dilemmas are construed differently – both from each other and from the various ways in which we would tend to construe them now. Such a study might well plumb those past moments and cultural differences profoundly and offer a great deal of enlightenment about the depth and extent of their otherness from us. In this way, the texts of the past, we might want to say, would be seen in their own terms, not in ours. By historicising we seemingly avoid what Foucault saw as an all-pervasive and narcissistic 'presentist' consciousness of the past; and we are kept aware, at the same time, of the contingency of our own distinctive perspectives on things.

This is a familiar, and relatively uncontroversial, sort of argument to advance in Anglo-American literary circles these days, with a good deal of sense on its side. Less familiar is a recognition of the potential danger inherent in characterising the literature of the past as *above all* 'different' or 'other' or the site of Foucauldian temporal 'ruptures' – the danger that it will end up as apparently *having nothing to say to us*. Gadamer makes this point with great force in *Truth and Method*:

We have seen, in considering the origin of historical thinking, that in fact it makes this ambiguous transition from means to end, i.e. it makes an end of what is only a means. The text that is understood historically is forced to abandon its claim that it is uttering something true. We think we understand when we see the past from a historical standpoint, i.e. place ourselves in the historical situation and seek to reconstruct the historical horizon. In fact, we have given up the claim to find, in the past, any truth valid and intelligible for ourselves.[4]

Gadamer mainly has in mind nineteenth-century historicism here, but the same foreclosure and semantic loss are evident in more contemporary kinds, not least in those genealogical and new historicist approaches largely spawned by Foucault.[5] It is a foreclosure on what Gadamer calls 'application' in the texts of the past, a loss of potential meaning 'for ourselves'. Gadamer's concern is that we can shut our ears to this potential in the very act by which we so strenuously attempt to hear the past in its own terms. That is, the means by which we seem to offer the past most scholarly and imaginative respect can be an unconscious mode of disrespect of a patronisingly present-minded kind. In this sense, historicism can be itself deeply ahistorical.[6]

Such historicist approaches characteristically fail to recognise the historically constituted framework of preconceptions, customs, and traditions that the critic *necessarily shares* with the literature of the past. One of the great virtues of Gadamer's work is to point out that *we only understand this literature at all because of what we share with it.* Shared traditions are presupposed in every act of understanding, which should be seen as an ever-active circular negotiation between critic and the traditions to which he or she belongs, often unconsciously:

The [hermeneutic] circle ... describes understanding as the interplay of the movement of tradition and the movement of the interpreter. The anticipation of meaning that governs our understanding of a text is not an act of subjectivity, but proceeds from the communality that binds us to the tradition. But this is contained in our relation to tradition, in the constant process of education. Tradition is not simply a precondition into which we come, but we produce it ourselves, inasmuch as we understand, participate in the evolution of tradition and hence further determine it ourselves.[7]

We only grasp the ontology of understanding the past when we grasp the 'communality that binds us to tradition', where tradition is properly seen as an actively evolving language of assumptions, preconceptions and values (including ethical ones) that we modify as we participate within it. The other side of Gadamer's story is that 'to understand is to understand differently'.

Recognising the 'communality that binds us to tradition' is essential if literary discourse is to keep contact (albeit ever-'differently') with the ethical richness, intelligence, and practical wisdom of our culture's most prized stories. We will be best attuned to what these stories have to say to us if we emphasise that 'communality' with them which is, in effect, their abiding contemporaneity-within-change. This is my deliberate heuristic emphasis in what follows. As is obvious in Gadamer's formulation, such an emphasis on underlying continuities involves no necessary ahistoricism or belief in timeless human essences. Indeed, anti-foundationalist moral philosophy assumes the historically contingent nature of those broad but distinctive ways of conceiving of the good which, within a given civilisation, define possibilities for a good life or for right actions. These seem to crystallise at certain historical moments (for example, in the New Testament or the Romantic periods) and are constantly being reshaped over time, but preserve within them sufficient continuity to be called moral traditions.

The particular historical picture my argument depends on (centred on the mutual interactions between two of these traditions) is one with extremely broad contours reaching across the whole of post-Enlightenment European civilisation. Post-Enlightenment moral selfhood can be best understood as a dialogue between Judeo-Christian and Romantic-expressivist traditions. The evidence for this claim will be the sense it makes of the novels examined in the following chapters.

CHAPTER 6

'Bound in Charity': 'Middlemarch'

The motto at the head of chapter 42 of *Middlemarch* is one of those surprises that turn out to be more and more interesting the more you think about them:

> How much, methinks, I could despise this man,
> Were I not bound in charity against it!
>
> (Shakespeare, *Henry VIII*)

As it happens, the speaker in Shakespeare's play is Cardinal Wolsey, and this elegant piece of popish casuistry is aimed at Surrey who is busily trying to relieve him of the great seal of England. But when these lines become the motto of chapter 42, 'this man' becomes the Reverend Edward Casaubon, and the whole effect is of an anarchic joke – against George Eliot herself. The moral constraints that apply in the novel itself are being wryly mocked, for George Eliot is firmly committed to doing something much 'higher' than despising. The mockery releases the liberating possibility of actually loathing 'this man' frankly and to the full – a possibility that corresponds to a gathering need audible in the narrating voice, not to be 'bound' in feeling by anything at all. By the middle of the novel, reminders that 'poor Mr Casaubon' had a point of view too sound increasingly forced, and scarcely check the vexed undertones of narrative complaint against him. Such feelings, which have no place in the novel's final *moral* vocabulary, tend in the end to empty that vocabulary of its force. Being *bound* to it, as George Eliot is, ultimately dries up charity altogether.

This is not to imply that George Eliot's charity, or the more usual terms, 'compassion', 'fellow-feeling', and 'sympathy', are of no importance or interest. Quite the reverse. A renewed ethical criticism in the 1990s will inevitably need to return to such words, even though they are now much more problematic than they were in the 1950s and 1960s following *The Great Tradition*. These terms are problems now because they have been characteristically viewed in the Nietzsche-dominated 1970s and 1980s as nothing much more than the stock Victorian emotivist intensities, shocked into being by a glimpse of the vast edges drear and naked shingles of a faithless world. Even Eliot's supposed defenders have presented 'sympathy' and 'compassion' as 'social feelings' – that is, as part of a conservative commitment to the maintenance of existing society.[1] Meanwhile most of the interesting Eliot critics of the last fifteen years have steered around her explicit moral terminology and focused very profitably on such things as her neglected feminism.[2]

These problems are raised acutely in J. Hillis Miller's account of Eliot in *The Ethics of Reading*. Miller's view is that George Eliot's affirmative ethics cannot ultimately distinguish itself from cynicism:

Extremes meet in their common baselessness. The cynicism which measures all people by a zero and finds them all equally poor comes to the same thing as the positive measure which gives my neighbor an infinite value, so generating a resolution to do good, to love him or her. It comes to the same thing yet comes to a very different thing in its effects, which makes all the difference between the maintenance and the dissolution of society. The cement of society is the fiction that my ugly, stupid neighbour is lovable.[3]

This is a sub-Nietzschean reading of Eliot's ethical theory and practice that sees her sympathetic or loving valuations of her neighbours as mere fictional colorations imposed on the reality of their ugliness and stupidity – all in the interests of holding together a potentially anarchic miscellany of individuals in the one society. In the previous paragraph Hillis Miller has made the point in a slightly different way by saying that all 'emotive evaluation is performative. It makes something happen which has no cause beyond the words which express it.' Anglo-American philosophers reading this will not have trouble in placing it: ethical statements are radically different from factual ones; they are ultimately 'emotive', their point being to cause other people to act in certain ways. Miller's argument, in short, for all its deconstructive sophistication in seeking to reduce George Eliot's substantive views to a set of figural confusions, boils down to the familiar naturalist suppression of ethics. The argument is itself mired both in what Alasdair MacIntyre called 'emotivism' and Richard Rorty 'positivism' – in which reality is conceived as the realm of fact and reason, whereas value belongs to a fictional, but subtly coercive, world of mere emotion. Writing on ethics in the mid-eighties, Miller had perhaps less excuse than John Carey for his seeming innocence of well-known developments in anti-foundational moral philosophy.

I also see feeling/emotion as an important issue for Eliot, but Miller is mistaken in seeing her as a mere emotivist. As we see in *Middlemarch*, her moral commitment has a significance and consequences of a wholly different sort. For one thing, Eliot's morality is not simply on the side of cementing existing society together; it is much more ambiguous politically than this. Here, for instance, is one important formulation of it:

Also, profitable investments in trades where the power of the prince of this world showed its most active devices, became sanctified by a right application of the profits in the hands of God's servant.
  This implicit reasoning is essentially no more peculiar to evangelical belief than the use of wide phrases for narrow motives is peculiar to Englishmen. There is no general doctrine which is not capable of eating out our morality if unchecked by the deep-seated habit of direct fellow-feeling with individual fellow-men. (p. 668)

On the surface, 'fellow-feeling with individual fellow-men', when offered as a corrective to the subtle hypocrisies of evangelical adherence to 'general doctrine', might sound like the sort of moral recommendation you would expect from a high Tory. And there can be no denying that Eliot sees more virtue in high church Farebrother than low church Tyke. But looked at from a longer perspective, the banker Bulstrode (on whom the above passage is focused) is what Alasdair MacIntyre would call a 'character': he is constituted by the dominant set of political and economic discourses of George Eliot's own time, those of *laissez-faire* capitalism. He appears to embody, and comes to believe that he does (such is the diffuse power of the ideology), the virtues of independence and self-reliance of the self-made man. But in this he is not alone in any sense. Lydgate, Casaubon, and Rosamond Vincy all conceive of themselves as, and partly in a sense are, self-created individuals. To this extent they too are ideologically constructed out of the very same set of discourses. 'Fellow-feeling' is not simply to be seen as a Tory answer to middle-class evangelicalism. Eliot's focus is on something very much larger: it is on that all-pervasive nineteenth-century individualism which defines selfhood in isolation from society's 'webs of interlocution'[4] and tends to suppress awareness of connectedness, interdependence, and commonality with others.

For George Eliot, 'fellow-feeling' is not the imposition of wishful rose tints on my neighbour's factual ugliness; it is rather understanding him or her in a deeper way, one that is not blinkered or distorted by an excessively individualistic self/other binarism. It is important to notice that George Eliot's images of 'egoism' do not simply convey selfishness or even self-centredness; they imply a radical sense of personal uniqueness and self-importance:

An eminent philosopher among my friends, who can dignify even your ugly furniture by lifting it into the serene light of science, has shown me this pregnant little fact. Your pier-glass or extensive surface of polished steel made to be rubbed by a housemaid, will be minutely and multitudinously scratched in all directions; but place now against it a lighted candle as a centre of illumination, and lo! the scratches will seem to arrange themselves in a fine series of concentric circles around that little sun. It is demonstrable that the scratches are going everywhere impartially, and it is only your candle which produces the flattering illusion of a concentric arrangement, its light falling with an exclusive optical selection. These things are a parable. The scratches are events, and the candle is the egoism of any person now absent – of Miss Vincy, for example. Rosamond had a Providence of her own who had kindly made her more charming than other girls. (p. 297)

The candle-flame suggests that, not only does the ego configure events according to its own desires and needs, but each phenomenological world thus created will be almost solipsistically contained within its 'flattering illusion of a concentric arrangement'. The egoist's world is there seemingly *for* the self, unfolding as if a 'kind Providence' (or an unkind one) was creating it simply in answer to its wishes (or anxieties).

It follows from this that the world the egoist 'sees' will to some extent be a mirror of his wishes, fears and desires. For a Rosamond, human society will be a great looking-glass in which to see reflected her long adorable neck (p. 140); for a Casaubon, the scholarly world will reflect back the scornful mockeries of Carp of Brasenose, or so he is 'bitterly convinced' (p. 314); for a Bulstrode, there may be surprise in 'seeing a very unsatisfying reflection of himself in the coarse unflattering mirror' of Mr Vincy's mind (p. 159). The world of *Middlemarch* bears out Iris Murdoch's contention in *The Sovereignty of Good* that the ethical life begins in the very way in which we read the world in the first place. If we are egoists like Fred Vincy, half of what we see will be 'no more than the reflex of [our] own inclinations' (p. 147). Hence the stupidity and ugliness I 'see' in my neighbour may be no more than a reflex of some inclination of my own to see him in that way – perhaps to flatter myself, or perhaps to prevent me from recognising his claim to a more sympathetic sort of attention.

One of the great insights at the heart of *Middlemarch* is that until I understand that my dominant impulses are not entirely separable from the world as I construe it, I will continue to misconstrue it. Further, as is obvious in the candle-flame passage, while my dominant impulses are egoistic, I will characteristically misconstrue it as being providentially there for me. I will regard it, in short, as a kingdom of means for the satisfaction of my own ends. The novel is at pains to show that this is a mistaken way to regard it, if for no other reason than that this is the way everyone else tends to regard it – from the centre of their own very different candle-flame visions. It follows from this that I only transcend egoism when I come to understand that I am not unique and that I share this 'first-personal' candle-flame mode of existence with everybody else. My neighbour then ceases to be a mere stupid and ugly object in my world, but becomes another self in some ways like me, whom I can understand by an act of imagination, commonly called putting myself in her place. This might also be called 'empathy' or 'sympathy', but these terms do not boil down to a mere determination to emote lovingly in the face of my neighbour's factual unlovableness; they indicate a transformed mode of intersubjective understanding that in some sense transcends the radically individualistic self/other binarism that Marxists identify (with some justification) as alienated bourgeois consciousness.

The form of transcendence that most interests George Eliot is moral rather than political, however, and, as is already clear, its terms are in some respects very much like Kant's. A more immediate source, however, is Ludwig Feuerbach's *The Essence of Christianity*; I quote from George Eliot's own translation:

The inner life of man is the life which has relation to his species, to his general, as distinguished from his individual, nature. Man thinks – that is, he converses with himself. The brute can exercise no function which has relation to its species without another individual external to itself; but man can perform the functions of thought and speech, which strictly imply such a relation, apart from another individual. Man is himself at once I and thou; he can put himself in the place of another, for this reason, that to him the species, his essential nature, and not merely his individuality, is an object of thought.[5]

The other is my *thou*, – the relation being reciprocal, – my *alter ego*, man objective to me, the revelation of my own nature, the eye seeing itself. In another I first have the consciousness of humanity; through him I first learn, I first feel, that I am a man: in my love for him it is first clear to me that he belongs to me and I to him, that we too cannot be without each other, that only community constitutes humanity.[6]

These passages might be seen as a commentary on the moral import of the woman taken in adultery as told in John 8. When the Pharisees look into their consciences, they cease to see the woman simply as an objective Other; she becomes a *thou* revealing to them their own nature. And that is so because human separateness is not so radical as we commonly fall into supposing; deep self-reflection reveals that we represent to each other our 'essential' as opposed to our merely individual nature. Seeing *only* individuals in the world, monadic selves set in binary opposition to others, is a form of alienated consciousness; the relevant corrective truth is that 'only community constitutes humanity'.

These are deep and important insights for *Middlemarch* too. They are capable of being defended along anti-foundationalist lines, as Alasdair MacIntyre defends them (or reflections closely related to them) in *After Virtue*, as well as pragmatically, as I have suggested in my own account of John 8 in chapter 3. However, in both Feuerbach and George Eliot, these traditional Judeo-Christian insights have, not surprisingly (given when they were writing), a distinctively Kantian inflection. For Feuerbach, what 'I think only according to the standard of my individuality is not binding on another; it can be conceived otherwise; it is an accidental, merely subjective view. But that which I think according to the standard of the species, I think as man in general only can think, and consequently as every individual must think if he thinks normally, in accordance with law, and therefore truly.'[7] The idea that we are bound only by universalisable principles (emanating from our 'essential' rational nature) is Kantian – which goes with a characteristic devaluation of all merely individual 'needs and inclinations, whose total satisfaction is summed up under the name of happiness'.[8] Returning to the candle-flame passage in *Middlemarch*, it is clear that the ego's candle-flame visions, reflexes of need and inclination, are being similarly discounted by

Eliot in favour of a transpersonal vision of things that somehow sees the scratches of reality running everywhere 'impartially'. To see things thus is itself an achievement of what Kant calls 'impartial judgment'.[9]

Impartiality is the moral ideal informing the development and structure of *Middlemarch* at every level. The movement from one narrative strand of the novel to another, the shift from presented particulars to generalising commentary and the shift in focus from one character to another, all embody Eliot's aspiration to transcend any particular first-personal mode of experience with its candle-flame concentricities of need and inclination – in favour of something rather like what Thomas Nagel calls the view from nowhere. But it is in an earlier book that Nagel's terms are most strikingly similar to Eliot's:

Recognition of the other person's reality, and the possibility of putting yourself in his place, is essential. You see the present situation as a specimen of a more general scheme, in which the characters can be exchanged. The crucial factor injected into this scheme is an attitude which you have towards your own case, or rather an aspect of the view which you take of your own needs, actions, and desires. You attribute to them, in fact, a certain objective interest, and the recognition of others as persons like yourself permits extension of this objective interest to the needs and desires of persons in general, or those of any particular individual whose situation is being considered.[10]

Part of the similarity with Eliot is the idea that the attempt to be impartial is the '*crucial* factor injected into this scheme' – in other words, it is what turns reflection into specifically *moral* reflection. By 'moral', here and throughout this chapter especially, I mean the way Bernard Williams uses it in *Ethics and the Limits of Philosophy* to indicate a more or less Kantian system of thought and practice centring on obligation, rational choice, and will; whereas 'ethical' embraces *all* distinctions of worth raised by the question 'How should one live?' – including those Charles Taylor calls 'Romantic-expressivist'. In this sense, candle-flame visions are sub-moral, but certainly not non-ethical. As I have argued above concerning *The View from Nowhere*, this implied division of experience into moral/non-moral is a potential fissure in any work of art that embraces it. On the other hand, the artist's continuing effort to see each imagined situation 'as a specimen of a more general scheme, in which the characters can be exchanged' is a necessary brake on partiality of vision and will therefore be an important element in any imaginative work of abiding ethical interest.

Something closely analogous to the imaginative exchange of characters is central to the great achievement of *Middlemarch*. For example, in the Casaubons' honeymoon in Rome (chapter 20 again), George Eliot begins by drawing us skilfully into close identification with Dorothea's first-personal needs, desires, and interests – as a prelude to the deeper recognition of her husband's reality. We are introduced to Dorothea's craving for affection from her husband, and when that turns to despondency, we are told of her efforts 'to shake off what she inwardly called her selfishness' and turn 'a face all cheerful attention to her husband'. This is morally exemplary from the Kantian point of view; her efforts are directed towards treating Casaubon not as a means to her own happiness, but as an end in himself.[11] But, as Richard Freadman points out in his excellent book on Eliot and James, Casaubon 'cannot concede to others the status of ends-in-themselves'.[12] It simply does not occur to him to attend to his wife in like measure. His sense of moral duty seems to be trapped in the almost unreachable hall of mirrors of concern for right appearances; any small affection he may have had has dwindled into a 'conscientious' determination to be 'an irreproachable husband, who would make a charming young woman *as happy as she deserved to be*' (my italics). The oblivious *in*justice of this concern with Dorothea's deserts cannot fail to provoke the judgment that Casaubon's happiness is getting rather more attention than it deserves. And such a judgment might well be hostile were it not for the fact that Casaubon's grotesque scholarly precisions of phrase are taken right to the border of burlesque. Finally Dorothea's moral efforts give way to an overflow of feeling as she seizes on an outlet for her pent-up energies:

'And all your notes,' said Dorothea, whose heart had already burned within her on this subject so that now she could not help speaking with her tongue. 'All those rows of volumes – will you not now do what you used to speak of? – will you not make up your mind what part of them you will use, and begin to write the book which will make your vast knowledge useful to the world? I will write to your dictation, or I will copy and extract what you tell me: I can be of no other use.' Dorothea, in a most unaccountable, darkly-feminine manner, ended with a slight sob and eyes full of tears. (p. 232)

At this moment Dorothea's loss of volitional and intellectual control, her yielding to the desires and longings of the 'heart', appear wholly

admirable, partly because they are seemingly directed to the
fulfilment of Casaubon's deepest desires and longings – and partly
because it is already clear that such generous ardour is being wasted
on a man incapable of returning anything like it.

The very next paragraph, then, is a surprise:

The excessive feeling manifested would alone have been highly disturbing to
Mr Casaubon, but there were other reasons why Dorothea's words were
among the most cutting and irritating to him that she could have been
impelled to use. She was as blind to his inward troubles as he to hers; she had
not yet learned those hidden conflicts in her husband which claim our pity.
She had not yet listened patiently to his heart-beats, but only felt that her
own was beating violently. In Mr Casaubon's ear, Dorothea's voice gave
loud emphatic iteration to those muffled suggestions of consciousness which
it was possible to explain as mere fancy, the illusion of exaggerated
sensitiveness: always when such suggestions are unmistakably repeated from
without, they are resisted as cruel and unjust. We are angered even by the
full acceptance of our humiliating confessions – how much more by hearing
in hard distinct syllables from the lips of a near observer, those confused
murmurs which we try to call morbid, and strive against as if they were the
oncoming of numbness! And this cruel outward accuser was there in the
shape of a wife – nay, of a young bride, who, instead of observing his
abundant pen scratches and amplitude of paper with the uncritical awe of
an elegant-minded canary-bird, seemed to present herself as a spy watching
everything with a malign power of inference. Here, towards this particular
point of the compass, Mr Casaubon had a sensitiveness to match Dorothea's,
and an equal quickness to imagine more than the fact. He had formerly
observed with approbation her capacity for worshipping the right object; he
now foresaw with sudden terror that this capacity might be replaced by
presumption, this worship by the most exasperating of all criticism, – that
which sees vaguely a great many fine ends and has not the least notion what
it costs to reach them. (pp. 232–3)

This comes as something of a shock, but a salutary one because it
reminds us that Casaubon has needs, fears, and desires too, though of
a very different kind from Dorothea's. We see here that what
underlies that dry, pedantic, cautious exterior that we have been
partly amused and partly indignant at is a lonely and anguished
struggle with the most acute sensitivities – sensitivities so painful that
they are only held out of consciousness with difficulty, and therefore
liable to be triggered by anything that comes unwarily within range
of them. The imagining here is fully inward, which is to say that
Casaubon is being imagined, certainly for the first time in this
chapter, from within his own candle-flame vision of things. Which

brings home to us that we have been trapped into seeing him from within Dorothea's circle of needs and desires – as a means to satisfying or denying her ends, and not as a first-personal thou, as an end in the terms he would use himself. Right up until this 'exchange' of places between Dorothea and her husband, we simply have not wanted to know that Casaubon is also a thou, and not merely an ugly and humanly rather stupid object in her phenomenal world.

There is a readerly form of egoism in other words, and becoming aware of it enforces on us the realisation that we are capable of forgetting the commonality of 'sensitiveness' to hurts, yearnings, and anxieties. Implicit in this is the realisation of how judgmental we are capable of being, and how ubiquitous the judgmental unconscious is. At the same time, the passage establishes the equivalence of moral dignity between the characters; it is here above all we see that everyone has 'an equivalent centre of self, whence the lights and shadows must always fall with a certain difference' (p. 243). The power of this whole sequence draws deeply on Judeo-Christian traditions of universal human worth.

The art in this part of *Middlemarch* is especially strong and compelling. The reasons for this can be put in different ways. For a start we can say that Eliot's imagining here resists any simple moral binary opposition which would merely oppose Dorothea's altruism and Casaubon's egoism. Dorothea is here 'as blind to his inward troubles as he to hers', and, while this equivalence does not much matter, Dorothea's egoism is a guarantee that Eliot has not yet forgotten that the tendency to the judgmental unconscious, even in the morally scrupulous, is practically ineradicable. Equally important is the fact that Casaubon here embodies psychic impulses that George Eliot herself knew in an intimately first-personal way. Gordon Haight reports a telling episode in which Eliot replies unexpectedly to the perennial question of who Casaubon is based on:

When a young friend put the question direct: 'But from whom, then, did you draw Casaubon?' George Eliot, with a humorous solemnity, which was quite in earnest, nevertheless, pointed to her own heart. Perhaps she had in mind the morbid fear of criticism that she shared with him.[13]

The gesture may have been a way of indicating that Casaubon represents a possibility of every self, that of being unreachably frozen in a deeply fearful ego. But more likely is the suggestion Haight makes, that Casaubon's extreme sensitiveness to criticism comes out of Eliot herself, who, for example, so dreaded unfavourable reviews that Lewes used to keep them from her.[14] If this is so, then the Casaubon who lived in dread of Carp of Brasenose may be seen as partly the mirror-enclosed narcissist or 'social being' within Eliot herself. Which means that the imagining of Casaubon will be deep and compelling as long as George Eliot keeps pointing to her own breast. But forgetting this affinity with him will carry with it the danger that Casaubon will become her 'shadow' – a projection of things she wants to obliterate in herself.

Increasingly after chapter 20, Eliot's moral identifications do polarise and solidify; her imagining is no longer so impartial, and any 'exchange' (or what Bernard Williams calls 'role reversal')[15] between Dorothea's and Casaubon's view of things becomes more and more and perfunctory. As we shall see, the seeds of the novel's undoing lie in Eliot's failure fully to recognise the *ethical* force of first-personal candle-flame visions. All of this becomes most evident towards the end of Casaubon's life, especially in chapters 42 and 48. That does not mean that there is no imaginative interest in them; quite the contrary, as we see here at the beginning of chapter 48:

They usually spent apart the hours between luncheon and dinner on a Sunday; Mr Casaubon in the library dozing chiefly, and Dorothea in her boudoir, where she was wont to occupy herself with some of her favourite books. There was a little heap of them on the table in the bow-window – of various sorts, from Herodotus, which she was learning to read with Mr Casaubon, to her old companion Pascal, and Keble's *Christian Year*. But to-day she opened one after another, and could read none of them. Everything seemed dreary: the portents before the birth of Cyrus – Jewish antiquities – oh dear! – devout epigrams – the sacred chime of favourite hymns – all alike were as flat as tunes beaten on wood: even the spring flowers and the grass had a dull shiver in them under the afternoon clouds that hid the sun fitfully: even the sustaining thoughts which had become habits seemed to have in them the weariness of long future days in which she would still live with them for her sole companions. It was another or rather a fuller sort of companionship that poor Dorothea was hungering for, and the hunger had grown from the perpetual effort demanded by her married life. She was always trying to be what her husband wished, and never able to repose on his delight in what she was. The thing that she liked, that she spontaneously cared to have, seemed to be always excluded from her life; for if it was only granted and not shared by her husband it might as well have been denied. (pp. 515–16)

Leaving aside for the moment the question of the tone and what it
betrays about George Eliot's nearness to Dorothea now, the passage
provides the most searching insights into the Casaubons' married life.
Will's presence at Lowick church has made it clear – though precisely
how clear to Dorothea herself we cannot easily tell – that her habitual
round of devotions, tastes, interests and thoughts is not so much a life
as a mere existence, an entombment. Eliot's ethical thinking here is
capacious enough to include an expressivist understanding of the fact
that no activity, not 'even [Dorothea's] sustaining thoughts', nor
even her 'perpetual effort' to reach and to connect with Casaubon,
can be of much real moment when she is starved of the one thing that
could vitalise them. It is especially the place given to conscious moral
'effort' that points to the unusual strength of the ethical reflection
embodied in this passage. Dorothea's continual struggle to overcome
herself is not vaguely exalted as it usually is as her 'noble habit of the
soul' (p. 464); it is seen as the awful consequence of an overpowering
'hunger' for love. Her need is so strong that she is 'always trying to
be what her husband wished', which, given Casaubon, means always
suppressing a great deal of what she spontaneously cares for, likes,
and is. And Dorothea being Dorothea, this perpetual effort is one she
cannot help making. George Eliot faces squarely here the fact that
such effort can only sharpen Dorothea's hunger for the one thing that
could ultimately satisfy it: a love that would let her 'repose on his
delight in what she was'.

'Repose', 'delight in what she was' – such terms are far from any
purely moral valuation of desire or need. It is here that we see very
clearly the post-Romantic impulsions of the basic story beginning to
work themselves out. Within months of being married to a deeply
frightened 'social being' who cannot give Dorothea the right sort of
love, her existence begins to become a weary oppression, a slow
attrition, no matter what moral heroism she may seem to realise in
the face of it. At the same time it is made clear that Casaubon simply
cannot take delight in what Dorothea spontaneously is. One of the
most compelling things in the whole novel is George Eliot's
exploration of the twists and turns of mind by which Casaubon half-
perceives and half-creates everywhere signs of adverse judgment,
rejection, and scorn. In one way or another almost all of Dorothea's
spontaneous outgoing energies, her quick intelligence, her power of
judgment, her moral ardour, her ready affectionateness, and above
all her need for love, keep startling Casaubon with confirming

reflections of his own profound feeling of self-insufficiency, and so he cannot help wishing these things not to be. His deepest wish is to control by fixing limits to the range of things she can be, or at least manifest to his imagination, for on this subject Casaubon's imagination is at least as quick and as exquisitely feeling in its own way as Will Ladislaw's. All of this comes out with special force in Casaubon's last wish, the one he expresses in his will, to 'bind' Dorothea after his death not to marry Ladislaw.

Some of George Eliot's deepest interests can be located just here, in the ways in which it is right and possible for the spontaneous self to be bound, either by someone else or by things within itself; and in the need to bind another or oneself, either to actions in the world or to constricted images fixed in the imagination. All of these things come into play in chapter 48 when, anticipating his will, Casaubon asks Dorothea if she will follow his wishes after his death. It is not so much the future reality of Dorothea marrying Will that terrifies Casaubon (that, after all, is not something he can experience), as the very thought of it. This is not simply jealousy (if jealousy can be simple), but an inability to endure a pictured outcome that has framed itself even more swiftly and indubitably in his imagination than in Ladislaw's desires, for Casaubon is quicker than either of them to sense what capacities in each would find an answer in the other. It is the self-born image of precisely these things finding their free play and satisfaction that Casaubon cannot stand, since it reflects so cruelly his deepest fears about himself. That, at all costs, must be effaced as a possibility to be contemplated while he is alive (he does not seem to care that the will itself will suggest the possibility to anyone reading it after he is dead), and so, typical of the 'social being', he uses all his power in law as husband to try to bind Dorothea not to figure in it. The result is a grotesque over-kill that brings out, as nothing else can, the distorted, impotent energies of the fearful, inward-turned ego.

This Casaubon, the victim of destructive drives that warp almost all his conscious life, embodies some of George Eliot's finest creative thinking. Unfortunately, as this same chapter (48) shows, that is not all there is to be said, because the things that go wrong with the imagining of Dorothea after chapter 20 ultimately affect our sense of Casaubon too. The way Dorothea bounces back ('in a clear voice') from Casaubon's suggestion that she obey his wishes after his death has that 'childlike' rightness we are meant to approve of: 'but it is too solemn – I think it is not right – to make a promise when I am ignorant what it will bind me to. Whatever affection prompted I would do without promising' (p. 519). Like Will Ladislaw, Dorothea is partly something of an 'innocent' in the positive post-Romantic sense and so her uncoerced 'affection' is an important term for George Eliot. But, however attractive this answer to Casaubon may seem for the moment (not least because of its own affective spontaneity), we are soon made to see that it does not go quite far enough. The all-important case for George Eliot is where almost all the spontaneous 'promptings' come from the other direction, from hatred and resentment. And there, all such promptings must yield to the force of something morally 'higher', to 'compassion'; that, above all, is what Dorothea is bound by:

When Dorothea was out on the gravel walks, she lingered among the nearer clumps of trees, hesitating, as she had done once before, though from a different cause. Then she had feared lest her effort at fellowship should be unwelcome; now she dreaded going to the spot where she foresaw that she must bind herself to a fellowship from which she shrank. Neither law nor the world's opinion compelled her to this – only her husband's nature and her own compassion, only the ideal and not the real yoke of marriage. She saw clearly enough the whole situation, yet she was fettered: she could not smite the stricken soul that entreated hers. If that were weakness, Dorothea was weak. (pp. 552–3)

The struggle to decide this has brought Dorothea to the limits of her strength; she has had to put down intense dread and revulsion at the thought of the waste of years and of herself that would come from (as she thinks) Casaubon's demand to finish his work. And in deciding as she does, she cannot be sure that she is not simply being weak. At the same time, the intensities of tone leave us in no doubt that, as far as George Eliot is concerned, this is anything but weakness; for her it is the noblest kind of strength, the kind that overcomes its own strongest feelings for the sake of not wounding the other. But then that tone also makes us wonder whether something vital is not being left out – or whether, in short, there might not be a sort of weakness in the way Dorothea decides that she 'must' yield to Casaubon's wish. The emotional intensities of the writing seem to be a way of *insisting* on the rightness of Dorothea's decision, insisting partly because the reasons offered for it are not (as I think George Eliot obscurely realises) entirely cogent. Dorothea foresees that 'she must bind herself' because she was 'compelled', partly by 'her husband's nature' (more on this in a moment), partly by 'her own compassion' (something of a circularity since compassion is also what she is compelled *to*), and partly by 'the ideal and not the real yoke of marriage' (whatever this may be!). Such a tangle does not simply point to woolliness on George Eliot's part (after all, who has a better eye for woolliness than George Eliot?), but to something behind it all that is being willed or evaded.

What helps to reveal this is the way in which Dorothea (and here she and George Eliot are practically impossible to distinguish) pictures to herself the effect of refusing Casaubon. Above all, this is the thought that compels her: 'She saw clearly the whole situation, yet she was fettered: she could not smite the stricken soul that entreated hers.' Two things stand out here, the violence of 'smite', and the image of Casaubon as a vulnerable, suffering, 'stricken soul' that is appealing to hers. These same two things come up whenever Dorothea feels herself to be slipping out of the fetters of 'fellowship'. For example, a little earlier in this chapter:

And now, if she were to say, 'No! if you die I will put no finger to your work' – it seemed as if she would be crushing that bruised heart. (p. 521)

she was too weak, too full of dread at the thought of inflicting a keen-edged blow on her husband, to do anything but submit completely. (p. 522)

Characteristic of these moments is the mixture of impulses brought into play: fantasised violence towards Casaubon and fearful stifling of it; and, beneath that, the paralysing 'dread' of transgression against him, and of his icy severity, which everywhere blocks and deflects her hostility. We see these impulses at work here in the excess, the element of unreality, in the images of smiting, crushing, and inflicting a keen-edged blow, all of which tells us that, as much as they may be picturing an impact on Casaubon, they also have a deeper, unconscious strategy: to coerce Dorothea herself. To imagine refusal as a deed of gratuitous cruelty inflicted on a hurt, vulnerable, entreating 'soul' is actually to turn the violence back upon the self that could even contemplate such a thing. The real violence is reflexive: such images are a means of inflicting a keen-edged blow on her own rising feelings of horror at what she somewhere realises she is going to do anyway. For the truth is, as her way of thinking here shows, that Dorothea is 'fettered' at a level deeper than any of her conscious struggling to decide can touch or see. The 'whole situation' is just what she cannot see 'clearly'; she simply cannot let herself, because beneath all her conscientious, other-centred *reasons* for acting as she does there is a willed commitment, or rather clinging, that she cannot begin to inspect or to struggle against. Dorothea is an important example of what I have called 'the libidinal unconscious': beneath everything, she is bound by 'compassion', hand and foot.

These moral struggles, surrenders, and self-evasions of Dorothea's in her attempts to live her married life with Casaubon in the most generous kind of way are profoundly interesting, even though it is clear that George Eliot herself could not (or would not) grasp the whole significance of what she was imagining. There is not the slightest indication that she understands the ways in which Dorothea unconsciously bullies herself into submission – quite the contrary, her admiring tone gives every indication that she does not. And that goes with something even more telling: the place given to feelings such as those Dorothea has after Casaubon has repulsed one of her attempts to comfort him (in the Yew-Tree Walk):

She was in the reaction of a rebellious anger stronger than any she had felt since her marriage. Instead of tears there were words:–

'What have I done – what am I – that he should treat me so? He never knows what is in my mind – he never cares. What is the use of anything I do? He wishes he had never married me.'

She began to hear herself, and was checked into stillness. Like one who has lost his way and is weary, she sat and saw as in one glance all the paths of her young hope which she should never find again. And just as clearly in the miserable light she saw her own and her husband's solitude – how they walked apart so that she was obliged to survey him. If he had drawn her towards him, she would never have surveyed him – never have said, 'Is he worth living for?' but would have felt him simple a part of her own life. Now she said bitterly, 'It is his fault, not mine.' In the jar of her whole being, Pity was overthrown. Was it her fault that she had believed in him – had believed in his worthiness? – And what, exactly, was he? – She was able enough to estimate him – she who waited on his glances with trembling, and shut her best soul in prison, paying it only hidden visits, that she might be petty enough to please him. In such a crisis as this, some women begin to hate.

The sun was low when Dorothea was thinking that she would not go down again, but would send a message to her husband saying that she was not well and preferred remaining up-stairs. She had never deliberately allowed her resentment to govern her in this way before, but she believed now that she could not see him again without telling him the truth about her feeling, and she must wait till she could do it without interruption. He might wonder and be hurt at her message. It was good that he should wonder and be hurt. Her anger said, as anger is apt to say, that God was with her – that all heaven, though it were crowded with spirits watching them, must be on her side. (pp. 463–4)

Perhaps nowhere in the novel does Dorothea's suppressed anger and hostility towards Casaubon express itself as fully and frankly. She strikes against him in the need to wound him as he has wounded her: 'He might wonder and be hurt at her message. It was good that he should wonder and be hurt.' Just here in these sentences, and elsewhere throughout the passage, George Eliot herself gets so caught up in the flow of Dorothea's dammed-up anger that she keeps breaking into a semi-dramatic manner rather like the one Lawrence uses, especially in the Will and Anna parts of *The Rainbow*. That mode of imagining is a way of implicitly admitting not simply the power of the anger, but also its right to be, because it is also, at the same time, an authorial-exploratory mode that is searching out a side of the truth that only feelings like anger or resentment have the power to irradiate and disclose: 'And what, exactly, was he? – She was able enough to estimate him.' So she was, while her blood was up: 'she who waited on his glances with trembling, and shut her best soul in prison, paying it only hidden visits, that she might be petty enough to please him'. There Dorothea has hit on an expressivist *ethical* truth of far-reaching consequence that none of her moral attempts to see Casaubon as an equivalent centre of self, or a poor battered 'soul', has been able to reach. As we have seen, imprisoning most of her best impulses is exactly what she has done in order to try to constrict herself into the wifely thing he wishes for.

But then that ethical truth is no sooner out than the whole drift of the passage is checked by a new note: 'In such a crisis as this, some women begin to hate.' Evidently not Dorothea, we gather. The way this reminder of Dorothea's unusualness and nobility cuts across what has gone before suggests that George Eliot is not entirely convinced that we will still believe in these qualities now we have seen Dorothea in this mood. She herself is uncomfortable with where things have led, as is made plain by the way she slides into sub-Kantian *moral* terms that begin to make Dorothea's overflowing anger seem like a corrupt *conscious choice of the will*: 'She had never deliberately allowed her resentment to govern her in this way before … ' Once she has slipped into seeing things in these terms, the only real choice for a Dorothea is deliberately *not* to allow such feelings to express themselves, which means by an act of will overthrowing or repressing them. And in due course this is what happens. After some meditation on Casaubon's 'sorrows', 'the resolved submission [does] come', she conquers herself, and 'the noble habit of the soul reasserts itself' (p. 464).

At the point at which George Eliot slips into sub-Kantian terms she demonstrates precisely why I have been insisting that narrative repression of the expressive demands of desire (and thwarted desire) is a form of the *ethical* unconscious. When Eliot suddenly introduces her vocabulary of delinquent choice we sense the presence of a predilection in her that cannot let the full significance of Dorothea's resentment and submissions express themselves – in ways that would have obvious bearing on the question 'How should a human being live?' And this happens precisely because too much is ruled out of account by Eliot's commitment to a specifically *moral* vocabulary. As Bernard Williams so persuasively argues, practical ethical deliberation 'involves an *I* that must be more intimately the *I* of my desire than this [Kantian] account allows'.[16] He goes on to raise a psychological question that is crucial in the world of *Middlemarch*: 'How can an *I* that has taken on the perspective of impartiality be left with enough identity to live a life that respects its own interests?'[17] George Eliot does not entirely evade the question of how Dorothea's 'noble habit of the soul' squares with her long-term interests. She somewhere seems to realise that, pursued for much longer, such self-effacement can only lead to some form of psychic crisis, as is shown in the diagnosis that Lydgate makes of Dorothea's state not long after Casaubon's death: 'He felt sure that she had been suffering from the strain and conflict of self-repression' (p. 534). This is spot on. And, given how she is here, how much more self-repression could Dorothea imaginably take? If we suppose, as we are invited to, that Casaubon had lived for another fifteen years or more and Dorothea had spent those years 'in helping and obeying him' (p. 520), how could she possibly have avoided either destroying herself in 'the strain and conflict of self repression' – or else coming to see that there was something wrong with such a 'habit of the soul'? And, more to the point, had George Eliot not killed off Casaubon when she did, how could she possibly have avoided seeing the limits of the moral vocabulary that her imagination is fettered by? Clearly Eliot is bound by 'compassion' too.

This helps to explain, I think, a good deal about the Dorothea parts of *Middlemarch*: such as why Casaubon's early death is such a

significant evasion; and why Eliot loses her critical perspective on
Dorothea just at the point at which Dorothea realises, with all its
implications for her, that Casaubon is an equivalent centre of self –
when her moral vision, in short, becomes Dorothea's. At that point,
George Eliot's imagining becomes fatally binary and she seems to lose
all sense of the things that are so finely and fully realised early on in
Dorothea's choice of Casaubon, the unconscious self-delusions that
come partly from an even deeper adolescent fear of life. From about
chapter 20 onwards Dorothea's characteristic suppressions, such as
her blindness to the plain fact that Will Ladislaw loves her, and to the
fact that Casaubon is keenly alive to it all – all of these become
expressions of an adorable high-minded innocence. But they can only
become that because Dorothea's blind spots are analogous to her
creator's. Eliot herself is clinging to a moral master-narrative in such
a way that she will not, perhaps cannot, admit to some of the
adulterous energies latent in the triangular tale she is telling. This is
the reason why Dorothea's love for Will while Casaubon is alive keeps
getting blurred into selfless ardour for justice, not just by Dorothea
but by Eliot too – becoming love, supposedly, only after Casaubon's
death; and why Will's love for her is constantly being blurred (if
there is enough imaginative substance there to blur) into a pure
recognition of Dorothea's pure adorableness, a kind of giving credit
where it is due; and why Casaubon's feelings about both of them are
constantly being discounted as those of suspicious egoism.

The bonds of 'compassion' impinge on George Eliot's imagining
of Casaubon at every point. The 'stricken soul' and 'bruised heart'
who figures in Dorothea's self-remonstrating thoughts is continuous
with the figure that George Eliot puts before us. As we have seen,
where the art is most vigorous, such as in chapter 20, it is the sudden
sight of this figure, flayed by suspicion and self-doubt, that makes us
check the assured censoriousness that George Eliot has trapped us
into feeling. But fresh moral refocusing of the kind that breaks down
habitual response cannot easily sustain itself, either for Dorothea or
for us. In the end, Dorothea has to make an effort to summon it in
order to try to squeeze from her heart a pang of sympathy. And that
goes with a fatal softening of Casaubon:

Dorothea sat almost motionless in her meditative struggle, while the evening
slowly deepened into night. But the struggle changed continually, as that of
a man who begins with a movement towards striking and ends with
conquering his desire to strike. The energy that would animate a crime is not

more than is wanted to inspire a resolved submission, when the noble habit of the soul reasserts itself. That thought with which Dorothea had gone out to meet her husband – her conviction that he had been asking about the possible arrest of all his work, and that the answer must have wrung his heart, could not be long without rising beside the image of him, like a shadowy monitor looking at her anger with sad remonstrance. It cost her a litany of pictured sorrows and of silent cries that she might be the mercy for those sorrows – but the resolved submission did come; and when the house was still, and she knew that it was near the time when Mr Casaubon habitually went to rest, she opened her door gently and stood outside in the darkness waiting for his coming up-stairs with a light in his hand. If he did not come soon she thought that she would go down and even risk incurring another pang. She would never again expect anything else. But she did hear the library door open, and slowly the light advanced up the staircase without noise from the foot-steps on the carpet. When her husband stood opposite to her, she saw that his face was more haggard. He started slightly on seeing her, and she looked up at him beseechingly, without speaking.

'Dorothea!' he said, with a gentle surprise in his tone. 'Were you waiting for me?'

'Yes, I did not like to disturb you.'

'Come, my dear, come. You are young, and need not to extend your life by watching.'

When the kind quiet melancholy of that speech fell on Dorothea's ears, she felt something like the thankfulness that might well up in us if we had narrowly escaped hurting a lamed creature. She put her hand into her husband's and they went along the broad corridor together. (pp. 464-5)

Here again, the very terms in which George Eliot envisages the possibility of Dorothea 'telling him the truth about her feeling' show that for her there can be only one possible outcome to Dorothea's 'meditative struggle'. To tell him would be like striking him – or, even more revealingly, like committing a crime in a situation where the two possibilities, of committing it or of not committing it, have been balanced on the fulcrum of full consciousness and require equal energy of will to animate either of them. Such figures, particularly the legal one, take away from Dorothea's angry 'feeling' any ethical rights or significance it might have. Seen in these terms, it hardly seems to be 'feeling' at all but perverse volitional 'energy'. The moral task that Dorothea is implicitly set by these terms is to find the 'energy' to tip the scales in the way they should be tipped – which means (being the person she is) precisely trying to summon or to excite in herself the *right* feelings. And so, 'with sad remonstrance' comes the thought that always helps, the thought of Casaubon's suffering 'heart': she goes back to 'her conviction that he had been asking [Lydgate] about the possible arrest of all his work, and that the answer must have wrung his heart'. But it is crucial to notice here that it is not simply a spontaneously arising thought about Casaubon that finally wrings Dorothea's heart; nor is it a thought leading her to discover underlying feelings. It is a 'litany of pictured sorrows' that can only come by her own effort of will. She has to make herself picture them ('It cost her a litany ... ') which means, in effect, that she has to make herself feel for the sorrows what she does not, in the ordinary sense, really feel. Nobody who knows the kind of religious meditation on which hers is based will want to judge what she does here too harshly, but it is clear in this case that these 'pictured sorrows' can only be creating an imaginary and highly tendentious conception of Casaubon. That imaginary Casaubon is the 'stricken soul' and the 'bruised heart' whose point is to make the heart of the faithful wife melt in compassionate sorrow. The word for that sort of excitation of feeling (no matter how worthy the object) is sentimentality.

It is one thing for Dorothea to sentimentalise Casaubon (she, so to speak, has to try to live with him), but quite another for George Eliot to do it. The Casaubon we find at the end of this chapter looks up at Dorothea with a 'gentle surprise' and speaks with a 'kind quiet melancholy', a bit stiffly, it is true, but certainly kindly and gently, meeting her need for response in a way he has not ever done before. True, fearful, self-preoccupied egos like Casaubon's need not always be suspicious and repellent; but the thing that is revealing here is the strangely providential way in which Casaubon suddenly answers to Dorothea's meditational image of him. He becomes the Casaubon in those 'pictured sorrows', a kind of 'lamed creature' (George Eliot's image) whom Dorothea has 'narrowly escaped hurting'. Casaubon does not remain like that for long, admittedly, but this is not simply a momentary imaginative lapse either, because its clear effect is to seem to justify Dorothea's submission. And, given the prominence that this little scene gets by virtue of being the ending of Book IV (the half-way point of the novel), its intended argumentative weight can hardly be overestimated. To have the two of them walking hand in hand 'along the broad corridor together' at such a crucial point is to give a specious feeling of possibility that entirely glosses over what have been so compellingly imagined: all those forces at play between them that make their marriage, to borrow Lawrence's word, an inter-destruction. The gentle 'lamed creature' who takes her hand is the man who simply cannot help making Dorothea 'shut her best soul in prison', and that is far too much to forget at a point such as this one. All this suggests that there is a close relationship between two things in *Middlemarch* that are usually thought of as separate, or even opposed: George Eliot's moral vision and the sentimentality that weakens the story of Dorothea, especially towards the end.

The signs of danger are there even where there is no hint of gush, for example, in the famous passage at the end of chapter 21 that irradiates so many of the novel's particulars with the broad and strong light of general truth:

We are all of us born in moral stupidity, taking the world as an udder to feed our supreme selves: Dorothea had early begun to emerge from the stupidity, but yet it had been easier to her to imagine how she would devote herself to Mr Casaubon, and become wise and strong in his strength and wisdom, than to conceive with that distinctness which is no longer reflection but feeling – an idea wrought back to the directness of sense, like the solidity of objects – that he had an equivalent centre of self, whence the lights and shadows must always fall with a certain difference. (p. 243)

The danger lurks in the idea that Dorothea had yet to learn 'to conceive with that distinctness which is no longer reflection but feeling ... that he had an equivalent centre of self ... ' The formulation does not distinguish between at least two quite different ways in which 'reflection' can become 'feeling', which imply two quite different ways of regarding such 'feeling'. In one case, reflecting on someone can reach and reanimate buried feelings towards them, or even activate wholly new ones – as we are shown so forcibly in the passage in which Casaubon's sensitivities are revealed in chapter 20. Ultimately, such 'moral feeling', as we call it, comes to obviate the need for reflection in similar situations. But equally, as Dorothea's meditational struggles show, reflection can be a way of actively and self-coercively creating feelings that for some reason have to be felt, so in some sense can be seen as forced or 'unreal' feelings.

It is important to notice that these two different conceptions of thought-induced feeling come from different traditions. The first is part of what one might broadly term the 'classical' tradition, which holds to a quite legitimate way in which some feeling is born of reflection – in the establishment of the virtues. Very roughly, Aristotle's idea is that, although the virtues may begin in reasoning and choice, they become part of us by repeated exercise until finally we can speak of the 'right feeling' (one form being 'fellow-feeling') that is associated with *phronesis*.[18] Iris Murdoch shows she is part of the same tradition in her famous discussion, in *The Sovereignty of Good*, of a woman coming to think and so feel differently about her daughter-in-law.[19] More recently Martha Nussbaum has shown the great interest and value of this classical view by reminding us of the reverse process – that feelings are 'discriminating responses closely connected to beliefs about how things are and what is important'.[20] They are discriminating, presumably, because ethical reflection *has* become feeling; when the virtues are established, we do not have to reflect any more about many of the discriminations we make – as if by purely spontaneous feeling. It is clear then that this important view of feeling sees it as at least partly socially constructed, to use Rom Harré's term; we learn, largely from our culture, how to feel or when to emote. These phenomena are not simply responses of unmediated libido or biology.

The 'social constructionist' is therefore both an ancient and a very contemporary view of emotion, and it does not take much thought about the variety of human responses to given situations to see that it is a necessary one. It is often contrasted to a 'naturalist' (mostly Romantic)[21] view which sees emotion as more or less primal, pre-social, and 'deep' and therefore an expression of our true nature. According to this view, we should trust emotion to reveal to us our deepest, often unconscious, beliefs and insights – that is, those repressed by socialisation. Such a Romantic-expressivist conception can be found in the Tolstoyan notion of the 'heart' and in the distinction D. H. Lawrence makes in 'A Propos of *Lady Chatterley's Lover*' between 'real feelings' and 'mental feelings' (that is, socially derived ones):

How different they are, mental feelings and real feelings. Today, many people live and die without having had any real feelings – though they have had a 'rich emotional life' apparently, having showed strong mental feeling. But it is all counterfeit. In magic, one of the so-called 'occult' pictures represents a man standing, apparently, before a flat table mirror, which reflects him from the waist to the head, so that you have the man from head to waist, then his reflection downwards from the waist to head again. And whatever it may mean in magic, it means what we are today, creatures whose active emotional self has no real existence, but is all reflected downwards from the mind. Our education from the start has *taught* us a certain range of emotions, what to feel and what not to feel, and how to feel the feelings we allow ourselves to feel. All the rest is just non-existent. The vulgar criticism of any new good book is: Of course nobody ever felt like that! – People allow themselves to feel a certain number of finished feelings. So it was in the last century. This feeling only what you allow yourselves to feel at last kills all capacity for feeling, and in the higher emotional range you feel nothing at all. This has come to pass in our present century. The higher emotions are strictly dead. They have to be faked.[22]

There is a rhetorical drive here that makes for over-simplicity (the term 'mental' tends to consign the whole 'classical' tradition to oblivion!), yet the central point Lawrence makes about mental feelings, particularly in what he calls 'the higher emotional range' (which includes love and compassion), is plainly relevant to George Eliot. As we have seen in the case of Dorothea, the mind can fake feelings, if it has to, or create an apparent 'active emotional self' that is actually a reflection of its own impulses – a reflection of what it needs or adheres to, or sees as right and fitting, or will 'allow', or will not 'allow'. We see this repeatedly:

But in Dorothea's mind there was a current into which all thought and feeling were apt sooner or later to flow – the reaching forward of the whole consciousness towards the fullest truth, the least partial good. There was clearly something better than anger and despondency. (p. 235)

As we see here, the 'current' into which Dorothea's 'thought and feeling' would sooner or later flow is the result of 'reaching forward', that is of moral *effort*, to feel in a certain ideal way. In this case the effort involves the suppression of 'anger' and 'despondency', in Lawrence's terms 'real feelings' which, as we have seen, cannot in the long run simply be overridden. Such feelings may not themselves be ultimately 'primal' or entirely free of social construction, yet clearly *some* Romantic-expressive account of feeling becomes dialectically necessary whenever there is strong commitment to moral rationality. The kind of mind that could frame the generalisation, 'we are all of us born in moral stupidity', with such authority and decidedness is a mind that will often want 'feeling' to fall into line. It is the decidedness that is the telling thing – after all, as George Eliot well knew, egoism is not the only thing, nor perhaps even the most important thing, to remark about the infantile self. (One wonders what Blake would have made of that generalisation of hers!) It is the very partiality and strength of her ethical conviction that carry with them the danger that 'feeling' will not always be, in Lawrence's sense, 'real feeling'.

A book that does make these necessary further distinctions between different kinds of ethical 'feeling' and motive is *Anna Karenina*, and for this reason, among others, it offers a much fuller truth than *Middlemarch* about mercy, pity, and love – one that Blake probably would not have baulked at. There, the dangers of moral purpose are brought to definition in (among other places) the interplay between Kitty and Varenka in Part 2, chapter 35. Kitty has realised that, in her attempts to serve others selflessly in the way that Varenka does, she has been false to herself and to others:

'Oh, it's so idiotic! So hateful! There was no need whatever for me to... Nothing but sham!' she said, opening and shutting the parasol.
'But with what object?'
'To appear better to people, to myself, to God – to deceive everyone. No, I won't descend to that again! I'll be bad; but at any rate not a liar, a humbug!'
'But who is a humbug?' said Varenka reproachfully. 'You speak as if...'
But Kitty was in one of her gusts of fury. She would not allow Varenka to finish.
'I am not talking about you, not about you at all. You are perfection. Yes, yes, I know you are all perfection; but how can I help it if I am wicked? This would never have happened if I weren't wicked. So let me be what I am, but I won't be a sham. What is Anna Pavlovna to me? Let them go their way and me go mine. I can't be different... And yet it's not that, it's not that.'
'What is not that?' asked Varenka in bewilderment.
'Everything. I can't act except from the heart, but you act from principle. I liked you simply, but you most likely only wanted to save me, to improve me.'
'You are unfair,' said Varenka. (p. 255)

There is no simple backing of Kitty in this passage (she is being a bit 'unfair', not least to herself), nor any simple judging of Varenka (her steadiness and presence are a real force), yet it is clear that the art is here searching out the limits and the costs of the kind of self-denying goodness that comes from 'principle'. The novel is wise and capacious enough to understand that such self-giving, for all its efficacy and fineness, can be a subtle evasion of life – and it is this, in Varenka and discovered also in herself, that Kitty is suddenly aware of. This is the 'sham', the self-deceiving love and concern for others that come from adherence to 'principle' and not from the 'heart'. Kitty is wrong, as Varenka points out (and as she herself half-knows), when she says that Varenka probably only wanted to save her or improve her; but her distinction is precisely the right one: 'I liked you simply' is a gesture towards the real feeling that draws them to each other, the feeling that comes frankly, and without prompting or any spiritual claims, from the 'heart'. As her father's return has reminded her, that (at least for Tolstoy) is the only trustworthy source of mercy, pity, and love.

'I liked you simply' – that (like the prince's return) comes as a breath of fresh air amid the spiritual intensities of Madame Stahl and Varenka. And the novelist who can see its central value in relation to so much else, including the farther reaches of Christian self-abnegation, does not overvalue principled 'compassion' or mistake it for something else. Where this becomes particularly evident is in his imagining of Karenin. Like Casaubon, Karenin is something of a 'social being': he is deeply afraid, mostly self-preoccupied, unspontaneous, needing to be unimpeachable in everything because he fears the world's scorn above all things and half-imagines he sees it everywhere. But it is impossible to sum him up in that way as he changes markedly in the course of the novel, especially after he knows he has lost Anna's love or affection. For the fact is Anna is fond of him, to put it no higher, as we see in a small incident near the beginning:

'I don't see how a man like that can be exonerated, even though he is your brother,' said Karenin severely.

Anna smiled. She knew he said that expressly to show that family considerations could not deter him from giving his genuine opinion. She knew this trait in her husband's character and liked it. (p. 126)

Whatever Anna may want, her deepest living self has already found its centre in Vronsky; yet her response to Karenin here is also, in Kitty's sense, from 'the heart'. And here we see one important thing that that means. Her smile and the feeling it manifests are drawn from her by a quality in Karenin she knows well and cannot help liking. They come without effort as a response to *him*. And Anna's response to Karenin is part of Tolstoy's own; without it, that slightly self-satisfied and self-righteous tone might lead us to overlook what really is likeable in such an awkward attempt to be sincere.

Significantly, this quality is absent from George Eliot's imaging of Casaubon: pitiable, contemptible, laughable he may be, but he is hardly ever remotely likeable or lovable, unless 'love' there means something like compassion or charity or pity. This absence is significant, not on the (sentimental) grounds that there must be something likeable about everyone, but because it points to one of the subjects on which George Eliot is most insistent: that is, the nature, the validity, and the appropriateness both of Dorothea's feelings for Casaubon and of his reactions to those feelings. Dorothea is supposed to love him and to waste her strong 'affection' upon him. It is his unresponsiveness to that 'affection' that makes him, for George Eliot, practically unforgivable: 'He distrusted her affection; and what loneliness is more lonely than distrust?' (p. 480). And what loneliness, by implication, could be more *deserved*? For that is the implication: given what Dorothea keeps offering him, it is his own fault if he cannot trust it. But then that implication raises the question: is it entirely Casaubon's own fault? And, even more important, what is it that Dorothea *does* offer him? We can easily find a ready enthusiasm for helping him with his work, and ardent concern for him when his health fails, much pity and compassion for his anxieties and disappointments, and beneath all this a great hunger for 'affection' from him. But where do we find Dorothea actually feeling 'affection' for something in him, where it would be possible to say that she, like Anna, 'knew this trait in her husband's character *and liked it*'? The only reason that this matters is that George Eliot herself is convinced that Casaubon is given the very best that any husband could be given:

She nursed him, she read to him, she anticipated his wants, and was solicitous about his feelings; but there had entered into the husband's mind the certainty that she judged him, and that her wifely devotedness was like a penitential expiation of unbelieving thoughts – was accompanied with a power of comparison by which himself and his doings were seen too luminously as a part of things in general. His discontent passed vapour-like through all her gentle loving manifestations, and clung to that inappreciative world which she had only brought nearer to him.

Poor Mr Casaubon! This suffering was the harder to bear because it seemed like a betrayal: the young creature who had worshipped him with perfect trust had quickly turned into the critical wife; and early instances of criticism and resentment had made an impression which no tenderness and submission afterwards could remove. To his suspicious interpretation Dorothea's silence now was a suppressed rebellion; a remark from her which he had not in any way anticipated was an assertion of conscious superiority; her gentle answers had an irritating cautiousness in them; and when she acquiesced it was a self-approved effort of forbearance. (pp. 455–6)

All of this is intended to show how Casaubon's suspicious egoism turns even these 'gentle loving manifestations' into instances of mere outward dutifulness that conceal rather less 'loving' attitudes and impulses towards him. But then Casaubon is surely closer to the truth about Dorothea than George Eliot supposes. As we have seen, 'her wifely dutifulness' often does require something 'like a penitential expiation of unbelieving thoughts', because in her heart Dorothea does 'judge' Casaubon, at times with irresistible hostility. And in her acquiescence there *is* 'a self-approved effort of forbearance'. 'Self-approved' is very penetrating. There is a quality of faintly self-approving righteousness in almost all those 'loving' actions of Dorothea's; they are shaped at least as much by a conscious virtue of hers (a need to serve in some great and generous way) as they are by any objective need for them in Casaubon. And '*effort* of forbearance' is exactly right too, for much of her 'tenderness and submission', as we have seen, is only made possible by an effort to overcome feelings of 'suppressed rebellion' and 'resentment'.

The striking thing here (compared with the passage in chapter 20) is that George Eliot seems unable to see much value in Casaubon's sense of things, and one reason why she does not, or cannot, is that a half-'suppressed' 'resentment' seems to be part of her own response to Casaubon. This is the significance of the tone of the passage discussed earlier:

She was *always* trying to be what her husband wished, and *never* able to repose on his delight in what she was. The thing that she liked, that she spontaneously cared to have, seemed to be *always* excluded from her life; (p. 516, my italics)

Compare this with Dorothea's 'rebellious anger' in another passage discussed above:

What have I done – what am I – that he should treat me so? He *never* knows what is in my mind – he *never* cares. What is the use of *anything* I do? (p. 463, my italics)

There is a clear continuity between the two tones, so that it is impossible to tell in the first where Dorothea begins and George Eliot ends. The feeling in both is resentment rather than anger because of the sense of powerlessness that goes with a note of self-pity: 'always trying' is going to get nowhere because 'he never cares', so 'what is the use' of expressing it? Implicit in that is the belief that the other is the stronger one, the one who is responsible for the way she feels and is – all she can do is suffer it. Already the feeling is half-suppressed and diffused away from the self into rather impotent appeals against the injustice of it all.

Here again, that Dorothea feels all this about Casaubon is understandable, but that George Eliot cannot see the *partiality* of that way of feeling means that her art is only offering us a half-truth. Casaubon certainly is partly responsible for the way Dorothea feels; he is an oppressor. But equally, Dorothea is a self-suppressor; her 'what is the use ...'? is a way of containing the feeling, of damming it up, so that she will 'always' go on 'trying' and resenting Casaubon for not responding – all that rather than be openly angry with him and so, in her eyes, show herself to be an 'egoist' after all. The moment we challenge George Eliot's explicit insistences, we see at once that the marriage is interdestructive: Dorothea can no more help 'trying to be what her husband wished' than he can help wishing her to be other than she is. But then, if the fullest view is to be taken, is this not precisely what Dorothea wishes about him too? 'If he had drawn her towards him she would never have surveyed him ... but would have felt him simply a part of her life' (p. 463). If only he had been different. Significantly, the novel never prompts us to ask about the effect of this wish on him, or about the kind of companionship that 'poor Casaubon' was hungering for, or about the thing he liked and spontaneously cared to have – not the pity he shrank from, nor the compassionate submissions he did not ask for, nor the moral ardour that alarmed him, nor the effort at forbearance he so rightly suspected, nor the suppressed judgment and rebellion, but an affection that would let him repose on a delight in what he was. Only this, presumably, could have helped make Casaubon different – more trusting in his own impulses and less defended against others'. Such possibilities hardly seem to occur to George Eliot.

If we ask why they do not occur to her, the answer seems to be that her resentment of Casaubon is just like Dorothea's. It too is dammed-up hostility towards a figure like Tom Tulliver in some ways, a hostility that is not able to express itself except in a diffused, half-suppressed kind of way because it can have no legitimate place in her moral scheme. And, because it is denied, it comes out (as resentment will) as a constant tacit appeal against the injustice of Casaubon being the way he is, suspicious, unresponsive, and harsh. In this George Eliot actually denies her best insights about him by implying that his whole mode of being is ultimately a matter of moral choice.

The end result is the last one you would expect from George Eliot, and that is a complete seizure of real imaginative sympathy towards him. And what finally produces it is precisely Eliot's moral *commitment* to 'compassion'. For the whole truth about 'poor Casaubon' is much more complex (and pitiful) than George Eliot, for all her 'compassion', can allow herself to recognise.

CHAPTER 7

Forgetting and disorientation in 'Anna Karenina'

As Jane Adamson has pointed out, it is George Eliot's characteristic bent to remember that all her characters are 'equivalent centres of self' but sometimes to forget the extent to which 'the lights and shadows must always fall with a certain difference'.[1] *Middlemarch* is a very great novel partly because it keeps reminding us of human connectedness, interdependence, and the commonness of our lot; but its greatness is uneven because at crucial moments the novel loses sight of the importance of individual need and desire. In its commitment to a master-narrative of moral sympathy and impartiality, *Middlemarch* has no terms in which it can grant *ethical* legitimacy to those non-sympathetic feelings which individuals need in order to defend themselves. The lack of such a language, as I have argued, ultimately eviscerates morality, at moments even twisting its generous ideals into their opposites. Without an adequate ethical vocabulary of need and desire, the novel itself, as Lawrence would say, will be pulling down the scale to its own predilection and so preventing that 'trembling instability of the balance' which is the ultimate 'morality' of novelistic discourse.

We find such an adequate language in Tolstoy's notion of the 'heart'. In *Anna Karenina*, the 'heart' is partly a source of feeling, but one which includes both those 'classical' moral feelings that are the virtuous traces of reflection and choice as well as those gnawings of expressive desire and need that are so often suppressed by reflection and choice. The 'heart' is a kind of unconscious mind, where *all* that we have 'forgotten' is somehow remembered and lies in wait for us. Crucially that 'all' includes both sorts of unconsciousness I have been preoccupied with here *without distinction* – that is, unconsciousness both of human likeness and of those individual longings that are often too painful to remember. The Tolstoyan 'heart' is the fullest embodiment of what I have called the ethical unconscious.

The ethical fullness of *Anna Karenina* depends on the fact that it embraces no final vocabulary of human worth, no final set of evaluative distinctions, either of a moral or of an anti-moral kind. If, as Charles Taylor so suggestively argues, identity is a kind of orientation in moral space, then the power of Tolstoy's art comes from his capacity as an artist to revise that identity, to keep it provisional, before the demands of his art. The ethical greatness of *Anna Karenina* is precisely its offer to the reader of profound *disorientation* in moral space. Its 'impersonality', so different from Kantian 'impartiality', provides imagined lives of the deepest ethical interest because neither identity-defining commitment, nor its ubiquitous 'shadow', come into play unchecked. To a greater degree than any other novel considered here, *Anna Karenina* grounds its story of innocence and social being in 'uncertainties, Mysteries, doubts'.

D. H. Lawrence's view of *Anna Karenina* is well known: Tolstoy the true artist celebrated the spontaneous passionate life in Anna and Vronsky, whereas the embryonic old Leo, the fearful moralist and social being, envied them, making the vulgar social condemnation of them figure as divine punishment; and so he justified his cowardice, his sense of fault or failure, with a rigid metaphysic. Whatever grain of truth there may be in this, it is perverse and reductive, as several critics have shown. None the less, even some of the most searching accounts of the book have continued to see it essentially in these terms, not grasping the real problem, which is that *Anna Karenina* makes the terms themselves, and the oppositions they imply, ultimately inadequate.

Some have also applied to Tolstoy's novel the so-called 'abiding antitheses' between 'social beings' and 'innocents' (from Lawrence's Galsworthy essay).[2] And much about *Anna Karenina* really is lit up by these terms. Karenin, for instance, has more than once been seen as a purely 'social being', and it is not hard to see why. Think of him trying to keep up appearances as he leads Anna from the racecourse; or the way he is deflected from his so-called 'spiritual inclinations' by the world's sense of him after he has forgiven Anna and Vronsky; or how often he takes his bearings from what he reads in other people's eyes. And beneath all that there is a deep-seated fear of those 'mocking eyes' he sees all around him – at the levee, for instance; but he goes on anyway calmly expounding his new financial project item by item to the government official he has buttonholed, as ever cut off, in some fundamental way, from the life of his real feelings. So the account could go on, through all the 'innocent', courageous figures like Anna and Vronsky, Levin and Kitty, opposing them to those who are ultimately ego-bound and afraid, such as Koznyshev and Varenka, and in this way catching a good deal that is true about the book. But to press these terms harder against *Anna Karenina* is to see for a start that the Lawrentian 'antitheses' cut right across the fine grain of its thinking, and that the novel's whole substance and distinction, its 'subtle inter-relatedness' (Lawrence's own phrase), can only be understood by noticing the distinctive terms of its thinking. For example, Karenin again, at the levee:

'And how strong they all are, how physically sound,' he said to himself, looking at the powerfully-built gentleman of the bedchamber with his well-groomed, perfumed whiskers, and at the red neck of the prince in a tight-fitting uniform, whom he had to pass on his way out. 'It is truly said that all is evil in the world,' he thought, with another sidelong glance at the calves of the gentleman of the bedchamber. (V, 24, p. 544)

This shows Tolstoy's own grasp of the point Lawrence makes against him – how a 'metaphysic', a consciously held set of beliefs, can be an unconscious means of obscuring a feeling of failure, holding at bay the realisation of one's cowardice. And yet Tolstoy's characteristic emphasis is significantly different. As so often in *Anna Karenina*, it falls on the way in which blocked feelings and memories come to transmute much of the experienced world into arresting psychic symbols, which resonate with meaning in terms of those feelings and memories. Karenin's instantaneous perception of those shapely calves as yet another example of the evil of the world suppresses a whole chain of psychic moves connected in the first place to Anna and Vronsky, but beyond them to an even deeper tendency to self-distrust and self-contempt that events have merely confirmed. If Karenin's life, as almost everyone else at the levee perceives, is closing down (as opposed to Levin's, in the previous chapters, which is beginning to open up even as his brother dies), this is principally why: practically everything Karenin sees and thinks and does will be part of a struggle to forget what cannot, in the deepest sense, be forgotten. So all his indefatigable work, his endless memos and reports, like his religion, is more than ever out of touch – 'listened to', we are told, 'as if it were something long familiar and the very thing that was not needed' (p. 543).

But Karenin's reports are only an extreme case of something that

recurs in a number of forms in the novel: absorbing work that is to
some degree a form of forgetting – Koznyshev's Pan-Slavism, for
example, or Vronsky's painting and his hospital-building, Kitty's
zealous good works at the spa, even Levin's mowing. All of these are
seen as more or less subtle forms of sleep, giving relief from some
suppressed need or sense of failure gnawing at the heart; and all are
to some degree out of touch with relevant realities.

While the conscious mind can forget, there are things the heart
cannot. Or, rather, the whole novel is an exploration of what, given
that (as Anna says) there are as many different hearts as there are
heads, can and cannot be forgotten; and an exploration of the need
for, and the conditions under which, real forgetting of the things that
obsess the heart can take place. This includes a special form of
forgetting – forgiving, and being forgiven, and the whole range of
things that these can mean. It also involves remembering, and that
special Wordsworthian form of it Dirk den Hartog writes about in
Dickens and Romantic Psychology,[3] in which the heart is put back into
'innocent' touch with the world and its own vital sources.

These are central considerations for Tolstoy, not like the comments
of Vronsky and his party about Mihailov's painting – 'only one
reflection in a million that might have been made, with equal truth'
(V, 11, p. 499). They organise the whole rhythm and movement of
the novel, and at every level. A telling example is Levin at dinner
with Oblonsky just before he proposes to Kitty. Oblonsky talks about
his current affair, but Levin for a variety of reasons can only become
judgmental, classifying women into two types, women like Kitty and
'fallen women' – a truly ominous phrase. Oblonsky presses him to
think harder, to try to put himself in his, Oblonsky's, place, yet Levin
becomes more and more clenched, more and more rigidly categorical
– as a prelude to remembering:

'If you want my opinion, I can only tell you that I do not believe there is any
conflict about it. For this reason: to my mind, love – both kinds of love
(Plato defines them in his *Symposium*) serve as a criterion. Some men only
understand one sort, and some only the other. And those who only
understand the non-platonic love have no need to talk of conflict. In such
love there can be no conflict. "Much obliged for the gratification, my
humble respects" – and that is all there is to it. And in Platonic love there
can be no conflict because in that love all is clear and pure, because...'

At that instant, Levin recollected his own sins and the inner conflict he
had lived through. And he added unexpectedly:

'However, perhaps you are right. You may very likely be ... But I don't know, I really don't know.'

'There, you see', said Oblonsky, 'you're very much all of a piece. It's both your strong point and your failing. You are all of a piece and you want the whole of life to be consistent too – but it never is. You scorn public service because you want the reality to correspond all the time to the aim – and that's not how it is. You want man's work, too, always to have a definite purpose, and love and family life to be indivisible. But that does not happen either. All the variety, all the charm, all the beauty of life are made up of light and shade.'

Levin sighed and made no reply. He was thinking of his own affairs and not listening to Oblonsky. (I, 11, pp. 55–6)

Levin, recollecting 'his own sins and the inner conflict he had lived through' (like the Pharisees in John 8), makes a connection between his experience and Oblonsky's that breaks down the simple judgmental binary pattern of his thinking, whose symbolic emphases have been shaped precisely by those actively forgotten feelings and experiences. And in that, Levin's expanded awareness points to the imaginative fullness of the scene itself: while so carefully defining the two men against each other, it never loses touch with what is common in their experience. For all that may be said about the Levin in Tolstoy, one of the most important strengths of the novel is the almost unfailing resistance it offers to any judgmental tendency in us to read its world as Levin first reads his experience, in terms of simple categorical oppositions. At the same time Levin's momentarily baffled 'But I don't know, I really don't know' goes close to the imaginative heart of *Anna Karenina*, since our own ethical imaginations are constantly being unbalanced and rebalanced by the very twists and turns of the lives in which they are so absorbed. That it should be Oblonsky (Stiva of all people) to set Levin right on a matter of conscience is not even the beginning of it, because what he says, so full of the 'charm' and 'beauty' he speaks of, is itself made up of 'light and shade'. The novel's 'beauty of life' is a simultaneous grasp of both what shines on Levin for the moment, illuminating him, and what is unconsciously cast, by the very direction and intensity of that light, into shade. The direction and intensity of the light derive from the fact that Oblonsky is both forgetting something and being subliminally reminded of it too: Dolly, and that shameful sense of himself the memory of her evokes. To speak of all the 'charm' of life's 'variety' as he does is to fudge such central issues as choice and responsibility in a way that Levin could not. The point is not, as

Logan Speirs suggests,[4] that Levin's and Oblonsky's 'moral attitudes are [being] compared' here. In imagining these two ethical possibilities Tolstoy is wholly inter-illuminating them, not merely what these men fix upon in the world or how they fix upon it, but also *why* they do it in that particular way. And the why in *Anna Karenina* comes from the shade of forgetting cast by the heart.

This scene is a mere moment, but its structure and movement, its various balancings and unbalancings, illustrate even here what Mihailov calls 'the indescribable complexity of every living thing' (V, 11, p. 499). Mihailov's phrase is about the whole picture, which brings to mind the far larger and more complex structures and movements of the novel itself. These involve changes and stabilities, growths and diminishments, that radically challenge the characters' need (and that of critics too) to forget whatever threatens the conscious values and ideas which make up the hard rind of their known, everyday identities.

The imagining of other people is a crucial part of this challenge, especially when these others are suddenly seen in a new light, or when they actually seem to change – as Anna does, for instance, when she falls in love with Vronsky. At that point, Karenin's crudely categorical cast of mind is tested by what does not seem to fit any more into its reductive order. Tolstoy likens this order to a bridge, constructed out of all the habitual decisions and rationalisations of conscious life, the point of which is to negotiate life without ever having to notice its frightening unfixity.

One of the fears that constructs the bridge is the one Karenin faces in Anna as he thinks about her behaviour at Princess Betsy's soirée, the fear even of the 'possibility' of change, especially in one so important to him as Anna. To recognise that possibility would threaten the very categories in which he can know her, or anyone (including himself), and so confront him with an 'abyss' of particulars, unsteady and uncontainable. Karenin shows the mind's need to defend itself against the shock of such a recognition, the need in this case to forget all that is 'separate' and other, even in, and perhaps especially in, the life of one so closely bound up in his:

Here, as he looked at her table, at the malachite cover of her blotter, and an unfinished letter lying on it, his thoughts suddenly underwent a change. He began to think of her, of what she was thinking and feeling. For the first time he really pictured to himself her personal life, her ideas, her desires; and the notion that she could and should have a separate life of her own appeared to him so dreadful that he hastened to drive it away. This was the abyss into which he was afraid to look. To put himself in thought and feeling into another being was a mental exercise foreign to Karenin. He considered such mental exercise harmful and dangerous romancing.

'And the worst of it all,' he thought, 'is that now, just as my work is nearing completion' (he was thinking of the project he was bringing forward at the time), 'when I need peace of mind and all my energies, this idiotic anxiety has to fall on me. But what is to be done? I am not one to suffer anxiety and trouble without having the courage to face them.'

'I must think it over and come to a decision, and put it out of my mind', he said aloud.

'The question of her feelings, of what has taken place or may take place in her heart, is not my affair but the affair of her conscience, and comes under the head of religion', he said to himself, feeling relieved at having found the category of regulating principles to which the newly-arisen situation rightly belonged. (II, 8, pp. 159–60)

Tolstoy, we should notice, can imagine 'the abyss' of Karenin's 'separate life' without turning away, as George Eliot does with Casaubon, to offer a general diagnosis of 'egoism' instead of grasping all that is at risk for such a figure in the apparently simple imaginative act of putting himself in thought and feeling into someone else's place. At risk for Karenin is nothing less than the whole structure of his conscious identity, what Michael Black calls his 'ego-shell'.[5] It is this shell, and not the important work, that is the real achievement of Karenin's life – the outer achievements are only means of solidifying it, holding it in place. As Tolstoy sees him, there is much within Karenin that is quite other than the detached, self-possessed, rational identity he has constructed and takes himself to be. There are among other things powerful self-pitying impulses, which make tears, especially in women, quite unbearable to him because they remind him of deeply hurt feelings he must hold back and which threaten to overwhelm him, to crack the shell open from within. For Karenin, unlike Levin, the pathways back to remembrance must be sealed off, and are until the famous moment beside Anna's supposed death-bed; this is why, for him, there *can* be no deepened or expanded imaginative engagement with life, no seeing others as equivalent centres of self, not even a baffled 'But I don't know, I really don't know', for in this sense Karenin *must* 'know'. Here Tolstoy sees clearly, as George Eliot sometimes does not, that so-called 'egoism' in a figure like Karenin will always spring from an urgent self-protective need. His sudden recollection of the important work that requires peace of mind comes along with a reminder of who 'I am' precisely because the known stable ego, the habitual 'I am', is threatened with dissolution. And the anxiety that goes with that can only be allayed by a form of knowing that thoroughly depersonalises the whole situation, that sees it not as 'my affair', but as an objective *case* to be grasped according to 'regulating principles' that already existed. His relief is that his pre-existing binary categories seem to contain the situation and so hold life once again in place, re-establishing the solidity both of the world and of the known, socially defined identity within it. He is the husband, head of the family, and she the erring wife; he can now cross the bridge with the clear duty to instruct and to correct her.

In this respect, Karenin is only one extreme of a continuum that includes every character in the novel. Levin with his two categories of women, Koznyshev with his mentalised sense of the peasants, Vronsky with his narrow, orderly sense of things, Anna herself, most grotesquely of all, just before her death – all at times need to make life fit into drastically reductive terms. The novel begins to draw attention to this need from the moment Oblonsky, waking up from his dream, reveals the binary categories into which his experience is habitually cast and which fix life in the shape he wishes it to assume – himself a 'handsome susceptible man of 34' and Dolly 'a good mother but she was already faded and plain and no longer young, a simple uninteresting woman'.

Oblonsky's waking up introduces a related set of metaphors – habitual consciousness as a kind of sleep, waking life as a dream. 'Oh dear, what am I to do?', Oblonsky asks when he remembers the situation he is in, and the novel straight away indicates the non-answer that everyone in it will enact: 'live from day to day; in other words, forget. But as he could not find forgetfulness in sleep, at least not until bed-time, nor return to the music sung by the little decanter-women, he must therefore lose himself in the dream of life' (I, 1, p. 16). This transposition of sleep and waking life underlines the importance of those little decanter-women whose music sounds a keynote for the whole novel:

'Yes, now, how did it go?' he thought, recalling a dream. 'Now how did it go? Oh yes! Alabin was giving a dinner in Darmstadt. No, it wasn't Darmstadt but some American place. Yes, but the dream Darmstadt was in America. That's it – Alabin was giving a dinner on glass tables – and the tables were singing *Il mio tesoro*. No, not *Il mio tesoro*, something better; and there were some little decanters who were women', he remembered.

Oblonsky's eyes began to sparkle merrily and he smiled as he continued with his thoughts. 'Yes, it was a nice dream – very nice indeed. There was a lot that was capital but not to be expressed in words or even thought about clearly now that I am awake.' Then, noticing the streak of light from one side of the heavy blinds, he cheerfully thrust his feet down to feel for the slippers which his wife had worked in gold morocco for his last birthday present. Next, without getting up, he stretched out his hand as he had done for the last nine years to where his dressing-gown usually hung in the bedroom. And then memory flashed on him how and why it was that he was sleeping not in his wife's room but in the study. The smile vanished from his face and he frowned.

'Oh dear, dear, dear!' he groaned, remembering what had happened. And he went over all the details of the scene with his wife, seeing the complete hopelessness of his position and, most tormenting thought of all, the fact that it was his own fault.

'No, she will never forgive me – she cannot forgive me! And the worst of it is that I am to blame for everything – I am to blame and yet I am not to blame. That is the whole tragedy', he mused, and recalled despairingly the most painful aspects of the quarrel. (I, 1, pp. 13–14)

As the border between sleep and waking is extended, so being awake, like the dream, is seen to have fine shades not easily 'expressed in words or even thought about clearly'. Oblonsky is not fully awake until memory flashes on him, and he recalls why he is sleeping in the study. Before that, while he is basking in the cheerful mood of the dream things have been in their usual places, slippers, dressing-gown, and himself in his wife's bedroom. And it soon becomes clear that Oblonsky's need for that 'cheerful mood' is quite invincible; things will soon be back in their usual places, even if, as in the dream, Darmstadt has to be in America and Dolly must become one of those little singing decanter-women. Oblonsky's everyday facts, the supposed fixities of his waking life (such as his sense of Dolly as a 'simple uninteresting woman ... [who] really ought to be indulgent') are as wishful in their way as the strange metamorphic impossibilities of dreams. The dream symbolises Oblonsky's wishes by humanising objects – how nice it would be if women *were* just decanters to be savoured, picked up, drained, and put down at one's pleasure! But then this is exactly what he tries to do in waking life, not least by objectifying women until, like Dolly, they rather inconveniently refuse simply to be put down.

This beginning hints that disorientation will be an important experience in the novel – and of the novel too. Things from here on are not going to be quite in their usual places for the reader either, because for all the characters the form of everyday forgetful consciousness is the dream, with its symbolic intensities and absences and its spurious internally consistent rationality. This becomes most marked where what needs to be forgotten is unbearably significant, as Anna is for Seriozha, for instance, or her whole former identity is for her. The culmination is Anna's last day where actuality takes on the haunting intensity of nightmare. Then the inner chaos of her self-torment flickers on the screen of the world as a 'clear', coherent vision of nihilistic disgust: 'Everything is false and evil – all lies and deceit!' (VII, 31, p. 800). This, together with her sense of all the eyes in the crowd staring at her, echoes Karenin's feeling at the levee, of running the gauntlet of mocking eyes. For both of them, the feelings the heart cannot forget stare back from the world, as they do in another way for Levin when he knows Kitty will accept him. In each case the eyes seem to validate a clearly apprehended, internally consistent, but drastically reduced and simplified reading of the world.

Tolstoy's art realises all these related de-realisings so compellingly from within partly because it never loses touch either with what is distinctive in each case or with what relates it to all the rest. Anna's 'plunge' into final forgetfulness comes full circle, without the slightest hint of predetermined design (at least in this), back to Stiva's waking up. In her last moment, on the border between life and death, Anna crosses herself and suddenly awakens from the nightmare of life: 'The familiar gesture brought back a whole series of memories of when she was a girl, and of her childhood, and suddenly the darkness that had enveloped everything for her lifted, and for an instant life glowed before her with all its past joys' (VII, 31, p. 801). There is nothing softening about this. The glow is dreadful in that (unlike the flickering candle by which she has been reading the nihilistic book filled with trouble and deceit, sorrow and evil) it lights up the ineradicable 'innocence' of her deepest ethical being: what in her cannot be, even now, other than responsible to life and makes her anything but simply a Stiva or a Karenin. The moment is dreadful because we see the inexorable inner logic that has led to it: this is the only way that Anna, being who she is, can for an instant wake up to be the whole self she would want to be, in the very act that cuts her in two.

This is why moments of awakening, not least in sleep itself, are of central importance in the novel. At such moments the characters are cut adrift by events and experiences that cannot be contained within the coherence of the dream-logic they need or wish to live by, and so they catch a glimpse of all that is not so 'clear' as the little candle of wish and need had made it seem. Levin's night in the fields in part 3, chapter 12, is one such, where 'the idea of renunciation', of a life shared with the peasants, comes to him as a heartfelt 'vision': 'The simplicity, the integrity, the sanity of this life he felt clearly ...' (p. 298). The joy he feels is reflected in the clouds, as Levin sees himself: 'Yes, and my views of life changed in the same imperceptible way!' What he cannot let himself see, until Kitty passes, is that this is an ominous image, pointing to the fact that conscious 'views', renunciations and decisions change and vanish like clouds. What is solid, and revealed just at that moment 'that usually precedes day break and the final victory of light over darkness', is Kitty, who embodies Levin's deepest wish for himself as she appears to him 'full of a subtle, complex inner life, remote from Levin' (p. 299). It is one of the most moving moments in the novel, and yet, for all its emotional amplitude, in every way earthbound and utterly uncloudlike in its grasp of the relevant realities. Kitty really is 'remote' from him and will in a way always remain so – she does not remember the moment in this way at all, if indeed she does remember it. And yet, as here, life can, and sometimes does, bring what is longed for, in the Tolstoyan phrase, 'from the bottom of the heart': this is surely one of the central possibilities the novel realises while it works out, in the same interrelating focus, the fates of Anna, Vronksy, Karenin, Seriozha, and all the others.

The fully awakened heart can be put back into 'innocent' touch with the world, able to see it in the way that Levin momentarily sees Kitty in the carriage, as subtle, complex, other, mysterious, and ever-moving (in both senses of the word) – that is, if life enables or allows the heart to be fully awake, and if one has the courage to take what it offers. This is the possibility Tolstoy explores in the marriage that begins the second half of the book. For Levin, there will always be something lacking, some elusive beyond, even at the end. Yet for Kitty it is otherwise. At her wedding, before the gaze of her parents, friends, and 'all Moscow', she is able to experience the man she loves as a being unknown, 'uncomprehended by her, to whom she was bound by a feeling of alternate attraction and repulsion even less comprehensible than the man himself' (V, 4, p. 478). At the same time, 'the old life', even the father so dear to her, seems a thing of indifference to her, like the rind in Lawrence's image of the established personality that falls away letting the new self, naked and undefended, drop into the unknown. The author of *The Rainbow* can hardly have been untouched by Tolstoy's way of putting it:

And now behold, anticipation and uncertainty, and remorse at repudiating her old life – were at an end and the new was beginning. (V, 4, p. 479)

Kitty can assent to the new life, wholeheartedly – that is the possibility she focuses. Anna, we are reminded by Dolly, 'had once stood there just as innocent in her veil and orange-blossom' (V, 5, p. 482), but she cannot assent in this way when a new life begins to stir her heart on the train-journey back from Moscow:

'What does it mean? Am I really afraid of looking at the facts? Is there – can there be anything more between me and that officer-lad than there is between me and the rest of my acquaintances?' She laughed contemptuously and took up her book again; but this time she definitely could not follow what she was reading. She traced on the window with the paper-knife, then pressed its smooth cold surface to her cheek and nearly laughed aloud, suddenly and unaccountably overcome with joy. She felt her nerves being stretched more and more tightly, like strings round pegs. She felt her eyes opening wider and wider, her fingers and toes twitching nervously; felt something inside her oppressing her breathing; and all the shapes and sounds in the wavering half-light struck her with unaccustomed vividness. Moments of doubt kept coming upon her when she could not decide whether the train was moving forwards or backwards, or had come to a standstill. Was it Annushka at her side, or a stranger? 'What is that on the arm of the seat, a fur cloak or an animal? And what am I doing here? Am I myself or someone else?' She was terrified of giving way to this nightmare-state. But something seemed to draw her to it and she was free to yield to it or to resist. (I, 30, p. 116)

This 'nightmare-state' is no mere judgmental signpost of Tolstoy's pointing to Anna's end, because the whole thrust of the experience is to take her towards frightening but deeper recognitions about herself. As she begins to allow herself to realise what Vronsky means to her, Anna faces questions of the most basic kind about all her former moral certainties: if she has these feelings, these needs, then what in her life is what? What is familiar and what strange? Nothing is in its usual place. Vronsky has awakened her to depths in herself, to a whole abyss of expressive possibility, she has never imagined. The strong derealising effect of the train journey is a striking metaphor for what she discovers in herself: a new vitality, at once joyful and terrifying, that so transforms her sense of 'orientation in moral space' that it is like waking up to discover that she is 'someone else' – quite other than the old self she thought she was.

Anna, being what she is, cannot simply draw back into the safety of that old identity in all the many ways we see others doing, not least Varenka and Koznyshev when they have so much less at risk. She yields to this renewal in herself, to its vitalising and de-stabilising power, because those habitual boundaries and configurations correspond to a whole range of realities, emotional, personal and social, set in a complex stable order that must be disrupted if this new life is to have its way. Kitty's wedding partly reconstructs some of the stabilities at stake for Anna here. They are not merely 'social' ones in the external sense Lawrence's account would suggest – unless by 'social' we also mean ethical and religious feelings in Anna's heart, and there can be no easy (in Lawrence's phrase) thumbing of the nose at those.

Nor is Tolstoy thumbing the pan in quite the way some recent critics insist. Whatever might have been at stake for the old Leo in him, the artist in him can only have realised *his* full vitality at depths of imaginative engagement just as disorienting as Anna's 'moments of doubt', depths at which he has broken free from the husk of his established identity to face the question his art prompts us to face, too, as we respond to it: 'and what am *I* doing here?' Which in turn raises the even more disturbing, yet ultimately freeing, question implied in all dramatic imagining where it becomes truly impersonal: 'am I myself or someone else?' It has always been clear that Anna is the crucial imaginative challenge for the Christian moralist in Tolstoy, yet what has not always remained so clear is that it is only by *dissolving* his moral certainties that he can portray so inwardly the Romantic-expressive values represented by the new vitality in Anna. Only by taking a disorienting journey well beyond the boundaries of his conscious belief and routine identity can he realise fully who she is. This is why it does not get us very far to be reminded by K. M. Newton that 'Tolstoy is known to have rejected many of the assumptions of humanism' and so must have intended to condemn Anna.[6] Whatever Tolstoy believed or whatever his 'assumptions' were, the valuations made by his art can only be found there.

It is confrontation with change in the characters that is the crucial imaginative challenge for critics too. Here, what we are disposed to remember and to forget become most telling. Karenin's sudden 'feeling of love and forgiveness' at Anna's supposed death-bed is an important case:

Karenin grew more and more upset, until his emotion now reached such a point that he gave up struggling against it. He suddenly felt that what he had regarded as nervous agitation was on the contrary a blissful spiritual condition that gave him all at once a new happiness he had never known. He was not thinking that the Christian law which he had been trying to follow all his life enjoined on him to forgive and love his enemies; yet a glad feeling of love and forgiveness for his enemies filled his heart. He knelt down and laying his head in the curve of her arm, which burned like fire through her sleeve, he sobbed like a child. She put her arm round his head that was growing bald, moved closer towards him, and raised her eyes defiantly.

'There, I knew he would be like that! Now good-bye, everyone, good-bye ... They've come again – why don't they go away ... Oh, take these furs off me!' (IV, 17, pp. 438–9)

This has always been felt to be a key moment in *Anna Karenina*, one of those moments that have prompted critics to talk of Tolstoy's special 'moral' quality (Lionel Trilling), expressed particularly in his power to 'love' his characters (Trilling, J. P. M. Stern) even while he never loses sight of their limits.[7] Such formulations as these, perceptive as they may be, do not really take us any further than Matthew Arnold's account:

Hard at first, formal, cruel, thinking only of himself, Karénine, who, as I have said, has a conscience, is touched by grace at the moment when Anna's troubles reach their height. He returns to her to find her with a child just born to her and Wronsky, the lover in the house and Anna apparently dying. Karénine has words of kindness and forgiveness only. The noble and victorious effort transfigures him, and all that her husband gains in the eyes of Anna, her lover Wronsky loses.[8]

The problem with this is that it blurs and sentimentalises Karenin's response to the situation in a familiar Victorian way by making it seem the grace-inspired outcome of a 'noble and victorious effort'. We are not far here from some of the more unsatisfactory Dorothea parts of *Middlemarch*. F. R. Leavis shows what is wrong with Arnold's account and then sketches in his own:

'Karénine has words of kindness and forgiveness only. The noble and victorious effort transfigures him' – who would divine from that the disturbing subtlety of the actual presentment? The state of feeling actually produced in us is very different from that which Arnold suggests with his 'in possession of our admiration and sympathy'. The way we take the scene, its moral and human significance for us, is conditioned by all that goes before, and this has established what Karenin is, what Anna is, and what, inexorably, the relations between them must be. We know him as, in the pejorative Laurentian sense, a purely 'social' being, ego-bound, self-important, without any spontaneity of life in him and unable to be anything but offended and made uncomfortable by spontaneity of life in others … The reader, even at the moment when Karenin seems most noble and most commands sympathy and Anna's self-abasement is deepest, can hardly falter in his certainty that revulsion from Karenin is basic and invincible in Anna.

As for the 'noble and victorious effort that transfigures him', when (as Arnold puts it), 'he is touched with grace', the effect of the episode on us, even before we know that this is the way his admirer and consoler, the Countess Ivanovna will put it, is so embarrassingly painful because it is so much more complex than such an account suggests. Karenin's inability to bear the spectacle of acute distress and suffering (especially, we have been told, in a woman) doesn't impress us as an unequivocal escape from the ego: that disconcerting fact is what, added to Vronsky's repellent and horribly convincing humiliation, makes the scene so atrociously unpleasant.[9]

Certainly, as Leavis says, the scene is much more complex and painful than Arnold suggests: Karenin is not 'transfigured' in the sense that he suddenly reaches out to Anna and Vronsky with a 'kindness and forgiveness' that is nobly selfless. There is no 'unequivocal escape from the ego' (as Leavis terms it) in that sense. But still, short of that, there is a transformation in Karenin in which his ego-defences fall significantly away and he is able to trust for the first time to the flow of those deeply hurt, self-pitying feelings that have been dammed up for so long within him. The tears are not in the first place tears for Anna; they are infantile, tears for himself. We cannot miss that in the way he lays his head in the curve of Anna's arm; nor can we miss the bald spot on this head, a reminder of what is so grotesque about this infantile surrender. There is no question of saint-like transfiguration here, yet equally there can be no real love or forgiveness, and certainly no 'escape from the ego' in any sense, until he can submit to the feelings that are released in him here. And when it comes, enabled by Anna's loving gaze, the release is strong and inevitable, sweeping aside that 'nervous agitation' which was the experience of blocked feeling and expressing itself with the joyful relief of a whole being reaching towards its own health. There is no hint of 'noble effort' or anything remotely morally strenuous about

Karenin's response to Anna, nor anything especially to do with 'grace' in the theological sense, and Tolstoy is perfectly clear-eyed about the ways in which this 'love and forgiveness for his enemies that filled [Karenin's] heart' is an untested feeling, centred on himself. Yet, until Karenin's 'heart' is engaged, as it is here, there can be no spontaneous reaching out beyond himself as he does with Vronsky's baby.

Arnold is right to the extent that Karenin is changed here, though he is not transfigured in a wholly unexpected way. Anna had obscurely known 'he would be like that' and, such is the fullness of Tolstoy's imagining, so had we. Tolstoy's distinction in this novel can be seen in the fact that a Karenin can change while remaining himself and without the slightest hint of the kind of sudden idealisation that Arnold's account might suggest. Leavis does not appear to notice this important change in Karenin partly because he too sometimes tends to think of characters in novels in essentially static and finalising terms. His first move in answering Arnold is to remind us how all that has gone before in the novel has 'established what Karenin *is*, what Anna *is*' (my italics): Karenin is 'a purely "social" being', 'ego-bound' and 'without any spontaneity of life in him'. Such terms can only be contradicted by seeing what is happening to Karenin in this part of the novel, and it is partly to Leavis' credit that he does just this when he writes of Karenin with the baby:

Positive sympathy does indeed enter in for us, to render the full complexity of life in that marvellous way of Tolstoy's, when we suddenly have to realize that even in this repellently 'social' being the spontaneity can come to life, and something unquestionably real assert itself. There is the tenderness that takes him by surprise in his feelings towards the baby, Vronsky's child.[10]

The question that this raises is just how 'the spontaneity can come to life' in someone who is 'without any spontaneity of life in him'. Where has the formerly non-existent 'spontaneity' come from?

This points to the fact that terms like 'ego-bound', 'social being' and 'spontaneity of life', necessary as they may be, are being offered as a *final* ethical vocabulary, and so simply *cannot* be adequate in the discussion of character in a book like *Anna Karenina*. Tolstoy's imagining always includes the possibility that egos, even those as deeply afraid as Karenin's, can shed, or at least break open, their shells. The reverse possibility is explored in Seriozha, where we see a once open and spontaneous self close off from the world rather than perpetually face a loss greater than it can bear. As usual, Oblonsky blunders into the centre of things: '"Do you remember your mother?" he said suddenly.' Seriozha's response, when Oblonsky has gone, shows his relationship to Karenin: '"Leave me alone! What business is it of his whether I remember or don't remember? Leave me alone!" he said, addressing not his tutor now but the whole world' (VII, 19, p. 760). What we are being shown here is how egos become bound, how 'repellently "social" beings' come about: for them, 'spontaneity of life' is too painful, too permanently fixed upon a single experience, to be something they can tolerate, either in themselves or in the world. Which means that they must hold the world at a distance, and at the same time look to it for rigidities and externalities they can live by. It will be fear, but not simply cowardice, that will make Seriozha, like Karenin, 'too much aware of social reality'.

Anna Karenina comes to apprehend, through the various lives it creatively explores, that 'spontaneity of life' is not simply something one happens to have or not have, nor simply something one chooses to live by or not live by – though neither nature nor choice is irrelevant. But it *is* something that can be enabled by loving or by being loved in the right kind of way by the right person, just as it can be disabled by loss of that person. It is Anna's 'ecstatic gaze', which (whatever its source in her) seems for a moment to prefer him to Vronsky, that lets Karenin momentarily forgive himself and the world for all that he (like Seriozha) holds against it; only then, relieved from shame and hostility, can he turn the undefended feeling self, with its gross, long pent-up needs, to the world. The self that is thus born turns out to be the weeping, orphaned child that Karenin has always been, as Anna knew, the very image of which he so cherishes in Anna's soon-to-be orphaned baby. At least until Anna recovers. Then, her gaze becomes a look of fear and evasiveness, and Karenin begins to notice the look of scorn in other people's eyes. Gradually the shame and hostility return, making it harder and harder to trust his impulses, and so the old ego-shell of the 'social being' re-establishes itself, more complete and more repellent than ever. What makes this episode even more complex and painful than is usually recognised is that Anna's recovery stifles the very possibility beginning to come to life in Karenin.

But if this episode is not, as the whole novel is not, merely complex and painful, it is because the innocence that is figured in the unprotected child, and in such a distorted way in Karenin's responsiveness to the child, also embodies a central quality of Tolstoy's imagination. We can see it in his imagining of Karenin. For all his unillusioned grasp of what is, and must remain from Anna's point of view, 'invincibly' repugnant about Karenin, Tolstoy never closes off the possibility of a degree at least of personal restoration, of Karenin regaining a kind of 'innocence' too.

It is not always so with George Eliot and Lawrence, for whom 'innocence' is also a key term. In *Middlemarch*, for instance, though George Eliot imagines Casaubon as a 'small hungry shivering self', she does not make it clear how that is related to the childlikeness we are meant to approve of in Dorothea and Will Ladislaw; or how egoism (imaged as an infant taking the world for its breast) *becomes* childlike 'innocence', or vice versa, or indeed if there can be any vice versa. With Lawrence, apart from *The Rainbow* and *Women in Love*, much the same is true. Nobody, not even Tolstoy, has matched the power of Lawrence's realisation of what it means to be 'innocently' at one with the great continuum of the natural universe – it is there in novel after novel right up to *Lady Chatterley's Lover*, and in the poems too. Nor perhaps can he be matched in his grasp of the wilfulness, nullity, and destructiveness of the 'social being'. But as to how they are *dynamically interrelated*, how one becomes an Anton Skrebensky or a Sir Clifford Chatterley in the first place, or how one might grow into something more if one happened to be one of them – on all of this Lawrence usually only points to the social or psychic evils they represent, and implies in the characters an unconscious choice to be as they are. 'It is only from his core of unconscious naïveté that the human being is ultimately a responsible and dependable being', Lawrence writes in his introduction to *Cavalleria Rusticana*. 'Break this human core of naïveté – and the evil of the world all the time tries to break it... – and you get... a merely rational creature whose core of spontaneous life is dead.'[11] Well, it might happen that way; but, as Tolstoy shows in Seriozha, it might also be that another ultimately 'responsible and dependable being', following her 'spontaneous life' as she must, will break this 'human core of naïveté' in one closely related to her – not 'the evil of the world' at all, but the person who goes on loving him more than anyone else.

This is where Tolstoy's idea of 'innocence' is fuller than Lawrence's, for he shows that, to be complete, 'innocent at-oneness with the great continuum of universe' must include the social continuum too. 'Only community constitutes humanity', as Feuerbach says; and it is a truth as important in *Anna Karenina* as in *Middlemarch*. Kitty and Levin's wedding, right at the heart of the book, expresses the ideal, without idealising it. Here, at the beginning of their marriage, we see expressed in the couple the great 'central relation', what Lawrence was to call 'the quick and the central clue to life'.[12] Tolstoy would undoubtedly have seen the force of that formulation. Yet around his couple Tolstoy places parents, family, friends, reaching outwards to the edge of their world – 'all Moscow' is there, in short. And, whether or not the couple understand it at the time, the presence of all of them is an important part of the meaning being expressed by the occasion too. They may not be the *central* clue to life, but they are part of the clue, none the less, and a necessary part, as Vronsky and Anna find out in their different ways. They discover, and we through them, that the great 'central relation', even if it is right in itself (as theirs is essentially), cannot be abstracted from the rest. Children, and the sort of work that is a calling, to name only two things, are not 'contingencies' (Lawrence's word), radically sep-arable from the centre. They are parts of another continuum that reaches right into the centre from the edges of the known social world, and which embraces a whole structure of affirmations, beliefs, supports, enrichments, responsibilities – all those things that con-stitute a culture, and which in turn are not radically separable from the structure of moral feelings and ideas that shape the key experiences of the heart: loss, shame, and a love that really does forgive and forget. In this sense, we are all 'social beings' – 'innocently' alive only to the extent that all the relations in which we have our being enable or allow us to be. If that points to tragedy for some, it also points, for others, to the possibility of human redemption.

CHAPTER 8

Two ideas of innocence in 'The white peacock'

In his first book Lawrence dramatises his own discovery of artistic and ethical identity – in some 'strong evaluations' which are at once post-Romantic, sub-Nietzschean and idiosyncratically Lawrentian. The remarkable thing in this very early book is that you can see Lawrence's own conscious 'metaphysic', along with its characteristic distinctions of human worth, already in place. Significantly, *The White Peacock* centres on the vision of a Fall from rural 'innocence' into post-industrial 'social being', conceived very much in the terms he would use almost twenty years later in the Galsworthy essay. He is much preoccupied with childish narcissism, dependence, and cowardice, for instance, especially in the face of sexual challenge, and these are constantly being explained, indeed over-explained, in terms of a framework of ideas about the supposedly disabling nature of civilised consciousness. Right from the start, Lawrence's own work exhibits the dangers of a conscious 'metaphysic' in a novel, and many of his own problems (as well as many of his achievements), even here, spring from the sheer expressive power of his explicit vision of nature and modern civilisation as opposed values.

At the same time *The White Peacock* encompasses much that is at odds with its stated themes – and with the accounts of thematising critics.[1] The Romantic part-truth that the novel insists on, that there is a healthy animal instinctiveness which is in 'innocent' connection with the natural world, is ever in tension with more complex apprehensions realised in the human drama it sets before us. The unfulfilled connection between Lettie and George survives their marriages to others only to deny each of them more limited fulfilments. Both remain incomplete, unable to face what they have lost, and George especially shows another kind of 'innocence' – the tragic kind that destroys those, like Anna Karenina, who are too large-hearted to suppress central needs of the heart. Lawrence seems to want to *say* through the novel that only the 'innocent' can really love, whereas his art creatively discovers that only those actively loved can remain 'innocently' alive.

These are two quite distinct notions of 'innocence'. The first is the explicit Edenic one of Annable's monologues and focused in the chapter-titles 'Dangling the Apple' and 'The Fascination of the Forbidden Apple', which construe George as a pre-industrial Adam and the Fall as modern civilisation, especially in the form of the white peacock, modern overspiritual woman. Lawrence never altogether abandoned this (by itself) over-simplifying master-narrative of modern history; it keeps turning up right up to his last where it gains sway in the monologues of an even more notoriously opinionated gamekeeper, Mellors. Yet, where the art is strong, here and throughout Lawrence's work, 'innocence' is imagined as fundamentally social and interactive: only the right sorts of human relationships can bring and keep the whole man alive. Wherever Lawrence's work is most significant, especially for our post-Nietzschean age, it never entirely loses touch with the Feuerbachian truth that 'only community constitutes humanity'. *The White Peacock* discovers, though in a narrower sense than *Middlemarch* and *Anna Karenina*, that we are all in the end *necessarily* 'social beings'.

In this sense the novel fruitfully deconstructs its conscious Nietzschean ethic of singleness and self-responsibility. And in the figure of Cyril, the semi-autobiographical narrator, it suggests some of the personal conflicts informing its explicit theorising. Cyril represents Lawrence's first and most ambiguous attempt to shake free from the 'social being' in himself. In dramatising this personal struggle, *The White Peacock* helps to suggest why such figures as Leslie Tempest, Anton Skrebensky in the *The Rainbow*, Gerald Crich in *Women in Love,* and Sir Clifford Chatterley continue to obsess Lawrence – like a series of Jungian 'shadows'. The struggle to get such figures right, to transcend the judgmental terms in which they characteristically present themselves to him, was always to be a crucial ethical challenge for his art.

Much recent attention has been given to various nineteenth-century 'traditions'[2] on which Lawrence's work has drawn, and it is not surprising that the novel most illuminated by this criticism is his first. *The White Peacock* resounds with more or less explicit echoes of its author's reading – Hardy, Schopenhauer, Huxley, Haeckel, Ibsen,

Nietzsche, George Eliot, Tolstoy, and many others speak through the lips of Cyril Beardsall and his circle in an often rhapsodic mixture of intellectual excitement and exuberant display.

Not all of these are shaping influences of the profoundest kind, while there are more important imaginative sources that hardly surface in any explicit way at all. One early reviewer was reminded of *Wuthering Heights*, 'especially in the character of the woman, who is able to love, in differing fashion, two men at once'.[3] The connection is a significant one. Lettie's two loves, like Catherine Earnshaw's, are set against each other in a far-reaching exploration of the competing claims of natural and social bonds. The terms of the exploration are remarkably similar. When Lettie plays on the piano, preoccupied after her meeting with George Saxton in the wood, Leslie Tempest says: 'I suppose you want me out of the way while you sentimentalise over that milkman' (p. 170). The adolescent, peeved tone may not be Edgar Linton's, but the response to sexual threat is much the same as when Heathcliff turns up at Thrushcross Grange after his long absence; Linton says: 'What, the gypsy – the plough-boy?'[4] In both cases fear of a sexual affinity that cannot be contained within the recognised legal and social bonds is expressed in an impotent recourse to social power. Such purely conventional judgments are withered into insignificance by a surrounding natural realm (just outside the country house, on the heath, or in the wood) in which ploughboys and milkmen have a vitalising rootedness. Unlike their sexual rivals, Edgar Linton and Leslie Tempest seem to belong to the civilised, indoor world, and are no longer at one with what Lawrence in the Galsworthy essay called the great natural continuum.

In these ways, Leslie points forward to a long line of 'social beings' in Lawrence's fiction, such as Anton Skrebensky, Gerald Crich, Rico Carrington, and Sir Clifford Chatterley, all of them men of social position, and all of them in a characteristic way imaginatively and vitally deficient. As I have noted, much of the later work is already present in embryo here. Leslie becomes a mine-owner, for example, and an advocate of machinery taking over the work of men. And more importantly the novel is reaching towards an understanding of the connection between those things and his relationship with Lettie. Leslie's is a frightened, possessive love like that of so many later men of position in Lawrence's novels. Typically the spontaneous play of conversation or action in an episode, especially when Lettie and George are together, is ended by his arrival, his feet crunching on the gravel like a not wholly unwelcome fate come to claim her. In a variety of ways the novel emphasises his need to bind her, to confine her vitality and to subdue it. The image that runs through their rather adolescent love play is the hunt, like the rabbit chase, with Leslie in pursuit of Lettie's freedom and life.

Lawrence's art already has its eye on the unconscious will beneath such possessiveness, the will to kill these qualities it loves in her. Leslie searches for the image of himself in her eyes:

'Then just be comfortable. Let me look at myself in your eyes.'
  'Narcissus, Narcissus! – Do you see yourself well? does the image flatter you? – or is it a troubled stream, distorting your fair lineaments.'
  'I can't see anything – only feel you looking – you are laughing at me –. What have you behind there – what joke?'
  'I – I'm thinking you're just like Narcissus – a sweet, beautiful youth.'
  'Be serious – do.'
  'It would be dangerous. You'd die of it, and I – I should –'
  'What!'
  'Be just like I am now – serious.'
  He looked proudly, thinking she referred to the earnestness of her love. (pp. 86–7)

The dialogue here focuses a great deal. Leslie's need of Lettie is narcissistic, a need to see himself steadily confirmed in her love. Anything other than that reflection will be intolerable; he will do what he thinks he has to in order to keep it there. But the free life of feeling cannot be kept static in the way Leslie needs it to be. It is a stream, ever in flux, which means that Lettie, if she submits to his love, will have to suppress her vitality and live an imprisoned, attenuated existence – like Dorothea with Casaubon, or Anna with Karenin, or Catherine with Edgar Linton. And, like all of these, Lawrence also imagines such a love as at once possessive and dependent, protectively patriarchal and infantile. The 'social being' is not simply, as he later put it in the Galsworthy essay, over aware of objective reality; he imagines him in his novels as the egoistic or narcissistic infant of *Middlemarch* taking the world as an udder to feed his supreme self.

Where Lawrence pushes forward beyond Brontë, Eliot, and Tolstoy is in his continual imaginative interest in the figure of the man as infant, the lover as son. Karenin breaks down and reveals the infantile self behind the social shell only at a moment of crisis, whereas Leslie shows himself to be a boy of tears all along. The regressive nature of his love is plain when he has the accident and enjoys being weak in Lettie's caring arms (pp. 196–7).

Lettie obscurely knows, as Catherine Earnshaw does, that she is marrying the wrong person – not the man for whom her love resembles the eternal rocks beneath, but the one for whom her love is changeable, like the trees. Here again Lawrence pushes further forward than his predecessors, even in this first book:

After the evening at the farm, Lettie and Leslie drew closer together. They eddied unevenly down the little stream of courtship, jostling and drifting together and apart. He was unsatisfied and strove with every effort to bring her close to him, submissive. Gradually she yielded, and submitted to him. She folded round her and him the snug curtain of the Present, and they sat like children playing a game behind the hangings of an old bed. She shut out all distant outlooks, as an Arab unfolds his tent and conquers the mystery and space of the desert. So she lived gleefully in a little tent of present pleasures and fancies.

Occasionally, only occasionally, she would peep from her tent into the out space. Then she sat poring over books, and nothing would be able to draw her away; or she sat in her room looking out of the window, for hours together. She pleaded headaches; mother said liver; he, angry like a spoilt child denied his wish, declared it moodiness and perversity. (p. 145)

Here is the germ of a good deal of *The Rainbow*, especially the early married life of Will and Anna Brangwen, which shows that a relationship in which one partner is possessive and dependent will be constantly changing, oscillating between separation and submission. Remarkably, this whole emotional rhythm is caught here in the image of the stream, even though it is one that will not be fully realised in a novel until the stream becomes the formal shaping principle dissolving the old stable ego into its allotropic, moment-to-moment states.

On a larger scale, for both Brontë and Lawrence the stream of seasonal change, of death, growth to maturity, and renewal, is strongly felt as the natural actuality of human lives – except where there is a fear of it, a need to evade it, or a disturbance strong enough in any given life to arrest it. *The White Peacock*, for all its immaturity, is centrally preoccupied with adolescent fear of life (as Brontë certainly is not) especially the wish, which Lettie, Leslie, and all the central characters have, to live like children in a timeless snug Present. Where it is most imaginatively open, the novel and its stronger characters keep glimpsing the harder, more bracing and impersonal world beyond, strikingly imaged here as a desert 'out space', and elsewhere in more clearly Brontëan terms as 'the winds of life outside', 'the black keen storm'. Lettie, peeping out from her tent, or looking out from her 'small indoor existence with artificial light and padded upholstery' (p. 291), is too cautious to wrench open the window as Brontë's heroes do and let in the storm.

Lawrence shows his 'modernity' in his consciousness of a yet larger stream, that of historical time. In *Wuthering Heights* the 'busy world' in the form of Lockwood comes and goes, leaving the world of the Grange and the Heights essentially untouched. In *The White Peacock* Nethermere has been long invaded. The busy world is right there in the valley, and its presence in the form of artificial light and all the rest is felt, right from the beginning of Lawrence's work, to be related precisely to the kind of timidity that cannot spontaneously wrench open the window. Those that eventually do, like Lou Carrington or Connie Chatterley, do so only after a crisis and long struggle. Their burden of over-consciousness, which includes their consciousness of being so burdened, affords them no easy access to the larger heroic world in which Brontë's lovers move and act on their impulses for good or ill with unselfconscious abandon.

There are moments where such life seems possible for George Saxton, especially at the beginning – as when he's in the fields mowing, chasing rabbits, drowning cats or crushing bees. The problem with the novel's imagining of these moments is the narrative over-consciousness of their significance. 'Leave them alone', says Cyril to George when he is playing with the bees. 'Let them run in the sun. They're only just out of the shells. Don't torment them into flight' (p. 2). The scene is powerfully evoked, but overshadowed with heavily ironic point: on the previous page Cyril has said: 'Your life is nothing but a doss. I shall laugh when somebody jerks you awake.' George is duly jerked awake, as is the reader – to a meaning that is almost always thinner than that grasped by the imagined particulars.

George's failure to take Lettie is the central action, or inaction, on which the novel turns. George is supposedly a victim of history. Uprooted from his traditional farm life, made 'conscious' by Cyril and Lettie, he is caught in an evolutionary no man's land, neither conscious enough to fulfil his higher powers nor yet any longer unconscious enough to act with the instinctive toughness and indifference of the birds and animals. Cyril tells him that he might have had Lettie had he had the courage to risk himself and to make

his own destiny; Lettie tells him that he could have taken her if he
had been prepared to fight and to sacrifice himself – like the dead
wood-pigeon they come across, which had died fighting for its mate.
These Nietzschean admonitions seem to bear Lawrence's stamp,
especially since they are vindicated by a Darwinian natural universe
that is yet not so cruel and indifferent as to withhold instructive
parallels. The Annable story, for all its ambiguity, is fundamentally
a fable pointing in the same direction. If George had been more of a
'good animal' he would simply have taken Lettie. Annable shows
what it is in Lettie's terms to act like a 'man', shaping things in one's
own way (p. 211). Instead, when he is put to it, George shows himself
to be a boy, like Leslie, with eyes 'full of misery and a child's big
despair' (p. 195).

The failed love of George and Lettie is dramatically compelling not
because of the insistent larger historical pattern (which is ever
gesturing towards a reductive, unconvincing reading of events that
centres on the uprooting of George), but because *both* of them fail to
enable the other to act as they each want to. When he is in the woods
and about to meet Lettie, George confesses to Cyril that he is afraid
of not being able to speak naturally 'like birds, without knowing
what note is coming next' (p. 162), and so he tries to recover some
spontaneity by looking at some Beardsley prints (of Atalanta and
Salome!) that Cyril has given him. Yet when he's face to face with her
the seizure is always more complicated. Lettie's refusal or inability to
entertain consciously and explicitly the sexual meaning of George's
proposal (pp. 166–7), and her need to misunderstand it in other
terms as a call for 'help' or a need of her money, are not the responses
of a wanton over-spiritual Salome so much as those of an adolescent
terrified of the challenge of the very thing she so ardently desires. As
is so often the case in this novel, the young novelist's conscious artistry
betrays itself in a muted allusiveness ('This is one of my flippant
nights', says Lettie, echoing Hedda Gabler, one of the roles she is
constantly being cast in) that is fundamentally at odds with the life it
is actually imagining. Lettie is decidedly not flippant here, much less
the 'wilful' 'modern woman' (p. 74) she is so often said to be, but a
somewhat virginal girl falling back on the safer social apparent-
solidities rather than risk the unknown 'out space' of her real sexual
'wants'. Lawrence's art *can* grasp (it is fixated on it here, we might
say) the need of all the characters to be overwhelmed by a franker,
more self-certain desire, a more adult one. It is not of course simply

Leslie or obligation that has 'fixed' Lettie here, unable to move forward, but the presence in George of a corresponding need to be encouraged, to have his 'wants' openly reciprocated. The interesting thing about George's and Lettie's failures in the wood is that they are mutual and interactive: in each, the same conflict finds its mirror in the other.

The degeneration of George and Lettie in part III is presented with unexpected tragic power. This section was written later than the rest, and the characters seem subtly more grown-up, the art sparer and more confident. Lettie's hiding from life in the conventional role of mother, and George's various distractions that end up with the bottle, do not leave either of them utterly extinguished. There is a core of irrepressible vitality in each of them that still finds its response in the other when they meet. Lettie remarks: 'You have changed ... but you are not another person. I often think − "there is one of his old looks, he is just the same at bottom"'' (p. 300). '[A]t bottom' he is still 'innocent', not in the external sense that he is a still unfallen pre-industrial Adam, but in the sense that beneath all the self-destruction (giving rise to it, in fact), is a fundamental openness that will not let him live equably unfulfilled. The unremitting intensity of his dissolution is the most telling sign of his stature: like Heathcliff, he remains for years 'the same at bottom', unable to forget his 'heart's love'.

The power of this last section, seen in George's meetings with Lettie and their ambiguous challenges to each other, his losing struggle with Meg, his visits to Cyril, comes from Lawrence's steady apprehension of the kind of frustrated need eating away at him. At this point in the novel, Annable's way of explaining the world (in terms of being a good animal, resisting the rotten fungus of civilisation and the white peacock of overspiritual woman) seems insupportably crude. Lettie combing George's hair in 'Pisgah' is the same tease she has always been, but the art undermines utterly any suggestion of false dichotomy between culture and nature. The sexual attraction between them, now that Lettie feels safe to experience it more overtly, expresses itself in and through the social limits set by the occasion, and on George's side reaffirms his sense of Lettie as a 'light' to his life. For him, as for Tom Brangwen whom he resembles in many ways, there is an instinctive need for a woman who will be a 'symbol of that further life which comprised religion and love and morality'. It is this that Meg cannot be for George and which explains why he 'can't give her any of the real part of [himself], the vital part that she wants' (p. 301). Whether or not Lettie really could have answered to the vital part of George is not something we can easily decide. It is clear, though, that this formulation involves a much more capacious idea of 'life' than Annable's frankly regressive animalism does, one as much associated with the expansive energies of the soul, with its mysterious 'out space' as it is with finding a response to male pride of the body. Lawrence's imagination, if not his spokesmen, already had before it the ideal of the whole man alive, in body and in soul.

The alcoholic wreckage of George at the end is disturbingly convincing – yet, like so much else in the book, curiously bifurcated. When he goes to visit his invalided friend and watches him wash, Cyril feels the tragic degeneration of the man all too keenly. The destroyed body (focused in such details as the bluish hands, the slow movements and the thin arms) renders unforgettably the destroyed man, cut off from his friend by an apparent indifference that is seen to be a soul-corroding shame. In that shame the innocent core of the man is still there, aware of what it has come to, but powerless to change. The phrase 'dull eyes of shame' (p. 321) sounds another note, however, a more external one with a faintly Temperance edge, that seems to be implying that the shame is well deserved. It has sounded before, notably when George has started to get drunk in the Ram Inn. There too the note cuts across an implicit understanding that the drinking is an attempt to obliterate a whole higher world of things that he feels he cannot have and so has to forget. To say, as Cyril does, that George is 'indulging himself like a spoiled child' (p. 142) is to withdraw from that ampler understanding and to become judgmental. At the end, the effect is even more jarring:

He talked stupidly, with vulgar contumely of others, and in weak praise of himself... George continued his foolish, harsh monologue, making gestures of emphasis with his head and his hands. He continued, when we were walking round the buildings into the fields, the same babble of bragging and abuse. I was wearied and disgusted. He looked, and he sounded, so worthless. (p. 323)

At such moments as this, the teller seems to draw attention to himself as distinctly untrustworthy, his stated judgments being at odds with those implied by the whole tale he is telling. The problem is that there are no other placing signs to suggest that he is meant to be so, no discrediting errors like Lockwood's judgment of Heathcliff as 'a capital fellow' to bring his unreliability into the foreground. Part of the problem with Cyril is that he is too shadowy and far too rarely inspected by the drama at which he is ever-present in a quasi-omniscient way. On the other hand, Cyril is not a pure transparency either. He is aware of himself at moments as both unsatisfied and acutely unsatisfactory, but not in ways, apparently, that are intended to refract the light he casts on the action. Quite the contrary, when Cyril tells George that he needs to risk himself, a chicken is likely to show how to do it by walking into the fire.

There is the closest possible relation, in other words, between Cyril and the mind responsible for *The White Peacock*. One important outcome of this is that Cyril's personality suggests some of the psychic tensions and conflicts informing the narrative and shaping it from beneath. For a start, there is a close connection between the novel's overconsciousness of the meaning it is setting before the reader (one contemporary reviewer aptly characterised it as 'sicklied o'er with the pale cast of thought') and Cyril's own ever-vigilant consciousness. Characteristic of Cyril is his reaction when George starts to get drunk at the Ram; while ashamed that his body is not perfectly in control, he finds that he is 'acutely conscious of every change' in George and himself; 'it seemed as if I could make my body drunk, but could never intoxicate my mind, which roused itself and kept the sharpest guard' (p. 203). Cyril is, on balance, pleased with this sharp guard here, drink being in question, even though George's reckless abandonment to the moment, speaking dialect and taking Meg in his arm, is that of a larger-hearted, altogether warmer and more generous spirit – which Cyril somewhere recognises too. For the most part, Cyril is happy enough to look on, to participate in the action vicariously, relishing other lives and drawing them into his own heightened inner life of imagination, perception, and judgment. His wish is to turn it all into art, into a great 'poem' of life that implicitly exalts the onlooker to a level where presumably he need give no account of himself. Only occasionally is this serene assumption pricked, when, for example, George does not react as he does to the 'surging of the ocean of life' in London. George is moved instead by a woman tramp sleeping under Waterloo Bridge:

'Give her something,' he whispered in panic. I was afraid. Then suddenly getting a florin from my pocket, I stiffened my nerves and slid it into her palm. Her hand was soft, and warm, and curled in sleep. She started violently, looking up at me, then down at her hand. I turned my face aside, terrified lest she should look in my eyes, and full of shame and grief I ran down the Embankment to him. We hurried along under the plane trees in silence. The shining cars were drawing tall in the distance over Westminster Bridge, a fainter yellow light running with them on the water below. The wet streets were spilled with golden liquor of light, and on the deep blackness of the river were the restless yellow slashes of the lamps. (p. 282)

The disturbance to Cyril is disproportionate; it is as if being suddenly thrust into the action and, above all, being seen, looked at in the eyes, by one who is normally merely the stuff of his vision, involves a kind of exposure that goes much deeper psychologically than the immediate experience that triggers it. It suggests that the role of seer is a way of not being too immediately touched by such hands, of holding such implied claims of common humanity at bay. Notably Cyril's narrative regains its composure again in the vision of the wet streets 'spilled with golden liquor of light', though the disturbance remains, as a feeling now contained, in the 'restless yellow slashes of the lamps'.

At moments Cyril catches himself looking on, making no immediate connection with the life around him:

I sat by my window and watched the low clouds reel and stagger past. It seemed as if everything were being swept along. I myself seemed to have lost my substance, to have become detached from concrete things and the firm trodden pavement of everyday life. Onward, always onward, not knowing where, nor why; the wind, the clouds, the rain and the birds and the leaves, everything, whirling along – why? (p. 83)

At such times Cyril recognises the connection between his usual detached mode of moving, centred in thought and imagination, through the firm everyday world, taking the shape of the life around him, and a sense of being himself unformed, without identity, not yet come into being. As ever in this novel, the wind blowing the clouds is a suggestive image of the movement of life, in every sense moving 'onward' into an unknown future, with Cyril himself divided between wanting to yield to it, knowing this in some sense to be an imperative (to be the only way to come into being), and wanting to hang onto what he presently is. In this he is like Lettie and all of the central characters, fearful of the mysterious as yet untracked desert space of freedom into which they must move to discover themselves, and inclined instead to hide in one of the smaller enclosed spaces of the familiar social world.

Typically Cyril's place is between the two, sitting inside at the window looking wistfully out. These are moments of muted struggle, half-diffused into poetic heightening yet always revealing:

I sat at my window looking out, trying to set things straight. Mists rose, and wreathed round Nethermere, like ghosts meeting and embracing sadly. I thought of the time when my friend should not follow the harrow on our own snug valley side, and when Lettie's room next mine should be closed to hide its emptiness, not its joy. My heart clung passionately to the hollow which held us all; how could I bear that it should be desolate! I wondered what Lettie would do. (p. 66)

Here again the future looms as an unknown to Cyril, this time dominated by a premonition of emptiness, a world without his closest friends. The passage is remarkable partly because of the frankness with which he discloses his wish to cling 'passionately' to Nethermere, which his wish construes as a 'snug valley' – the warm cradle of the sensibility that paints its friend's occupation rather quaintly as 'following the harrow', and his sister's room as a place of 'joy'. And yet the writing also indicates an obscure awareness of the ultimately stifling nostalgia in which that kind of sensibility cocoons itself; the snug valley of one sentence becomes in the next 'the hollow which held us all'. The ambiguities of 'hollow' and 'held' nicely focus what the prose is realising: what Cyril's friends are all holding onto is holding them back, in a life they have outgrown, like an empty shell.

In an immediate sense the hollow that is holding Cyril is Woodside, the world of Mater, which is also the hollowest part of *The White Peacock*. Set beside the warmer, stormier domestic life of the Ram, the family scenes at Woodside seem in obvious ways imaginatively thinner, more self-consciously literary, at times even embarrassingly unreal. At the same time, the resemblances between both and Lawrence's own family life as it emerges in *Sons and Lovers* are, in different ways, strong and suggestive. The Beardsalls are a kind of upper middle-class version of the Morels, transported out of Bestwood to a respectable country house, with the figure of the drunken father almost written out of the story. Looking back with the later book before us, it is not hard to guess at the pressures informing this transposition. Paul Morel used to pray every night that his father would die; Cyril Beardsall's creator makes it come true, even without the prayer being uttered. Many such things (including Lawrence's use of his mother's own maiden name, Beardsall) conspire to suggest

that Woodside is a world of imaginative wish-fulfilment for the young
novelist who is still, in every important sense, his mother's son.

The White Peacock also shows the imaginative price to be paid for
being too closely identified with his mother's most cherished
aspirations. The refinement of Woodside seems over-rarified from the
moment we enter it to find Cyril's mother at the keyboard in the
drawing-room playing 'a coy little tune' that 'teased me with old
sensations, but my memory would give me no assistance' (p. 6).
Typically the interest of the moment is deflected from anything that
these acutely sensed 'old sensations' might reveal by a stiffening in
the prose, which sets hard in well-bred formality. This stiffness is
particularly noticeable when the father is introduced:

The marriage had been unhappy. My father was of frivolous, rather vulgar
character, but plausible having a good deal of charm. He was a liar, without
notion of honesty, and he had deceived my mother thoroughly ... When he
left her for other pleasures – Lettie being a baby of three years, while I was
five – she rejoiced bitterly. (p. 33)

The phrase 'rejoiced bitterly' is alive with response in a way that the
rest of the paragraph is not; the judgmental condemnation of him
makes no attempt to get beyond the most external understanding.
The father is simply beyond the pale morally and, almost indistinguishable from that, socially. If anything, the word that tells
most harshly against him is 'vulgar'. Mere immorality might after all
be redeemed, but his vulgarity removes him from among those who
might be respectably acknowledged. The prose is effectively dis-
owning him, which is what mother and son later do to the man
himself at his death-bed. '"Only a cousin?" [his landlady] guessed,
and looked at us appealingly. I nodded assent' (p. 36).

This denial of the father seems to be innocent of any intended
irony, yet he does not detach himself from the narrative quite as easily
as Cyril might wish. When he is shown the body, like the disapproving
wife in 'Odour of Chrysanthemums', Cyril's pettier conventional
thoughts are cut adrift for a moment in the tide of something larger:

By the glimmering light of the two tapers we could see the outlined form
under the counterpane. She turned back the hem, and began to make
painful wailing sounds. My heart was beating heavily, and I felt choked. I
did not want to look – but I must. It was the man I had seen in the woods
– with the puffiness gone from his face. I felt the great wild pity, and a sense
of terror, and a sense of horror, and a sense of awful littleness and loneliness

among a great empty space. I felt beyond myself, as if I were a mere fleck drifting unconsciously through the dark. (p. 37)

The moment is striking because of the way Cyril's habitual moral vantage-point in regarding his father, apparently securely based on his mother's valuations, is suddenly lost in a more immediate response to the man that seems to threaten his routine sense of who he himself is. The narrator is disoriented in moral space. Pity and terror overwhelm him, and remarkably the imagined experience seems to overwhelm the habitual limits of Lawrence's prose, giving rise to a more supple, fluid, expansive rhythm that is responsive to the immediacy of the new feelings in Cyril. The mature Lawrence's capacity to keep probing 'the dark' beyond and within himself, casting the meaning of 'myself' into doubt, is glimpsed here in this rendering of Cyril's sudden intuition of his 'awful littleness' in relation to 'the great empty space' of things. And here Cyril does, as it were, move outside the window of vigilant, over-conscious selfhood, as the mode of awareness responsible for the late-Victorian poeticism 'glimmering light' is dissolved in the flow of a larger creative current, one that finds itself, in a sense, moving like Cyril himself 'unconsciously through the dark'. In the end Cyril comes back to his usual self, and significantly it is his mother's clasp that returns him – to a less frightening, more conventional sense of things.

Like the father himself, these feelings provoked by him are apparently forgotten, yet they emerge in the novel anyhow, in displaced, projected ways. The men in the book to whom Cyril feels nearest are physically strong and seem to offer a warmth and protectiveness in which he feels safe. Cyril's otherwise seemingly disproportionate attachment to the improbable figure of Annable has an obvious emotional centre: 'He treated me as an affectionate father treats a delicate son; I noticed he liked to put his hand on my shoulder or my knee as we talked' (p. 147). Whatever 'homoerotic' element there may be here (and there are hints that Cyril's feelings for Annable are troubled enough to bring him thoughts about 'the discipline of life' (p. 152)) the form of their relationship is that of affectionate father and delicate son. The adjectives are significant, as the delicate son of Lawrence's more straightforwardly autobiographical novel did not consciously think of his own father as particularly affectionate at all. Yet the story of that father is, in general outline, not unlike Annable's, the story of a young man with

pride of body married to a spiritual woman above his own social
station who at first loves his body but then tires of it. Annable is a kind
of Walter Morel imagined articulate enough to tell his side of the
story. For the young Lawrence, the mother's son, it was a side of the
story dangerous to entertain, certainly not one that he could
consciously admit to as his own father's. And yet, perhaps for that
very reason, it was the side of the story that he could not help telling,
over and over again.

The story of George Saxton, as originally conceived (where he
marries Lettie),[5] was another version of it. But, even in the novel as
it stands, George is only partly Cyril's disintegrating friend and
partly, as Annable is, one who satisfies his yearning to be like the tiny
larks he comes across in the chapter 'A Poem of Friendship': 'In my
heart of hearts, I longed for someone to nestle against, someone to
come between me and the coldness and the wetness' (p. 220). George
answers this need, as the swimming episode makes plain:

> He saw I had forgotten to continue my rubbing, and laughing he took hold
> of me and began to rub me briskly, as if I were a child, or rather, a woman
> he loved and did not fear. I left myself quite limply in his hands, and, to get
> a better grip of me, he put his arm round me and pressed me against him,
> and the sweetness of the touch of our naked bodies one against the other was
> superb. It satisfied in some measure the vague, indecipherable yearning of
> my soul; and it was the same with him. When he had rubbed me all warm,
> he let me go, and we looked at each other with eyes of still laughter, and our
> love was perfect for a moment, more perfect than any love I have known
> since, either for man or woman. (pp. 222–3)

Here again the homoerotic element takes the form of a love between
father and son – there is an easy glide between Cyril thinking of
himself as a child and as a woman. The link between the two is highly
suggestive: both child and woman are imagined as passive, limp,
caught up by a confident, strong, active love that is protectively
adult. This is precisely what Lettie yearns for too, on Cyril's report;
she too wants someone to come between her and the elements, a lover
who has got some of the qualities of a father.

In his married life with Meg, George also resembles the father in
Sons and Lovers in obvious ways: his drinking bouts, his increasingly
peripheral importance, the children's antagonism towards him, the
mother's dominance. But Cyril is very far from viewing the marriage
from the mother's side. For the most part, George is not seen as the
author of all their trouble, but as a victim of the woman's will to

power. In the chapter 'Domestic life at the Ram', Cyril displays a clear animus against Meg's dominating maternity, which is shown as actively stifling any attempt on George's part, or on anyone else's, to raise the level of conversation above domestic trivia. She treats George like a servant, bullying him mercilessly: 'she humiliated him and was hostile to his wishes' (p. 275). The observation of Meg's not entirely unthreatened scorn and authority is extremely acute, and she is given compelling presence, even a kind of grace and nobility, in her ministrations to the baby, but, in her triumph over George, Cyril sees her as yet another particular example in what for him is an overwhelming general case:

A woman is so ready to disclaim the body of a man's love; she yields him her own soft beauty with so much gentle patience and regret; she clings to his neck, to his head and his cheeks, fondling them for the soul's meaning that is there, and shrinking from his passionate limbs and his body. (pp. 277–8)

It is easier to see these days that such general thoughts about 'woman' point to a serious partiality, in fact to their author's 'helpless, unconscious predilection' as he himself termed it in 'Morality and the Novel': 'But if you set out to write a novel, and you yourself are in the throes of the great predilection for love ... then you will write an immoral novel.' The young Lawrence's great predilection at the time was not love, but growing up. As he wrote to Blanche Jennings in 1908: 'One little thing I will say seriously. Laetitia [the novel's original title] was written during the year that I changed from boyhood to manhood, my first year in college. It is a frightful experience to grow up, I think, it hurts horribly.'[6] The ways in which it hurt are not hard to divine from the novel itself. Lawrence was in the process of wanting to move, like Cyril's clouds, 'onward', out of the domain of childhood, which meant trying to shake free, especially from those communal self-definitions and feelings of belonging to which he was clinging and which were holding on to him all too powerfully. It meant, in Nietzsche's terms, being cruel to such childlike impulses in the service of manly self-responsibility and expressive integrity, taking control of one's destiny. And yet, as the novel also suggests, the regressive yearnings keep reasserting themselves, longings for safety and continuity, for the protective, unchanging, ever-affirming love that can be found ultimately only in a mother's eyes. And there lay the supreme danger – the fatal need,

like Leslie's, to find such a steady reflection in the eyes of the woman
he loves.

For Lawrence, the imperative to move 'onward' involved the most
fundamental conflicts. It is these that help to explain the drift of the
book's conscious theorising, its case against the most troubling things,
motherhood, men who are children, and its explicit ethic of animal
toughness, manly indifference, and responsibility, as well as its
concern to explain the disappearance of these virtues in an
overarching historical narrative. It is important to notice at the
outset of Lawrence's career something that remained true: his
explicit polemics, as with many writers, were often extensions of
struggles within himself. As Middleton Murry first argued in *Son of
Woman*, the psychic tendencies most deeply explored and resisted in
his novels are Lawrence's own. A Jungian 'shadow', in other words,
ever hovers over Lawrence's 'social beings'. Revealingly, there is
more than a little of the 'social being' in Lawrence's alter ego in *The
White Peacock* – for example, his mildly snobbish disdain of Meg's
naive pleasure in a puppet-show at Nottingham. Cyril casts himself
into the role of the urbane young man of taste and well-bred
sophistication: 'It was rather vulgar, and very tiresome' (p. 247).
There is some insistence on the point of breeding. Even the father's
degeneracy retains several small signs of respectability. His things, we
are told in one or two places, were 'good', and he departs leaving a
not-unrespectable £4,000. The insistence reminds us that Lawrence
could all too easily imagine a much less well-heeled vulgarity than
Mr Beardsall's, together with the attitudes of those who might have
used that withering word about a case much closer to home. To this
extent, the novel is written with half an eye on its metropolitan
readership. The reviewer in the *Morning Post* who asked in as-
tonishment: 'do they really discuss Ibsen and Aubrey Beardsley in
farmhouses in the Trent Valley?'[7] was in a sense reacting on cue. The
author of the book's glittering, self-conscious allusiveness must have
been half hoping for such a compliment.

But there was, even in *The White Peacock*, much more to the young
Lawrence than this. There are numerous moments, such as when
Cyril is looking at the Beardsley prints, where his 'soul leaped out
upon the new thing. I was bewildered, wondering, grudging,
fascinated. I looked a long time, but my mind, or my soul, would
come to no state of coherence. I was fascinated and overcome, but yet
full of stubbornness and resistance' (p. 159). One of the things that is

always surprising in rereadings of this novel is the presence here and there of passages that might well have been taken from one of the later novels, passages that show precisely this capacity to be fascinated and overcome by experience, when the sharp guard of reflective consciousness gives way to a much more deeply receptive state of mind. Such moments are not the 'poetic' ones, the lush, densely descriptive passages about peonies and snowdrops that are so characteristic of this book and which always suggest a mind in a state of full conscious coherence, knowing exactly where it is going. The more interesting ones seem to develop when the primary focus is at first elsewhere, such as when George feeding the pigs is momentarily upstaged by the pig that gets left out (p. 198); or when, at the Ram, Cyril's glum misogynist thoughts about being neglected by Emily at baby's bath-time suddenly give way to a new thing:

'Ha! – Ha–a–a!' she said with a deep-throated vowel, as she put her face against the child's small breasts, so round, almost like a girl's, silken and warm and wonderful. She kissed him, and touched him, and hovered over him, drinking in his baby sweetnesses, the sweetness of the laughing little mouth's wide wet kisses, of the round, waving limbs, of the little shoulders so winsomely curving to the arms and the breasts, of the tiny soft neck hidden very warm beneath the chin, tasting deliciously with her lips and her cheeks all the exquisite softness, silkiness, warmth, and tender life of the baby's body. (p. 277)

The second sentence keeps surging on, out of strict syntactical control, under the pressure of a rising need to capture the essence of the experience, as the exploratory–descriptive focus moves over the baby's body, like Emily enthralled and overcome by its delicious 'sweetness'. This is not too far from parts of *The Rainbow* in its vivid surrender to the living moment of response; tightness and intellectual control give way to the rapid pace of accumulating periods that dramatise the flow of feeling. It may have been with passages such as this one in mind that Lawrence could still say in 1925, having just finished rereading the novel: 'I haven't changed fundamentally.'[8]

In obvious ways the Lawrence of *Sons and Lovers* showed that he had not changed fundamentally, yet it is clear that no Cyril– Lawrence could have written that. The author of that book had moved 'onward' and farther inward, to face squarely things about himself that were half-hidden, diffused, not least by an understandable need to present an acceptable self to the literary world. The result is an immense gain in reality and life, where the posture of finding things 'vulgar and tiresome' yields more and more to a capacity to relish such things as the 'sensuous flame of life' playing over the dancing miner's body. To discover and to admit kinship with him was a great step forward, one that took the confidence not to be 'too much aware of objective reality'. Casting off that sheath of outgrown values let him open up altogether new possibilities.

CHAPTER 9

Into the ideological unknown: 'Women in love'

The main argument of political literary theorists against the traditional literary canon is by now perfectly familiar and more or less respectable in the academy: such works univocally speak the ideology of a hegemonic class, further silencing such groups as blacks, women, and the working class. This is why 'surface' ethical exposition of the good/evil binaries within canonical works is worse than useless, since it merely perpetuates and legitimates existing structures of power. Nor does psychological criticism fare much better for a political theorist such as Jameson, for this is merely a sub-genre of the ethical, substituting 'myths of the re-unification of the psyche' for the 'older themes of moral sensibility and ethical awareness'.[1] The canonical texts are said to repress their ideological function, consigning it to their unconscious where it can only be retrieved by political analysis. To this extent they are mad texts, dangerously so, because, unless we are capable of analysing them politically, they can only offer, as Lennard J. Davis says, to reinforce in us 'those collective and personal defences' which are our 'neurotic' constructs of the world.[2] Using Freud's famous essay, 'Remembering, repeating and working through', Davis argues that in reading novels we merely 'repeat' repressed narratives which, in the long run, impair our capacity to know 'what really is'.[3]

Just why it should be supposed that political analysis alone can confront us with non-ideological reality is rarely made clear in the criticism I have been citing. The question that is so often asked remains unanswered: what privileges Marxist history? This question reveals in such theory a not very thinly disguised will-to-master-narrative that mirrors closely its own account of the hegemonic narrative it wants to supplant. As Dirk den Hartog has suggested, this usurpation of the old authority looks very much like an Oedipal reaction.[4] The point of making this observation is that almost

everywhere political discourse has found its identity, not by coming
to terms inclusively and dialectically with humanist criticism and the
texts it helped to canonise, but by attempting to marginalise all of
them. This comes out plainly in the apparent disinclination or
inability of many theorists to look with care and disinterest at the
works they are adducing; instead they offer straw-man accounts of
them that grossly underestimate their complexity and intelligence.

As I have been arguing, a significant sign of the intelligence of
many canonical works, such as *Middlemarch, Anna Karenina,* and
Women in Love is their understanding of the narcissistic or neurotic
impulses often involved in insurgent theorising: Casaubon's wish, for
instance, to possess a Key to All Mythologies; or Karenin's need to
picture threatening otherness simplistically and distortedly in order
to contain it; or the merely reactive will in Gerald Crich's mechanistic
rationalism, which remains unconsciously bound to his father's
troubled Christian philanthropy, the very principle it struggles to
efface. Gradually over the past fifteen years or so, this sort of ethico-
psychological insight has tended to become the unconscious of a more
and more predominantly theoretical literary discourse. And once
again, this is not something that would have been lost on the
canonical authors themselves. As Ursula Brangwen says to the artist
Loerke: 'As for your world of art and your world of reality ... you
have to separate the two, because you can't bear to know what you
are.' The capacity of art to reveal what artists in that sense *are* in their
works is irreducible, and the impulse to theorise the revelation away,
together with the sort of criticism that would highlight it, is itself
always going to be psychologically revealing. This suggests yet
another *raison d'être* of the canonical works and of humanist criticism
– as subversive Other to the suppressive will of hegemonic Theory.

As I show in chapter 5, this role of literature has been grasped by
some deconstructionists, who have understood that the canonical
texts are often the most powerful demystifiers of the ideologies they
have been said to promote. This at least gestures in the direction of
noting the complexity of such works, and it points to the reason why
readings such as Lennard J. Davis gives these texts are simply
inadequate:

It might be worth considering the normative ways in which characters in
novels change. Usually the change is from unfeeling to feeling (Gradgrind,
Casaubon, Dombey), from crime to moral realization (Moll Flanders,
Fanny Hill, Magwitch), from *naïveté* to world-weariness (Jude Fawley,

Dorothea Brooke, Raskolnikov), from repression to mature sexuality (Lucy Snowe, Jane Eyre, Emma Bovary). Thus the consummate composite character used to be an unfeeling, repressed, naive outcast who becomes an integrated, feeling, moral, world-weary, sexually-mature being. Obviously, I am fooling around with categories a bit, but in a way the pattern of change is to transform the character from one of them to one of us. Again, the movement is normative, creating humans in the image of an idealized, middle-class image of themselves.[5]

Davis is arguing that these novels embody 'middle-class' ideology by showing characters changing themselves in a morally approved direction, thus reinforcing the idea that individuals, as opposed to social forces, bring about human betterment. The 'middle-class' ethical system expressed in the novels is therefore false consciousness (or ideology), since it does not involve a 'properly historical' (or neo-Marxist) view of human betterment. In so far as Davis' argument is not simply armour-plated against refutation (since only novels that embodied the neo-Marxist view could escape all taint of ideology), it depends on whether this particular ethical system, and therefore the ideology it is said to entail, can be validly attributed to the novels themselves. Here it is important to notice the precise *character* of the ethical signification attributed to these novels, which is registered in a series of simple binary oppositions: unfeeling/feeling, crime/moral realisation, *naïveté*/world-weariness, repression/mature sexuality, one of them/one of us. Such binaries are inadequate because, in almost every case, so many questions of ethical interest and import are *already* begged by *each* term. Where, for example, do Casaubon's or Gradgrind's or Dombey's occasional over-cathected responses come from if they can be described, *tout court*, as 'unfeeling'? What sort of 'world weariness' is it that we find in Jude Fawley, Dorothea Brooke, and Raskolnikov – that would not, on closer analysis, turn out to involve some reflex of what is gestured at in the word '*naïveté*'? How would we distil 'mature sexuality', at any point, from 'repression' in either Jane Eyre or Emma Bovary? In ways that have crucial ethical import, many of the apparent moral binaries in works of abiding imaginative interest keep collapsing into each other.

As Lawrence himself argued in his *Study of Thomas Hardy*, the ethical interest of most of these novels lies partly in the ways in which they question the moral systems they might superficially be taken to be supporting:

Yet every work of art adheres to some system of morality. But if it be really a work of art, it must contain the essential criticism on the morality to which it adheres. And hence the antinomy, hence the conflict necessary to every tragic conception.

The degree to which the system of morality, or the metaphysic, of any work of art is submitted to criticism within the work of art makes the lasting value and satisfaction of that work.

A few pages later, Lawrence expands on the same point:

It is the novelists and dramatists who have the hardest task in reconciling their metaphysic, their theory of being and knowing, with their living sense of being. Because a novel is a microcosm, and because man in viewing the universe must view it in the light of a theory, therefore every novel must have the background or structural skeleton of some theory of being, some metaphysic. But the metaphysic must always subserve the artistic purpose beyond the artist's conscious aim. Otherwise the novel becomes a treatise.[6]

All too often ideological analysis produces straw-man readings precisely by taking works of art as univocal treatises, seeing only 'the conscious aim' and not the 'artistic purpose' (its sources in part unconscious) that transcends the intentional 'system of morality' or 'theory of being' of the author. This involves reading not simply for static hermeneutic structures or systems of signification, but also for _process_, for art as discovery, exploration. When he points to the lack of a properly '_dynamic_ intentional structure' in Jameson's reading of Conrad's _Lord Jim_, Jacques Berthoud is making a similar point.[7] Whatever static binary oppositions the author may start out with, one test of the true classic is the degree to which the work either clings to them or entertains doubts, uncertainties, dialogic 'criticisms', which allow these terms to interact, become unstable, fluid, even altogether to change places. _Women in Love_ is interesting and important as a work of art not because it expresses a Romantic ideology of 'innocence' versus 'social being', or opposes preconceived 'good' human possibilities to 'evil' ones, but because it explores these things in their dynamic interrelatedness.

It follows from this that a work such as _Women in Love_, far from simply confirming a structure of ideological ethical fixities, contributes to what Alcorn and Bracher call 'blurring or dissolving various artificial boundaries on the reader's cognitive map'.[8] Moreover, _Women in Love_ especially foregrounds, in the lives it represents, the ways in which fixed ideas, modes of what it calls 'knowing' (that is, consciously constructing) the world, are actually a defence against repressed feelings and realisations. The novel's searching is a good deal directed towards understanding the conditions under which such defences can be dropped and one can move into what it terms 'the unknown'. It is a novel very much about transformation, selves in process, about both reinforcing psychic resistances and 'working through' them. At the same time, in a process analogous to, and reflecting, the represented ones, the novel's ultimate 'artistic purpose' can be seen as a 'working through' of that overinsistent will-to-vision which keeps threatening Lawrence's art even in *The White Peacock*, but most especially from *The Rainbow* on.

Most accounts of *Women in Love*, such as the one in Dan Jacobson's *Adult Pleasures*, stress the polarisation between two sets of characters, one struggling through to freedom and life, the other going down the slope, with the rest of the race, to various forms of death.[9] This view of the novel has a lot to be said for it. The opening dialogue, for instance, immediately presents a distinction between two ways of thinking about something – which turn out to be, more importantly, two ways of being.

On the one hand, there is Ursula, 'calm and considerate', deciding that she does not know whether she really wants to get married; for her, it will depend on what sort of man turns up, which cannot be known in advance. Her calm already hints at a fundamental trust, or underlying ease, in face of this unknown future. The prose is soon to suggest the shaping underlife from which these thoughts and words come. Though she feels curiously 'suspended', we are told, Ursula accedes to what she senses darkly at centre: a new potential life like an infant in the womb, held in by 'integuments', but pressing for birth. Leaving aside for the moment the ideological question of the sort of transformation-narrative this image might seem to imply, it is clear after a few pages that Ursula's capacity to be at ease with uncertainty is connected with a strong potentiality for growth. In this first page, her 'I don't know' and 'I'm not sure' are the first hints of that, and it is important to note that they indicate an openness, not least of *mind*.

Gudrun by contrast wants to be 'quite definite'; for her it seems possible that 'in the abstract' one might need the *experience* of having been married. The dramatic imagining also suggests that, despite this drive for definiteness, Gudrun is not, as Ursula is, really 'considering' possible consequences of marrying for the experience. When Ursula

points to the most likely consequence, that it will be the end of
experience, Gudrun 'attends' to the question as if for the first time.
Two things then happen; the conversation comes temporarily 'to a
close', and Gudrun, almost angrily, rubs out part of her drawing in
a way that indicates suppressed emotion. These little closures keep
occurring, and are always brought about by Gudrun. A bit later,
Ursula questions her about her magnificently stated motive for
coming back home – 'reculer pour mieux sauter':

'But where can one jump to?'
    'Oh, it doesn't matter', said Gudrun, somewhat superbly. 'If one jumps
over the edge, one is bound to land somewhere.'
    'But isn't it very risky?' asked Ursula.
    A slow, mocking smile dawned on Gudrun's face.
    'Ah!' she said, laughing. 'What is it all but words!'
    And so again she closed the conversation. But Ursula was still brooding.
    'And how do you find home, now you have come back to it?' she asked.
    Gudrun paused for some moments, coldly, before answering. Then, in a
cold, truthful voice, she said:
    'I find myself completely out of it.'
    'And father?'
    Gudrun looked at Ursula, almost with resentment, as if brought to bay.
    'I haven't thought about him: I've refrained', she said coldly.
    'Yes,' wavered Ursula; and the conversation was really at an end. The
sisters found themselves confronted by a void, a terrifying chasm, as if they
had looked over the edge.
    They worked on in silence for some time. Gudrun's cheek was flushed
with repressed emotion. She resented its having been called into being.[10]

Gudrun's conversational closures show a way of talking and thinking
– or rather, not thinking – that is at least as interested in the
impression it is making on others as it is in getting at the truth of
something. As the fashionable cynicism of 'What is it all but words!'
reminds us, this is the sociolect of glittering Chelsea bohemia. It is
what post-structuralism would call a discourse: the cynical 'words'
to some extent speak Gudrun. It is a discourse, above all, of power,
which is exercised precisely in clipping off whatever subject might
reveal one, give one away, show a chink in the armour. The chilly
formality of 'I've refrained' does this to Ursula, who until then
wants to go on thinking about the matter of father, to think it through,
not least for her own sake. Like everything else, the words add to
Gudrun's impressiveness, but they also instantly resist any possibility
either of closer contact with Ursula or, more significantly, of getting

at the blocked feelings that are obviously calling out for expression within herself. For Lawrence's imagining insists that the expressed 'words' of any individual or group, their sociolect or discourse, cannot really be understood as such without reference to the whole state of being they involve. Gudrun in a sense is in a prison-house of language ('what is it all but words'), but that is only intelligible in terms of the underlying 'repressed emotion' her particular language both manifests and helps to contain. It is a language of repression, of resistance, in other words, designed, like her stockings, to cover up magnificently. And, already, the novel is suggesting the price to be paid for this magnificence – thwarted energy, the feeling of everything withering in the bud.

In Hermione Roddice we see a similar thing in a more extreme case. As she walks into the church she shows the continuities between the drive for definiteness, the need to 'know', and the need to cover up vulnerabilities. The repeated 'knew' in she 'knew herself to be well-dressed ... knew herself the social equal ... knew she was accepted' dramatise an inner texture of thoughts which cloak sublinguistic states that the novel quickly puts before us. Hers is assuredly, if you like, a neurotic text in that the story it has to keep repeating about her and about the world is always going to be containment, rationalisation, compensation, projection, and so, on of what lies beneath. And it is worth pointing out that, in her, the novel puts clearly before the reader the ways in which 'aesthetic knowledge, and culture, and world-visions, and disinterestedness' (p. 17) can all be 'defences', ways precisely of blocking and resisting insight. *Women in Love* is a good deal about 'world visions' as false consciousness, symptoms of resistances that need to be worked through.

At the same time, the novel's own impulse is not to 'know' with this sort of drive for finalising definiteness. The central figures certainly are not, as most of the wedding guests are for Gudrun, 'sealed and stamped and finished with' (p. 14). The usual thematising readings (such as Jacobson's) fail to see the whole process of signification by which the novel questions its leading intuitions as it registers them. No sooner do we think we have a settled sense of the contrasts being drawn between Ursula and Gudrun than the novel turns about and re-*minds* us of what has also been implied in the imagining of them: that they are, as the chapter-heading says, sisters. Another characteristic of these little scene-closures is the way they serve to defeat ideological closure in our reading of them (construing

the issues simply as 'innocence' versus 'social being') by pointing to
what the women have in common: 'The sisters found themselves
confronted by a void, a terrifying chasm, as if they had looked over
the edge.' A little earlier: 'They both laughed, looking at each other.
In their hearts they were frightened ... The sisters were women ... But
both had the remote, virgin look of modern girls ...' (p. 8).

These sentences illustrate in miniature that dialectical interplay
between difference and similarity which is another aspect of the
'frictional to-and-fro' characteristic at every level of Lawrence's
thinking at its best. It is a *movement* of dramatic exploration and
signification that never lets differences harden into structures of static
opposition, but keeps turning back on them, threatening to dislodge
them. One moment we find Gudrun wanting to be quite definite, the
next we find her not wanting to be (p. 9) – and *Ursula* afraid of the
depth of feeling within her (p. 11) or saying to herself, in a way that
faintly echoes Hermione's intensely apprehensive projections about
Birkin in the church: 'The wedding must not be a fiasco, it must not'
(p. 18). This conventionality in Ursula, which Birkin will spend a lot
of energy trying to dislodge, is in part the self-protective 'integument'
preventing her at moments from peering over the edge into that
'void' or 'terrifying chasm' of the unknown faced by 'both' sisters. It
too manifests itself as self-concealing discourse (Ursula's being of the
less sophisticated 'things are just dandy' kind) especially when the
vertiginous chasm gets too close. 'I know!' she cries in response to
Gudrun's *reculer pour mieux sauter* – 'looking slightly dazzled and
falsified, and as if she did not know'. This tendency of Ursula's to lie
to herself looks false because of that vigorous life coming into being
within her, which simply will not be falsified. Gudrun is in better
control of herself than that, except at those moments when she
darkens and the held-in life appears on her cheek as a resented
'flush'. At such moments she and Ursula show themselves to be sisters
in a full sense.

It is important to reflect on what this sisterhood means. Nearly all
accounts of the novel, including Leavis' pioneering one, either
overlook or understate the degree to which, at least in all four major
figures, the novel keeps sight of that core of 'innocent' life in them
which remains *as a permanent possibility*. It is seriously reductive to say,
as Dan Jacobson does, that the 'others' (that is, other than Birkin
and Ursula, whom he calls the 'good' characters) 'can barely say or
do anything – make love, give to charity, paint, teach, talk – without

revealing or being said to reveal how advanced, how gangrenous, their condition really is'.[11] This ignores the fact that these figures can barely do these things or reveal their 'dissolution' without, at the same time, also revealing the thwarted or twisted *vitality* in them which continues to express itself in their deathward disintegration, in a sense as its very motive-force. Lawrence describes the process in a contemporary essay, 'The Crown' (1915):

Still the false I, the ego, held down the real, unborn I, which is a blossom with all a blossom's fragility.

Yet constantly the rising flower pushed and thrust at the belly and heart of us, thrashed and beat relentlessly. If it could not beat its way through into being, it must thrash us hollow.[12]

This underlines the dynamic interrelatedness established at the beginning of *Women in Love* between Ursula's 'unborn I' and that bud ('Everything withers in the bud.') which is the image of the same undeveloped possibility in Gudrun, a blossom very much 'held down', suppressed, by her Chelsea-nurtured 'ego'. What beats its way through into being in Ursula and Birkin is the same life-source that thrashes Gudrun and Gerald hollow.

In part this interrelatedness makes itself felt metaphorically: there is a far-reaching suggestive continuity between the flowers, say, that Ursula gives Birkin (in place of those rings) in 'Excurse', and the 'open flower' of Gerald's love in 'Snowed Up'. In each case, the implication is precisely the same: to be given over to the other is to be open both to the possibilities of transformation and of annihilation. The direction the process takes is seen to depend on a complex interactive enablement or disablement between the lovers, where each of these courses continues to be imagined in terms of the opposite possibility. The destruction of Gerald is so final precisely because, to the extent of his capacity for it, he is so open to Gudrun; his love-wound and his death-wound are one and the same thing: 'This wound, this strange, infinitely-sensitive opening of his soul, where he was exposed, like an open flower, to all the universe, and in which he was given to his complement, the other, the unknown, this wound, this disclosure, this unfolding of his own covering, leaving him incomplete, limited, unfinished, like an open flower under the sky, this was his cruelest joy' (p. 446). For Gudrun, being the object of Gerald's 'cruelest joy' feels like being torn open, a feeling that underlines the incapacities of both; yet with her too the imagery also hints at what might otherwise have been realised: 'She felt, with horror, as if he tore at the bud of her heart, tore it open, like an irreverent, persistent being. Like a boy who pulls off a fly's wings, or tears open a bud to see what is in the flower, he tore at her privacy, at her very life, he would destroy her as an immature bud, torn open, is destroyed' (p. 446).

This sort of writing, far from dismissing Gerald and Gudrun as 'gangrenous', presents their interdestruction as a tragic inevitability involving all that they are, including their most valuable possibilities. Gerald dies because he cannot be, as Loerke is and Gudrun becomes, merely 'indifferent'; his nature is, as we are told, 'too serious' (p. 445). At the same time, Gudrun seems to bury with Loerke a longing for belief in something more than her modish ironies will ordinarily allow. At unguarded moments, such as when (significantly) Gerald is asleep in bed beside her, she works through to a realisation of what, at centre, she longs for:

Her heart was breaking with pity and grief for him. And at the same moment, a grimace came over her mouth, of mocking irony at her own unspoken tirade. Ah, what a farce it was! She thought of Parnell and Katherine O'Shea. Parnell! After all, who can take the nationalisation of Ireland seriously? After all, who can take political Ireland really seriously, whatever it does? And who can take political England seriously? Who can? Who can care a straw, really, how the old, patched-up Constitution is tinkered at any more? Who cares a button for our national ideals, any more than for our national bowler hat? Aha, it is all old hat, it is all old bowler hat?

That's all it is, Gerald, my young hero. At any rate we'll spare ourselves the nausea of stirring the old broth any more. You be beautiful, my Gerald, and reckless. There *are* perfect moments. Wake up, Gerald, wake up, convince me of the perfect moments, oh convince me, I need it.

He opened his eyes, and looked at her. She greeted him with a mocking, enigmatic smile in which was a poignant gaiety. Over his face went the reflection of the smile, he smiled too, purely unconsciously.

That filled her with extraordinary delight, to see the smile cross his face, reflected from her face. She remembered, that was how a baby smiled. It filled her with extraordinary radiant delight.

'You've done it', she said.

'What?' he asked, dazed.

'Convinced me.'

And she bent down, kissing him passionately, passionately, so that he was bewildered. He did not ask of what he had convinced her, though he meant to. He was glad she was kissing him. She seemed to be feeling for his heart, to touch the quick of him. And he wanted her to touch the quick of his being, he wanted that most of all. (p. 419).

Here Gudrun is as given over to Gerald as she will ever be, and while the scene dramatises what is alive between them (it almost is a perfect moment) the imagining never loses touch with what must thwart that life. On the one hand, there's Gerald's regressive 'wanting' – the baby-smile hinting at the way in which, for him, the world is an udder to feed his supreme self. Before long, he will be exultant; she will feel used. At the same time, Gudrun's characteristic defences have only been able to fall because she is alone. Her thinking here has an exploratory freedom that it never seems to have in conversation; others, even her sister and her lover (perhaps especially these) always inhibit the open expression and so the true discovery of the fundamental needs we see displayed here. Afraid of giving herself away, she can only fully be herself by herself. And the clear price to be paid for being like that, for remaining enclosed in a defensive sheath of cynicism, is to remain an immature bud.

And yet (as Lawrence would put it, using his most significant connective) the imagining here is so inward as to present a problem with even that formulation. The problem is that Gudrun's defensive cynicism here is so close to the novel's own attitude to these political and social questions. We would not be surprised to hear *Birkin* saying all that about political England and Ireland. At moments he says things that are even more extremely disillusioned. At the beginning of 'Excurse', for instance, he thinks thoughts that show his kinship with the nihilism of Loerke:

His life now seemed so reduced, that he hardly cared any more. At moments it seemed to him he did not care a straw whether Ursula or Hermione or anybody else existed or did not exist. Why bother! Why strive for a coherent, satisfied life? Why not drift on in a series of accidents – like a picaresque novel? Why not? Why bother about human relationships? Why take them seriously – male or female? Why form any serious connections at all? Why not be casual, drifting along, taking all for what it was worth? (p. 302)

This could not be Loerke, partly because for him these would not have been questions but settled convictions. But there is something in what Leo Bersani says about the novel when he talks of Lawrence playing 'dangerously with similarities; we are always being asked to make crucial but almost imperceptible distinctions'.[13] This is overstated, as the present case illustrates: neither Loerke nor Gudrun would have gone on to reflect, as Birkin does, that they were 'damned and doomed to the old effort at serious living'. And yet there can be no doubt that Lawrence does endow many of the characters, including those who are usually thought of as objects of his critique, with his own characteristic thoughts. Bersani goes on to make a similar point when he says that 'Lawrence nonchalantly exposes what the realistic novelist seems anxious to disguise: the derivation of his work from a single creative imagination'.[14] There is nothing 'nonchalant' or merely modernist in this, however. What it shows is the strenuous innerness of Lawrence's dramatic thinking about the various life-possibilities his work is exploring: very little is merely external or notational in this novel, or left as unrealised 'metaphysic'.

Which is to say that there is very little in the novel that remains merely Other to the novel's thinking and feeling. One good reason for thinking of this as a canonical text is that, like *Middlemarch* and *Anna Karenina*, *Women in Love* is for the most part both supple-minded and imaginatively generous enough not to fall into the repressive ethical oppositions which, according to Jameson, are supposed to characterise such books. In these books the over-defended 'social beings' ever retain a core of innocence, a mostly unrealised capacity, and unconscious longing, for change and growth; while the 'innocents' must always struggle against defensive integuments in themselves if they are to beat their way through into being. The necessity for permanent struggle in these figures precludes the simple idealisation of them that George Eliot falls into with Dorothea towards the end of *Middlemarch*, for instance, or our thinking of them simply as 'good' characters. This is why it is a notable strength in *Women in Love* that Birkin, even as late as 'Excurse', is still tempted to chuck in the whole thing with Ursula and draw back into his shell, for the moment a Loerke look-alike.

Right from the beginning, Birkin has been saying other characters' lines in a way that reveals the repressed 'social being' in him. An extremely telling moment is at the wedding at Shortlands when Mrs Crich hints that she would like him to be Gerald's friend:

Birkin looked down into her eyes, which were blue, and watching heavily. He could not understand them. 'Am I my brother's keeper?' he said to himself, almost flippantly.

Then he remembered with a slight shock, that that was Cain's cry. And Gerald was Cain, if anybody. Not that he was Cain, either, although he had slain his brother. There was such a thing as pure accident... Or is this not true, is there no such thing as pure accident? Has *everything* that happens a universal significance? Has it? Birkin, pondering as he stood there, had forgotten Mrs Crich, as she had forgotten him.

He did not believe that there was any such thing as accident. It all hung together, in the deepest sense. (p. 26)

Assuming that Birkin is right and there is no such thing as pure accident, then what are we to make of Birkin 'accidentally' uttering Cain's cry, and then when he remembers whose cry it is instantly associating it with Gerald? It all suggests something that Freud, who did not believe in accidents either, would have seen as a significant slip, a revelation 'in the deepest sense' of an aspect of Birkin that he did not want to know about – the Cain in himself. One way in which Birkin is Cain is not hard to see; after all, he is a mass brother-murderer in his often-expressed wish that the rest of mankind would simply disappear. He has just said so to Mrs Crich:

'Not many people amount to anything at all', he answered, forced to go much deeper than he wanted to. 'They jingle and giggle. It would be much better if they were just wiped out. Essentially, they don't exist, they aren't there.'

Saying this kind of thing is obviously much more disturbing to Birkin than he can allow himself to know, which is one reason for resisting Dan Jacobson's assertion that Birkin is allowed by the novel to get away with this sort of sentiment without 'being accused by the narrative voice or the other characters of manifesting therefore a murderously diseased will'.[15] This overlooks a much more subtle form of placing: Birkin's annihilating wishes and Gerald's brother-killing as a ruthless mine-owner (thus annihilating his father's sort of troubled brotherhood) are being unmistakably linked.

In this and in other ways Birkin and Gerald are seen to be brothers in spirit if not in blood long before explicit *Blutbruderschaft* comes into question. As with the sisterhood of Ursula and Gudrun, this is so even when the imagining of them draws strong attention to difference. The dialogue that concludes 'Shortlands', for instance, has Birkin analysing Gerald's conventionality and opposing it to true spontaneity, when suddenly the focus shifts to what connects them:

There was a pause of strange enmity between the two men, that was very near to love. It was always the same between them; always their talk brought them into a deadly nearness of contact, a strange, perilous intimacy which was either hate or love, or both. They parted with apparent unconcern, as if their going apart were a trivial occurrence. And they really kept it to the level of trivial occurrence. Yet the heart of each burned from the other. They burned with each other, inwardly. This they would never admit. They intended to keep their relationship a casual free-and-easy friendship, they were not going to be so unmanly and unnatural as to allow any heart-burning between them. They had not the faintest belief in deep relationship between man and man, and their disbelief prevented any development of their powerful but suppressed friendliness. (pp. 33–4)

Here it is Birkin, as much as Gerald, who is showing that, as Birkin himself has just said, 'It's the hardest thing in the world to act spontaneously on one's impulses' (p. 32). This is only remarkable because in context it was a dictum directed at *Gerald's* supposedly Cainlike suppressed desire/fear of having his gizzard slit. Birkin's whole argument suppresses his own feeling for Gerald, which has a good deal to do with why it *is* such a provocatively cutting sort of argument. In yet another Cainlike way Birkin is denying that in himself which is common to both men; and he has the analytical knife out for Gerald precisely because, at some level, that brotherhood itself is deeply 'perilous' to him.

Brotherhood, commonality, movements of responsibility or pity for others, notably Hermione, are ever the threatening Other in Birkin's psyche. His conscious ethic is that of Nietzschean singleness and self-responsibility. The sentence on spontaneity continues: 'and it's the only really gentlemanly thing to do – *provided you're fit to do it*' (my italics). The problem is that most of mankind are evidently not fit. As he said to Mrs Crich, they 'just jingle and giggle. It would be much better if they were just wiped out.' But fortunately it does not have to come to that because, as he says, 'Essentially they don't exist, they aren't there.' Which is not simply saying all over again that they do not really *live*, spontaneously and with *übermensch* singleness. It is saying also that one does not have to take them into account. They do not matter; one can forget them. And Birkin does that, very largely, for he seems to 'know', in advance, that any larger political responsibility or social consciousness is a form of false consciousness – a strategy for avoiding the responsibility of looking closely into oneself.

Granting Birkin's point, that social consciousness can be a form of false consciousness, or unconsciousness, his own refusal to know about the jinglers and gigglers surely involves another form of false consciousness, which is what I have been calling here the judgmental unconscious. This is the pharisaical thank-God-I-am-not-as-other-men attitude that George Eliot has in her sights, especially in the figures of Bulstrode and Lydgate, when the whole burden of her imagining is to underline the moral responsibilities of mutual interdependence and intersubjective understanding, whereby we only begin to know others by looking into the depths of ourselves. Where Eliot's emphasis runs the risk of sentimentality, Birkin's 'disquality', in emphasising *dis*continuity (the other side of the truth about others), is always in danger of the sort of delusive belief in its own superiority and uniqueness which is the core of judgmentalism.

It is here that *Women in Love* itself is most open to criticism, because there are strong grounds for thinking that Lawrence largely backs Birkin in his thoughts about 'disquality'. One might say that his text fulfils Birkin's murderous wishes by hardly allowing these jinglers and gigglers to exist in it. Only a superior class of people does exist in *Women in Love*. Most of them belong to the artistic and intellectual avant-garde, but at centre-stage are those potentially able to beat their way through to new life. The novel leaves us in no doubt that it is a very tiny elite indeed, surrounded by a great mass (typified by Palmer the electrician, the middle-aged Will Brangwen, and the couple who take the Birkins' chair) about whom there is nothing interesting, and certainly nothing hopeful, to be said. The rest presumably belong to meaningless mediocrity or to the great industrial machine. It is usual to say at this point that Lawrence himself, surrounded by the originals of most of these characters, had lost any touch he once had with the world in which such ordinary people lived. This does not quite go far enough, because after all he was the author of one of the most compelling novels about English working-class and provincial life ever written – and (what partly accounts for this triumph) one written from within. That the Midlands colliers of *Women in Love* are caricatured as sexually potent underworld automata, imagined in the mass rather than as individual Walter Morels, needs another explanation: as in *The White Peacock*, Lawrence was denying his social roots, suppressing many things he knew – in the service of an ethic of individual self-transcendence.

Marxists have already had their say about this, and I do not think there is any point in denying the force of the case here. *Women in Love* does have a political unconscious; to this extent it is ideology-bound, symptom of a particular historical process. But this can only be the final word about the novel if one is prepared to grant, as I am certainly not, some sort of trans-historical privilege to Marxism that guarantees it against counter-deconstruction. In the absence of this,

one can only say that there are various different stories about what is
real and important – and about transformation. All, as Lawrence
freely admitted, have in them the bones of an ideology. What matters
for art is the extent to which that is criticised from within, subjected
to a dialectical pressure that will bring to light its characteristic
suppressions – in this way 'working through' them into what I can
only provisionally call an 'ideological unknown'.

Women in Love takes up the bold experimentalism of *The Rainbow* and
perfects it by grafting it back onto the formal stem of the 'old' novel.
Lawrence found the most uncompromisingly 'modernist' and
stylised sections of *The Rainbow*, which are shaped almost entirely
around alternations of inward response, difficult either to sustain or
to resolve, and he more or less abandoned the mode long before he
finished the book. These sections raised a more profound difficulty
too. For all their undoubted interest and power, the rhythmic
withdrawals and returns of Will and Anna come to seem claustro-
phobically overfocused on their own significance and, lacking the
imaginative resistances of a realistic surface, ultimately program-
matic. The paradox is that the most formally exploratory mode in the
novel is at the same time the most insistent on its own *terms* of
exploration: unlike the 'old' novel of Eliot and Tolstoy, it offers us no
other terms.

The heart of the problem with *The Rainbow* can be seen in
Lawrence's famous letter about the novel to Edward Garnett of 5
June 1914, where he outlines his limited affinity with Marinetti and
the Futurists:

I don't care so much about what the woman *feels* – in the ordinary usage of
the word. That presumes an *ego* to feel with. I only care about what the
woman *is* – what she *is* – inhumanly, physiologically, materially – according to the use of the word: but for me, what she *is* as a phenomenon (or as
representing some greater inhuman will), instead of what she feels according
to the human conception.[16]

Lawrence also carefully distinguishes himself from the Futurists in
this letter, but what is not usually noticed is that his own tone is
continuous to some extent with theirs: 'I only care about what the
woman *is*... inhumanly, physiologically, materially' is almost pure
1914-manifestoese, the sort of formulation that might have come out
of the pages of *BLAST*. A similar determination to make it new is at
the centre of *The Rainbow*. 'I *only* care' corresponds to its modernist

foreshortening or stylisation of experience that is achieved by jettisoning much of the 'human conception' of the 'old' novel. At the same time, it is important not to overlook the prominent 'me' in this sentence ('but for me'), which reminds us that this is his own distinctive vision of newness, that is, as distinct from Marinetti's or Pound's or Gaudier-Brzeska's or any of the other Cubists or Vorticists competing for the limelight in those heady brink-of-war days.

The formulation also raises substantive questions. If it is asked how one tells 'what the woman *is*' as distinct from what she herself '*feels*', the answer is given time and again in *The Rainbow*: one 'knows'. Lydia may not consciously feel the 'vacancy' at the heart of her existence, but Tom Brangwen, seeing her walk by, instinctively 'knows' of it. This sort of 'knowing', or 'blood'-knowing, is one of those vital capacities handed on from generation to generation: it is possessed as much by Ursula peering into her microscope ('she only knew that it was not limited mechanical energy') as it was by the ancestral Brangwens who 'knew the wave which cannot halt'. At the same time, the novelist's own way of apprehending experience in *The Rainbow* is clearly continuous with theirs. Tom's intuition of a connection between Lydia and himself largely expresses the novel's own:

It was coming, he knew, his fate. The world was submitting to its transformation. He made no move: it would come, what would come. (ch. 1)

Tom is proven to be more or less right about this, and in context the rightness of his 'knowledge' seems imaginatively compelling. But this is only because the novel gives no space here to other possibilities, such as (as is the case so often in *Middlemarch*) that the lover may be confusing projected need or wish with actuality – and that Lydia may feel that his intuition is wrong. Such possibilities presumably belong to the old 'human conception' that Lawrence no longer 'cares about' here: they are irrelevant to the foreshortened vision of things that largely controls the novel. Which is to say that the importance given to blood-knowing in some ways imposes an element of ideological closure in *The Rainbow*; or, to revert to Lawrence's own terms, the presented world of the novel in some respects lacks that implied internal 'criticism' of its 'metaphysic' which 'makes for the lasting value and satisfaction of that work'.

It is significant that, as we have seen, 'knowing' in *Women in Love* mostly means something very different: it is usually a form of *false* consciousness clung to in order to suppress subconscious realisations. At the same time, without rejecting the essential intuitions or formal discoveries of *The Rainbow*, the later novel goes back to a realistic surface of things that includes, crucially, an interest in what the person 'feels', as distinct from what she or he is 'known' to 'be'. One of the primary nodes of interest in *Women in Love* is often the gap between what is intuitively (that is, projectively) 'known' about one character by another, and what is in other ways revealed.

We see this in a particularly telling way in Gudrun's attempts to come to terms with Gerald. By the chapter 'Death and Love' it begins to become clear that her intense desire to 'know' him (led on by all that seemed desirably unknown about him) is actually a subtle form of resistance to his otherness. Right from the beginning, her response to him has been passionately visionary, alive with an imaginative energy that, for her, seems to be indistinguishable from sexual desire. She is momentarily taken out of her self-consciousness by what she sees as his arctic dangerousness, his wolf-like singleness, a conception which both genuinely lights him up for us and yet makes him curiously difficult to square with, for instance, the man Birkin loves. In short, there is an element of abstraction in Gudrun's Gerald, of assimilative vision, that is related to her own modernist carvings and beyond them to Loerke's futuristic friezes. In *Women in Love*, the stylisations of modernism are now themselves problematic – and deeply implicated in the mechanical reductions of the modern world.

As we see when Gudrun and Gerald kiss under the railway bridge (and she yields passionately to an *idea* of Gerald as the powerful 'master' of all the colliers), Gudrun's sexuality is bound up with imaginative appropriation, this being an ultimate sort of light-in-the-darkness, a form of control that can never lapse finally in surrender to him. She seems partly to recognise this:

She reached up, like Eve reaching to the apples on the tree of knowledge, and she kissed him, though her passion was a transcendent fear of the thing he was, touching his face with infinitely delicate, encroaching, wondering fingers. Her fingers went over the mould of his face, over his features. How perfect and foreign he was – ah how dangerous! her soul thrilled with complete knowledge. (pp. 331–2)

The thrill of Gudrun's exploratory way of trying to 'know' Gerald's face (we should never forget that she is a sculptor) is itself rendered exploratorily, in prose that focuses the limits of her knowledge.

Lawrence's imagining of her experience, unlike her sense of Gerald, is sympathetically inward.

Gudrun's fear of knowing Gerald in that way, of understanding 'the thing he was' (as the flow of Lawrence's sympathetic consciousness has given him to us), is linked with those conversational closures of hers in the conversation with Ursula at the very beginning of the novel. There we see that, for all her apparently dazzling originality, Gudrun is very much bound by the language of the society that she affects to despise. Unlike Birkin and Ursula, Gerald and Gudrun mostly talk in conventionalities, even at their most intense moments, which is associated with their inability either to push through or to lapse into new understanding:

'Why don't I love you?' he asked, as if admitting the truth of her accusation, yet hating her for it.

'I don't know why you don't – I've been good to you. You were in a *fearful* state, when you came to me.'

Her heart was beating to suffocate her, yet she was stony and unrelenting.

'When was I in a fearful state?' he asked.

'When you first came to me. I *had* to take pity on you – but it was never love.'

It was the statement 'It was never love', which sounded in his ears with madness.

'Why must you repeat it so often, that there is no love?' he said in a voice strangled with rage.

'Well you don't *think* you love me, do you?' she asked.

He was silent with cold passion of anger.

'You don't think you *can* love me, do you?' she repeated, almost with a sneer.

'No', he said. (p. 442)

The novel suggests that the conventional terms in which Gudrun and Gerald mostly talk to each other are partly a sign of a blockage from which their language can provide no release. The present is hostage to the past. In Freudian terms, Gudrun and Gerald seem merely able to 'repeat' the past to each other symbolically rather than 'work through' their mutual resistances to an understanding of the other's separate being.

In the case of Gerald, the Freudian terms are especially relevant because part of our sense of 'the thing he was' is provided by the story of childhood trauma that hovers over all accounts of him like a suggestive pathogenesis. It is merely suggestive because the novel reaches for no definite explanation about its importance in Gerald's life, but questions the various versions that enter the characters' heads. In Birkin's meditation on Gerald's shooting of his brother, two possible ways of regarding this episode are raised. At first, Birkin thinks of the shooting as an 'accident' that has 'drawn a curse across the life that had caused the accident'. But he quickly moves away from this more ordinary 'surface' explanation to ponder another one – that there is 'no such thing as pure accident', that 'everything that happens [has] a universal significance', such that 'it all [hangs] together in the deepest sense'. These are obscure reflections, and we can only make sense of them cumulatively as the novel goes on pondering them. From the hints that emerge, we see that this 'deepest sense' of all human actions is that they are obscurely willed, as in the extreme case Birkin envisages, of murderer and murderee, in which even the victim desires his execution. This is about as close *ad absurdum* as any *reductio* can be allowed to go, and it keeps us wondering about the state of the man putting it forward.

The novel by no means simply backs the idea that everything that happens is in some ultimate sense willed, though it by no means rejects it either: time and again events are shaped so as to disclose the 'deepest' will in them. And yet, as is already evident, the drive for single coherent vision, the drive to see things *simply* 'in the deepest sense' as opposed to a more ordinary, common sense, 'surface' way of seeing them, is something about which the novel is properly sceptical. It is constantly opening a space to see some things as accidental, including Gerald's childhood trauma, which is much more generous to him than Gudrun or Birkin sometimes are.

More specifically, Birkin's drive for coherence at the 'deepest' level of vision is portrayed as partly a variant of Gudrun's will to 'know' things, a will that obscurely resists entertaining their otherness. Especially at the beginning of Birkin and Ursula's various love-scenes, we see his sort of drive to 'know' partly as an elaborate *defence* against her, a way of fending her off. They are unable to connect; she slips into an embarrassed conventionality, he into a brutal intel-lectualising directness:

'How nice the fuchsias are!' she said, to break the silence
   'Aren't they! – Did you think I had forgotten what I said?'
A swoon went over Ursula's mind.
   'I don't want you to remember it – if you don't want to', she struggled to say, through the dark mist that covered her.
There was silence for some moments.

'No', he said. 'It isn't that. Only – if we are going to know each other, we must pledge ourselves for ever. If we are going to make a relationship, even of friendship, there must be something final and infallible about it.'

There was a clang of mistrust and almost anger in his voice. She did not answer. Her heart was much too contracted. She could not have spoken.

Seeing she was not going to reply, he continued almost bitterly, giving himself away:

'I can't say it is love I have to offer – and it isn't love I want. It is something much more impersonal and harder, – and rarer.'

There was a silence, out of which she said:

'You mean you don't love me?'

She suffered furiously saying that.

'Yes, if you like to put it like that.' (p. 145)

This is characteristic of Birkin: even as he talks of final pledges and being 'without reserves and defences, stripped entirely into the unknown' (p. 147), he is bristling with them, untrustingly throwing the theory in her face precisely as a way of holding off those things in her. This 'abstract earnestness' is exactly what would not enable Ursula to be stripped entirely, as Birkin, beside himself with deep fears, obscurely knows.

At the same time, Birkin's drive to theorise about this 'something more impersonal' has an importance that cannot simply be psychologised away. As he realises himself: 'There was always confusion in speech. Yet it must be spoken. Whichever way one moved, if one were to move forwards, one must break a way through. And to know, to give utterance, was to break a way through the walls of the prison, as the infant in labour strives through the walls of the womb' (p. 186). This reminds us why clinging to the conventional language of love (as Gudrun and Gerald do, and Ursula wants to) does not get anywhere. As we have seen, it is indeed a 'prison'; it is a repressed and ultimately repressive language that obscures the often ambiguous underlife of sexuality. For Birkin, to move forward to new life is partly to force one's way through into expression, to break through the current limits of thought and language to new vision, however crude or violent or confused or abstract the first attempts might be. *This* sort of breaking through (as opposed to the flow of *sympathetic* consciousness) applies in one way to the novel as a whole, but it applies in a particular way to Birkin, who clearly dramatises a similar impulse in Lawrence himself. He embodies Lawrence's own insurgent will-to-vision, the discursive drive of the essays and pamphlets that gets all too much free rein in the later novels.

It is revealing that Lawrence, in the famous letter to Garnett, sounds rather like Birkin when he is trying to explain something to Ursula and ends up sounding, as she would say, too 'cocksure'. In 'Mino' his terms are strikingly similar to those in the letter:

'I want to find you, where you don't know your own existence, the you that your common self denies utterly. But I don't want your good looks, and I don't want your womanly feelings, and I don't want your thoughts nor opinions nor your ideas – they are all bagatelles to me.'

'You are very conceited, Monsieur', she mocked. 'How do you know what my womanly feelings are, or my thoughts or my ideas? You don't even know what I think of you now.'

'Nor do I care in the slightest.' (p. 147)

The crucial difference between the letter and the novel is that in *Women in Love* the woman is there to talk back and to insist on the importance of those womanly feelings that Birkin says he does not care about. In doing so, she also insists on the importance of a more ordinary sense of 'knowing' – not blood-knowing, but mere acquaintance with facts, such as what she actually *does* think, as opposed to what he 'knows' her to be thinking, or not thinking.

The importance of Ursula to the imaginative process and power of *Women in Love* can hardly be overestimated. It is usual to say that the strength of Birkin as a creation (as opposed, say, to Mellors) is that he is constantly being revealed and illuminated, his views being tested, refined, and contradicted, by the drama of which he is part. And Ursula provides much of the internal 'criticism that makes the lasting value and satisfaction of [the] work of art'. Yet her part in the novel is very much more important than this. Not only is she Birkin's complement, his Other, the one in whom he finds what he is after; she is the one in whose realised resistant spirit Lawrence's own will-to-'utterance' finds its complement and Other too.

We can see this at the end of 'Mino', where Birkin and Ursula are in contact in a new way:

'Proud and subservient, proud and subservient, I know you', he retorted dryly, 'proud and subserved, then subservient to the proud – I know you and your love. It is a tick-tack, tick-tack, a dance of opposites.'

'Are you so sure?' she mocked wickedly, 'what my love is?'

'Yes I am', he retorted.

'So cocksure!' she said. 'How can anybody ever be right, who is so cocksure? It shows you are wrong.'

He was silent in chagrin.

They had talked and struggled till they were both wearied out.

'Tell me about yourself and your people', he said.

And she told him about the Brangwens, and about her mother, and about Skrebensky, her first love, and about her later experiences. He sat very still, watching her as she talked. And he seemed to listen with reverence. Her face was beautiful and full of baffled light as she told him all the things that had hurt her or perplexed her so deeply. He seemed to warm and comfort his soul at the beautiful light of her nature.

'If she *really* could pledge herself,' he thought to himself, with passionate insistence but hardly any hope. Yet a curious little irresponsible laughter appeared at his heart. (p. 153)

The 'curious little irresponsible laughter' that comes to Birkin here is a hint that something like the star-equilibrium he has been talking about is beginning to take place between himself and Ursula. It is important to note that, although it might signal the beginning of what he is after, it does not come simply because he has been after it. In that important sense it comes from beyond his conscious aim, from the 'unknown' to which at last he seems to be open.

Birkin is slowly transformed in these love-scenes. Ursula's unfearful loving mockery sets in train something like a Freudian 'working through' of his defences, his tendency to neurotic repetition, such that he comes slowly to understand that she is not like the Hermione he 'knows' and fears she is. The key sign of this is that his ideas fall away and are reborn as experience – experience all the more remarkable for being, at the same time, so ordinary. When Birkin can be quiet enough to allow it to happen, their relations take on a simplicity and an ordinariness that is itself extraordinary in the world of this novel: Ursula tells him about her past; they have tea; they joke with each other, tease each other.

It is important to see that this remarkable ordinariness (which is so valuable because it lies, so to speak, on the other side of the prison walls from which all of the characters long to be released) reveals a good deal about the art that embodies it. The transformation of Birkin in these love-scenes recursively mirrors the novel's own creative transformation of the psycho-ethical thinking from which it partly springs, into an art that goes 'beyond the artist's conscious aim'. Ursula's loving subversion of the preacher in him reflects the novel's 'working through' of the sort of prophetic will that came to express itself more and more in the latter half of *The Rainbow* as over-certain knowledge of what the world is like.

The world of *Women in Love* is much more mind-resistant than the
one that keeps disclosing its meanings to the student Ursula in the
earlier novel. Which is partly to say that the later novel's 'theory of
being', like Birkin's, is constantly being met dialectically by a 'living
sense of being' that refuses simply to be badgered into passive
agreement with it. The cats in 'Mino', for instance, altogether shrug
off not only the sort of anthropomorphising signification that both
Birkin and Ursula try (half-seriously) to force upon them (and which
readers commonly try to read into them) but they lie altogether
beyond human ken. Their apparent handiness to the characters',
and what is often taken to be Lawrence's, argument, dissolves when
the focus comes back to the 'uncanny fires' of the cats' eyes that are
constantly looking beyond or through the human beings into a
landscape that is utterly 'unknown'.

The cats' final unknowableness means that, so far as the human
drama is concerned, they are not part of that remorseless coherence
'in the deepest sense' which is often supposed to characterise *Women
in Love*. Their most important role is that they tempt the characters
(and us) to read them as symbolic, and then run off, fundamentally
unread and unsymbolised. To that extent they remain accidental to
the thrust of the drama, part of what might be called, not a realistic
surface, but a realistic depth, of things that keeps impinging on events
in ways that are utterly unexpected. Just at the point at which the
quarrel between Birkin and Ursula is about to flare up again, Mrs
Daykin comes in with a tray:

> '*You prevaricator!*' she cried, in real indignation.
> 'Tea is ready, sir', said the landlady from the doorway.
> They both looked at her, very much as the cats had looked at them, a little
> while before.
> 'Thank you, Mrs Daykin.'
> An interrupted silence fell over the two of them, a moment of breach.
> 'Come and have tea', he said.
> 'Yes, I should love it', she replied, gathering herself together. (p. 151)

The essential action here is what it always is for Lawrence, the ebb
and flow of vital feeling within and between the two lovers. By this
point in their quarrel, we sense that Ursula's 'real indignation' is on
the point of playing itself out and metamorphosing into something
quieter and more responsive to Birkin. Yet Mrs Daykin really does
impinge on this process, enforcing on both of them (and us) a vital
sense of relativity: compared to someone really on the outside of their

little world, they are, for all their momentary antagonisms, in profound connection with each other. And that implied realisation helps to precipitate the shift of feeling that is already coming into being between them.

It is one sign of what is so deeply convincing about *Women in Love* that its 'living sense of being' includes realistic rhythms of episode and accident as subtly reshaping cross-currents to the master-rhythms of love and withdrawal between the lovers. Here mutual defences fall away partly because the lovers are distracted by tea or because they get simply 'wearied out' – too fatigued to argue any longer. The transformed, 'worked through' quality of these moments is extremely important: Lawrence is defining an ordinariness that is significantly different from the mere conventionality of Gerald and Gudrun. At a given moment, tea with beautiful china can revive closeness for Ursula and Birkin as easily as the great living continuum of the fields can for Anna Brangwen. In *Women in Love*, realistic episode and detail are not simply subsumed and effaced as they are in the most modernist sections of *The Rainbow*, with its rather fixed pattern of variation within endless repetition. The imagining in the later novel is able to embrace much more of a world that, like Mrs Daykin and the cats, quite cuts across the rhythms of the lovers' connection.

The importance that small accidents and unexpected events have in *Women in Love* draws attention to the importance of the 'unknown' in the imaginative process that produced them. Lawrence is constantly working on an edge where precise ends are not pre-known – in such a way that decisive moments can spring into being (in the novel's own phrase) 'accidentally on purpose', out of the suggestive interstices of surface happenings. Birkin downing his champagne accidentally on purpose before giving the wedding-speech nicely illustrates the combination of willed ends yet unwilled means that characterises the artistic process of this novel. The 'ordinary' moments between Ursula and Birkin are, from their point of view, so poised and free and, in a certain sense, blessed, precisely because they seem to happen so spontaneously: one minute Ursula is attacking Birkin as a prevaricator, the next she is drinking tea and telling him about her people. At the same time, the art that embodies this moment is only 'right' because it too comes into being in an utterly unsignalled way that simultaneously takes up and clinches the deeper purposes that have been latent in the imagining of the whole scene and indeed the whole novel. The story Ursula tells of her mother and of Skrebensky shows the necessary connection here between the represented life and the art itself: in remembering them she is dramatising the return to conscious expression of latent purposes that go right back into the prehistory of *Women in Love* – to a time when this novel and *The Rainbow* were one story.

Looked at from this larger perspective, the will for the lovers to connect in some such way has been there all along (in both their minds and their creator's), and has been expressing itself even in their quarrelling. It is expressed especially in their quarrelling: though they are not conscious of it, their arguing, unlike that of Gerald and Gudrun, is part of the process of 'working through' their resistances to each other. And just as it is impossible for them to plan consciously the overcoming of these defences, so it is impossible for Lawrence to plan consciously the precise realisation of these unplanned moments that are at the same time a consummation of all that he has been 'in the deepest sense' striving to realise. In a real sense, such moments come out of an 'unknown' that keeps transcending, even as it completes, the artist's will-to-meaning.

The notion that art can in a certain sense transcend its so-called ideological underpinnings is not one that would be necessarily persuasive or even intelligible to someone committed to seeing *any* representation of personal transformation as 'neo-Freudian nostalgia for some ultimate moment of *cure*'.[17] Nor would pointing out that, in this novel, there is no 'ultimate moment', only continuing process. There is no answer here to those who insist ideologically that there can be nothing in a non-Marxist work of art but enfleshed ideology.[18] Yet *Women in Love* demonstrates that, to conceive, as some do, of embodied morality in a novel as a static system of binary oppositions is to miss the *dynamic* nature of intentionality as a restless process of undermining, interrogating, and repositioning the work's key terms. And to insist, as others do, that novels can only reinforce our resistances to non-ideological reality, is to miss the fact that some significant ones actually represent such resistances and are centrally concerned with the possibility of 'working through' them. Not only this, but as *Women in Love* also demonstrates, the dynamic intentionality of some novels is an embodiment of the 'working through' process itself, whereby discursive purpose issues in represented meanings that were unplanned and, in a relevant sense, 'unknown'.

CHAPTER 10

Lawrence and Lady Chatterley: the teller and the tale

Since Kate Millett's *Sexual Politics* Lawrence has been associated with another manifestation of ideology – the patriarchal sort that waged explicit counter-revolution against the feminism of his day. This association has so deeply affected the estimate of Lawrence prevalent today, it is important to recall the kind of reading it is based on. Millett, for instance, comments in this way on the passage in *Women in Love* in which the male cat cuffs the female:

Ursula draws the parallel, in case we missed it: 'It's just like Gerald Crich with his horse – a lust for bullying – a real Wille zur Macht.' Birkin defends such conduct and brings home the moral: 'With the Mino it is a desire to bring his cat into pure stable equilibrium ... It's the old Adam ... Adam kept Eve in the indestructible paradise when he kept her single with himself, like a star in its orbit.' And of course a star in Birkin's orbit is exactly what Ursula's position is to be; Birkin will play at the Son of God, Ursula revolving quietly at his side.[1]

It will be plain by now that such a reading of the scene depends on some questionable assumptions: that meanings in *Women in Love* are simple and transparent ('in case we missed it'); that Birkin is simply Lawrence's mouthpiece ('brings home the moral'); that Ursula, despite her own feminist consciousness, is there simply to revolve 'quietly at his side'. Millett reads the novel both selectively and as if it were an illustrative tract, static, moralistic, and binary (males right/females wrong), and so catches no glimpse of the restless process of exploratory questioning which is the distinction of the novel's art.

With *Lady Chatterley's Lover*, on the other hand, Millett is on firmer ground, and she demonstrates strategic acumen by beginning her account of Lawrence with his last novel. Here the polemicist in Lawrence does overpower the artist; and the polemicist, for all the strangeness of his vision of things, is inevitably more subject to ideology because there is less of substance pushing antithetically against the will-to-vision, or leading it into 'places unknown'. Fortunately we are now reasonably well placed to talk about these internal dynamics (or lack of them) within the creative process of *Lady Chatterley's Lover* because we have earlier versions of it which allow us to see the transformation of an unexpectedly powerful novella, published as *The First Lady Chatterley*, into Lawrence's painful and notorious last novel.

To turn from *Lady Chatterley's Lover* to *The First Lady Chatterley* is to have a sense of recovering the imaginative source of the later novel, the moment at which the act of imagining was at the same time one of discovering, defining and testing the ethical intuitions that were later to harden into doctrine. At the heart of all versions are complementary intuitions about what is most essential for human flourishing: on the one hand, a modern marriage of 'personalities' (or 'social beings') is thought to be deadening if it is not at the same time a passional bond, a 'blood marriage'; and on the other, a 'blood marriage', even where there is no marriage of minds or personalities, is something ultimately more sustaining. All versions are to some extent 'thought adventures', or thought-and-feeling-experiments, in which one kind of marriage is imagined in an interexploratory way against the other, with the figure of the wife (as ever) at the centre.

The authority of the first book partly comes from the way it explores the two sorts of 'marriages', between Connie and Clifford, and between Connie and Parkin, as *limit* cases, though without letting us think of them merely as cases. Here we come to see not only what is finally so withering about the relationship of Connie and Clifford, but also, for much of the novel, the very limited way it is alive; for it is a close, cultivated companionship in which minds *can* meet, and the novel by no means dismisses that even while it discovers why such companionship might not be enough. With Connie and Parkin, personal differences are as extreme as they could be. Class, for instance, remains an intractable reality, so that, even while the novel defines the sense in which their 'marriage in the wood' satisfies needs and desires that are ultimately more essential, the relationship is always seen to be problematical and incomplete. There is an imaginative integrity about *The First Lady Chatterley* that is evident in the way its insights are so searchingly tested against all the resistant realities. Essential though the passional bond may be when set beside intellectual and social compatibility alone, it is none the less, when abstracted from the rest, *not enough either.*

That Lawrence did not publish *The First Lady Chatterley* and kept reworking it as he did, suggests that he wanted to affirm his 'marriage in the wood' in an altogether more unambiguous way, such that it *would* be enough. In the final version he contrives to make it so by keeping his thumb on the pan, turning Parkin into an educated Mellors and Clifford into an egomaniac who is no companion for Connie. In this way *Lady Chatterley's Lover* certainly gains a great deal in clarity, force, and directness, but at the same time it violates both the imaginative integrity of the original tale and the ethical thought-and-feeling-experiment it represents.

The important differences between the two versions are best seen at the level of local detail. Here, for example, is an episode from *The First Lady Chatterley*, and below it is the corresponding episode in *Lady Chatterley's Lover*.

The front door of the cottage was shut, and nobody came. She walked round to the back and suddenly, in the yard, came upon Parkin washing himself. He had taken off his shirt, as the colliers do, and rolled his breeches on his hips and was ducking his head in the bowl of water. Constance retired immediately and went back into the wood, to stroll around for a time.

But in the dripping gloom of the forest, suddenly she started to tremble uncontrollably. The white torso of the man had seemed so beautiful to her, splitting the gloom. The white, firm, divine body with that silky firm skin! Never mind the man's face, with the fierce moustache and the resentful, hard eyes! Never mind his stupid personality! His body in itself was divine, cleaving through the gloom like a revelation. – Clifford even at his best had never had that silky, rippling firmness, the more than human loveliness.

It was with great difficulty she brought herself to go back to the cottage and knock at the door. She stood on the threshold and trembled inwardly. Previously, she had never even thought of him as anything but an instrument, a gamekeeper. It seemed to her almost wrong that he should have that pure body.[2]

So she went round the side of the house. At the back of the cottage the land rose steeply, so the back yard was sunken, and enclosed by a low stone wall. She turned the corner of the house and stopped. In the little yard two paces beyond her, the man was washing himself, utterly unaware. He was naked to the hips, his velveteen breeches slipping down over his slender loins. And his white slim back was curved over a big bowl of soapy water, in which he ducked his head, shaking his head with a queer, quick little motion, lifting his slender white arms, and pressing the soapy water from his ears, quick, subtle as a weasel playing with water, and utterly alone. Connie backed away round the corner of the house, and hurried away to the wood. In spite of herself, she had had a shock. After all, merely a man washing himself; commonplace enough, Heaven knows!

Yet in some curious way it was a visionary experience: it had hit her in the middle of the body. She saw the clumsy breeches slipping down over the pure, delicate, white loins, the bones showing a little, and the sense of aloneness, of a creature purely alone, overwhelmed her. Perfect, white, solitary nudity of a creature that lives alone, and inwardly alone. And beyond that, a certain beauty of a pure creature. Not the stuff of beauty, not even the body of beauty, but a lambency, the warm, white flame of a single life, revealing itself in contours that one might touch: a body!

Connie had received the shock of vision in her womb, and she knew it; it lay inside her. But with her mind she was inclined to ridicule. A man washing himself in a backyard! No doubt with evil-smelling yellow soap! She was rather annoyed; why should she be made to stumble on these vulgar privacies?[3]

The second passage is no mere revision of the first; it is a reimagining that changes the emphasis in several crucial ways. The first moves more swiftly and vibrantly in a way that registers the 'revelation' more completely as *Connie's* experience. The emphasis, the repetitions, the rapid crisis, convey a dilation of feeling so sudden and unexpected that her mind cannot quite take it in; and the 'inward trembling' is rendered in the movement of the prose. In the second, we are less aware of this flow of feeling; the repetitions and the emphases, particularly in the second paragraph, are not so much those of dramatised response as those of a certain kind of expository insistence. There is a drive for a precision which does not quite come, and, probably because it does not, the will to achieve it stiffens, pushing the passage towards abstraction. The 'shock of vision' in the third paragraph comes then as something half-asserted, but it is significant that we hardly notice this because the passage keeps moving into assertion of an altogether grosser kind: 'Connie had received the shock of vision *in her womb*, and she knew it; it lay inside her. But *with her mind* she was inclined to ridicule.' To intervene in the way indicated by the italicised phrases is not merely to schematise and to simplify Connie's response; the intervention narrows, and so profoundly alters, the significance of the revelation.

In the first, the significance is irreducibly what the whole passage gives to us; it is complex and organic. For Connie to respond to Parkin's body in that way is itself an implicit self-discovery, a discovery in herself of what Lawrence in 'A Propos of *Lady Chatterley's*

Lover' calls 'the body's life'. To discover this is to experience 'real feelings', 'real sensations', 'real passions' – as opposed to the cerebral sort Dorothea forces herself to feel for Casaubon and Sir Clifford makes himself feel for art. For Connie, in the wasting monotony of her life with Clifford, it is to become aware and alive in a new way. So the movement of the prose which gives us the flow of Connie's feeling is an important part of the meaning; to an extent, this way of feeling *is* the revelation. Which is not to say that it is a matter of new consciousness merely; to come alive in this way is precisely to come alive *to* someone in a way that quite transcends the self-enclosed awareness of seeing him as an instrument, a gamekeeper, or even as a 'personality'. Parkin is there for Connie as a strangely pure and naked being; she sees in him an unexpected sensuous beauty which goes beyond both sensuousness and beauty to reveal that quite unexpected life which is the 'body's life'. His body is both there as that to which Connie comes so responsively alive, and is itself an image of the responsive life she discovers.

The episode in *Lady Chatterley's Lover* means something quite different. In the first paragraph, where it is most impressive, there is little sense of quickening response. The keeper's finely sensual attractiveness is felt in the way his back, loins, and hips are caught in the writing; but at the same time the visual sharpness and clarity emphasise his distance, his otherness. Here his washing conveys something merely hinted at in the earlier novel: an unconsciousness and absorption that show him as utterly single and out of relation with any other being, including Connie. What is not conveyed in any way, though, is why this vision should hit Connie 'in the middle of her body' or in her 'womb'. The term is at once pseudo-anatomical jargon, like 'bowels', 'loins', 'thighs', which so often signals a characteristic kind of Lawrentian vagueness, yet at the same time conveys an intended meaning that is precisely anatomical. The vagueness and the pseudo-precision go together: the 'shock of vision' in Connie's womb is not something imagined (how could it be?) but a meaning wilfully imposed, which makes the significance of the scene at once more nebulous and much narrower.

Seen side by side in this way, the two passages show what I think is true of the novels as a whole: that the impulse at work transforming *The First Lady Chatterley* into *Lady Chatterley's Lover* is fundamentally a reductive one. The life we get in the first novel is more deeply and completely imagined, and the significance discovered in the imagining of it (registered in such key terms as 'the body', 'contact', 'connection', 'marriage') has a range, a wholeness, that is characteristically diminished in the later book into a narrow didactic preoccupation with sex itself. The corresponding terms in *Lady Chatterley's Lover* are precisely those for which the novel is notorious, those of the genitals and the sexual act. Here Millett is right. The reduction of Connie to a 'female' 'womb', the counterpart in her of that triumphant 'phallus' which will answer so fully to all that she presently lacks, does derive ultimately from an ideological hierarchy of oppositions. Millett's analysis is not reductive in this particular case because the centre of gravity has crucially shifted from Connie–Lawrence's explorations in one version to Mellors–Lawrence's narrow (and frankly patriarchal) answers in the final one.

The important shift between the two is the foreclosing on *Connie* as a complex centre of imagined response. In the passage from *Lady Chatterley's Lover*, Lawrence's intervention, 'in her womb ... with her mind', not only schematises and reinterprets; it declares valuations that are at one remove from those registered in the details themselves. To say 'with her mind' is to insist that it was *only* with her mind; and this valuing, or rather devaluing, is external to the particulars of the art. In the passage from *The First Lady Chatterley* the judgments are implicit in the very flow and cross-flow of Connie's feelings; they are creatively realised in the rendering of a mind suddenly enraptured yet simultaneously in conflict, struggling to absorb the vision, to place it against the gamekeeper she knows. Parkin's class-foreignness to her, felt as a slight sense of squalor (he washes 'as the colliers do'), the fierce moustache, the resentful hard eyes, the stupid personality, are all fully presented. In this moment of vision they are felt to be mere surface realities, but they are none the less a true part of the vision in that they represent all those realities that make her relationship with Parkin permanently incomplete. Here, Parkin's class-origins, his foreignness to Connie, together with his rather repellent social self, are grasped in a way which implicitly tests the depth and significance of the revelation. There is no impulse here to write these things down; the vision itself shows the reader how to value them.

Dramatic imagining such as this can be described as an *impersonal* thought-and-feeling-experiment to the extent that the writer's conscious identity, his habitual orientation in a space of moral or anti-moral *beliefs*, is somehow suspended or absorbed into the current of the life being imagined. Keats writes of the poet as a chameleon, ever assuming identities other than his or her own. This is the only way in which we can account for a Tolstoy, with all his baggage of well-known beliefs, being able to create an Anna, or a Lawrence here surrendering to the exigencies of his 'tale' – going against the grain of what he might want to happen in the name of what *has* to happen. The touchstone for such ethical inquiry will be the complex created reality of the centres of consciousness being imagined. This is why it is so important in *The First Lady Chatterley* that the novel's imagining has a character, a distinctive tone and way of moving, which comes from the fact that it is characteristically imagining the world as *Connie* experiences it (though not only in this way).

The scenes in the woods with Parkin, for example, have an innocence and directness that are partly Connie's own uninhibited, sometimes slightly naive, naturalness. Her slow, brooding, at times faintly ponderous, coming to life, with its strange, ever-renewing intensity, yet with its uncertainties and recoils, its constant shifts in seeing and feeling – all this describes a complex rhythm that is actually the inward structure of *The First Lady Chatterley*. It is less intense than the irresistible, all-engulfing tidal ebb and flow of parts of *The Rainbow*; it is more like the stream mentioned in the novel itself (in a passage about Clifford): 'Yet he never felt Constance really as another flowing life, flowing its own stream ... he never warmly *felt* her, not for a moment' (*FLC*, p. 34). By contrast Lawrence's art does create Connie, for the whole novel, as a flowing life, flowing its own stream. Connie's flowing life and the novel's are continuous – and it is precisely this continuity between natural and human life, and between different aspects of human life, that is one of the main themes of the novel. The image of the stream, with its steady, but by no means direct, course, with its eddies and cross-currents, may seem commonplace enough, but it happens to be just right for the fluidity of both the substance and manner of the novel's ethical searching and appraising.

While this fluidity is of a kind that can only be grasped adequately over several pages, there are brief passages that illustrate something of it, for example:

'And what do you think happened to *me*!' said Clifford, with arch importance.

'What?' said Constance.

'Miss Bentley actually called – sent in her *card*!' he cried it out in triumph.

'Never!' she cried, her eyes glowing. Clifford was utterly uninterested in her and her tale of rabbits. And she, she had torn herself away from the other one for nothing.

Clifford seemed in a perfectly good humour, as if there had never been any strain between them. She listened to him in perfect acquiescence: all about old Miss Bentley in a short and modish dress of tea-rose yellow. Some far corner of her critical feminine mind was interested. But her dynamic self was so bored, so bored, screaming with boredom.

She fled at last upstairs and sat down in a low chair by her window. What could she do? How could she recover her poise? – How lovely he was, really! How he had pounced on her! How humble she ought to feel, how grateful to him, for feeling this straight unerring passion for her! How lovely it was to be near him! How lovely he was. If only she were near him now, just even to smell the corduroy of his coat. So common, an old corduroy coat! Made stripes on one's face if one leaned against it. How ashamed she ought to be! – a gamekeeper, in her husband's employ! But his body! – the unspeakable pleasure of being near him. 'Ay!' she imitated in her mind the broad sounds of the vernacular. 'Ay! Ah should!' And she laughed a little, she liked it so much. It amused her down to her very toes.

But she could never live with him. No, No! Impossible! She was not a working man's wife. It would be a false situation. He would probably begin speaking King's English – and that would be the first step to his undoing. No no! He must never be uplifted. He must never be brought one stride nearer to Clifford. He must remain a gamekeeper, absolutely.

And herself? It would be absurd for her to become a gamekeeper's wife. Her piano, her paints, her books – leave them all behind? But even if she did, she wouldn't be able to leave her thoughts behind, and all she had acquired, the whole run of her mind. (*FCL*, pp. 79–80)

Connie has just returned from a chance meeting with Parkin in the woods. She had been there to escape Clifford, and though she meant to escape Parkin too, her coming across him there was not entirely accidental either. Throughout that earlier scene with Parkin, in the way that Connie sees herself as mere prey to the 'cunning', the 'savage instinct', the 'keen animal look of search in [Parkin's] eyes' (*FLC*, pp. 74–6), there is in her an unconscious shrinking from the recognition of her own desire. And when Parkin takes her, and she lapses into the unconsciousness of passion, she feels a loss of 'solidity', an imminent dissolution of the self she knows. She is obscurely afraid of it, and she hurries away from him half-aware that she is running away from the risk demanded by the awakening life within her, the risk of losing all that is known and solid and 'sensible' and 'poised' in the rising swell of the unknown. So she arrives back at Wragby desperately trying to recover her 'old self, her famous poise' (*FLC*, p. 79), not so much to conceal herself from Clifford as out of a powerful countervailing need to cling to the known and the safe. This brief scene at Wragby shows her that the known and the safe is also, in a crucial sense, the dead; she cannot go back either.

The fineness of this scene, and it is a characteristic one, lies in the special delicacy with which the smallest shifts in Connie's feelings are registered so as to convey a complex, partly unconscious process of sifting, adjustment, and decision. The completeness and subtlety of Lawrence's imagining here can be felt in the precision of tone which gives us such a fluid sense, not merely of that 'dynamic self' which the scene is in part defining, but of a whole mind moving in its mysterious wholeness. As soon as she is free of Clifford, Connie turns almost by reflex to what she was thinking of before Clifford started speaking: 'What could she do? How could she recover her poise?' But by now the questions have been emptied of their force in the implicit rediscovery of what that 'poise' is worth. And also implicit in that, and almost simultaneously coming out of it, is the discovery of what she had really been feeling, but which the questions had been suppressing: 'How lovely [Parkin] was really!' That comes with a feeling of release, of returning to something more essential in herself, something she cannot help being. And in the warm delight with which she recalls Parkin, a sense of relative importance is recovered by which Clifford and Wragby and the civilisation they stand for are defined and valued.

But this is never a final valuation. Also implicit in this paragraph, particularly as Connie's reverie runs to a delighted amusement at Parkin's way of speaking, is the recognition that it is passion recollected in a sort of tranquillity, at a distance. Significantly, it is only now, in the security of Wragby, that she can relive it all with such delight – significantly, because it suggests the extent to which that delight depends on a slight blurring of the real Parkin. Yet it is not quite pure delight either; there is also an undercurrent of uneasiness, surfacing only in the half-dutiful, but not entirely unfelt, reflex-thought: 'How ashamed she ought to be! – a gamekeeper in her husband's employ!' This is not quite the relevant point, we notice, but it signals the pressure of a gathering realisation that only emerges for her in the next paragraph, 'But she could never live with him', and terminates in the following paragraph at the real point:

'Her piano, her paints, her books – leave them all behind? But even if she did, she wouldn't be able to leave her thoughts behind, and all she had acquired, the whole run of her mind.'

Here we might recall Millett's complaint that in *Lady Chatterley's Lover* Connie is never 'given the personal autonomy of an occupation, and Lawrence would probably find the suggestion obscene'.[4] Her point is that, according to the patriarchal ideology speaking though Lawrence, the woman can only find her fulfilment and *raison d'être* in subordination to the man. However true this might be of the final version, as is evident here the first version is by no means dismissing the importance of such intellectual and artistic occupations as were thought appropriate for a woman of Connie's class and time. There is no hint of anything 'obscene' here about needs that could never be satisfied in a gamekeeper's cottage with Parkin.

It is the whole run of Connie's *mind* that Parkin could not satisfy, and this novel (unlike the final version) does not obscure the importance of the fact precisely because that 'run' of mind is given to us with such wholeness. But then the novel itself is larger in scope than even the whole run of Connie's mind. Clifford and Wragby may be, as far as her 'dynamic self' is concerned, a remote dead world for her, yet it is independently there, insisting on its own reality when Connie returns to find Clifford quite unexpectedly preoccupied with something else. And despite its rather boyish egoism, Clifford's telling of his own little meeting with Miss Bentley, the tea-shop lady with such a crush on him, has a certain refined satirical charm, which a part of Connie cannot help being mildly excited by. In this novel, unlike *Lady Chatterley's Lover*, Connie and Clifford *can* share such things, and the 'good humour', the surface ease between them, which depend on what they do share, are given their due ethical weight – a weight that Connie's underlying feeling of boredom by no means displaces. There is a subtle excess in Connie's feeling of being 'bored, so bored, screaming with boredom', which tells us that the reality of what is shared, and its value, go beyond Connie's momentary grasp of them. That kind of recoil has an energy which is suppressing something too. Connie is caught up in a fluid interflow of opposites, and as she moves between them the novel searches out and defines the worth of all the continuous realities of her life with a fineness and sureness of touch that make much of the novel as impressive in its way as anything Lawrence ever wrote.

For the reader who knows only *Lady Chatterley's Lover*, that claim might seem an unlikely one, yet time and again in *The First Lady Chatterley*, and especially in the forest scenes, we can be surprised by a particular kind of imaginative delicacy that was quite lost in the subsequent reworking. The finest example of all, to my mind, is this one:

After this she would go often after tea, as the evenings lengthened, and walk in the wood and sometimes sit in the hut. In the little clearing by the hut the coops were put out in a circle, and hens were sitting on the pheasants' eggs. Towards sundown the pheasants would come running furtively for the bit of corn the keeper had scattered, the cocks steering horizontal in all their brave plumage.

And Constance would sit very still, watching. And the keeper would come and go quietly, almost benevolently. He had accepted her presence and accepted himself as her male guardian angel of the woods. He never interfered with her and rarely spoke to her. But when she did not come for almost a week, he watched her when she returned. And it was a long time before he brought himself to say:

'You wasn't poorly, was you?'

'No! Nurse has been away for a week, so I stayed with Sir Clifford.'

'Ah see!'

She was delighted when the pheasant chicks began to run out on to the grass. They were so tiny and odd. She had to help to feed them. They would stand, with their tiny tremble of life, in her hand and peck from her palm.

She looked up at the keeper, and her blue eyes were bright and moist and wonderful.

'Aren't young things lovely!' she said, breathless. 'New young things!'

'Ay! T'little baby bods!'

He spoke almost condescending but understandingly. And his red-brown eyes had widened and looked strangely into hers.

She remained crouched among the busy, tiny little birds, and she was crying. She felt a great abandon upon her. And he, trying to go away from her, was spellbound. He could not go away from that soft, crouching female figure. In spite of himself, he went and stood by her, looking down at her.

'Y'aren't cryin' are yer?' he asked in a bewildered voice.

She nodded blindly, still crouched down upon herself, her hair falling. He looked down upon her folded figure, and almost without knowing what he did, crouched down beside her, knees wide apart, and laid his hand softly on her back. She continued to cry, breathing heavily. And the touch of her soft, bowed back, breathing heavily with abandoned weeping, filled him with such boundless desire for her that he rose and bent over her, lifting her in his arms. All that could ever be that was desirable, she was to him then. And she, lifted up, for one moment saw the brilliant, unseeing dilation of his eyes. Then he was clasping her body against his. And she was thinking to herself: 'Yes! I will yield to him! Yes! I will yield to him.'

Afterwards, he was gloomy and did not speak a word. He avoided her. Even when she was leaving, and she softly said: 'Good night!' and looked to meet his eyes, he would not look at her. And that was the only word spoken between them. (*FLC*, pp. 49–51)

Like all of Lawrence's best writing, this scene seems to develop in a way which is not wholly conscious of ends, and in that sense the art itself is partly continuous with the life Connie feels in the chicks and finds in herself and Parkin when he embraces her and she sees 'the brilliant, unseeing dilation of his eyes'. Here, in their coming together for the first time, Lawrence conveys, with a directness which is characteristically his, their quickening desire, all the more vitalising for its unseeing impersonality, rapidly absorbing and submerging the conscious self. In this novel that quickening has distinctive qualities of which the chicks, in their 'tiny tremble of life', are one precise image and example; their innocence and vulnerability are not merely similar to, but continuous with, just those qualities in Parkin himself, in the flowers crushed by Clifford's chair, and in the whole resurgence of life in the wood, of which Connie's coming to life is felt so forcefully to be a part. Thus, the complex but quite unexpected imaginative resonance between Parkin and the chicks is seen to be real and significant, despite Parkin's surface personality. When he answers Connie's remark about the chicks, he seems to need that slightly self-protective, self-controlling air of condescension, and he needs it partly because, like Connie, he too is moved, but also partly because he is half-afraid of the vulnerability which goes with it. There is something almost undefended about him – caught here in his tentative question about Connie's absence, in that recurrent note of bewilderment. These are inseparable from the strange caressing sensuousness of his dialect and an intuitive integrity that shows itself especially when he acts, as he does here, 'almost without knowing' what he is doing. When he caresses Connie's back his spontaneous sensuality is at the same time, without the slightest division of impulse, a profound kind of responsibility, a concern which is much more caring than Clifford's mentally derived 'kindness'. One of Lawrence's great intuitions is that, in itself, desire is essentially innocent – and can be healing and creative.

The art in this scene is therefore very different from the corresponding one in *Lady Chatterley's Lover*, which has been both highly praised (by Richard Hoggart) and strongly disparaged (by Kate Millett). For in that scene Lawrence's thinking often seems to be merely external. There, for example, Connie feels 'so forlorn and unused, not a female at all' when she sees 'the soft nestling ponderosity of the female urge' (*LCL*, p. 117) in the pheasant hens. In *The First Lady Chatterley* the 'great abandon' evoked in Connie by the chicks comes as something creatively discovered. The experience is primarily one of release, not merely from a weight of accumulated unhappiness, but from the unconscious self-resistance which has been at the centre of it. It is a release of what can only be called her 'real' bodily feelings, which tell her in an instinctive, nameless way what she needs. There is much more in Connie's weeping here than a thwarted 'female urge'. The deadness of her years with Clifford, the physical nearness of Parkin and all he has come to mean to her consciously and unconsciously, the 'breathing contact of the living universe' (*FLC*, p. 55) she has discovered in the woods, this sudden apprehension of the chicks' odd tiny newness which is so lovely and moving – all this is inwardly apprehended and brought into a richly significant relationship. The scene has a poetic integrity which recursively reflects that vital form of innocence valued in and by the scene itself.

The First Lady Chatterley is not always as admirable as this, though. It is a flawed book in a way that is reminiscent of *Lady Chatterley's Lover*. The problem is focused in Lawrence's attitude to Clifford. It is true that Lawrence is much more open to him here; apart from a few rather hysterical pages at the end, there is little to compare with the animus directed at him in *Lady Chatterley's Lover*. Yet even here, for the most part, Lawrence still does not, perhaps cannot, allow himself to imagine what it is to be Clifford. At moments he very nearly does, and these are extremely revealing, as here, for example:

'Clifford,' she said suddenly, looking up at him. 'You know I am fond of you. And I want always to be fond of you. Never mind what has happened to your legs. You are you.'

'I am I!' he repeated. 'I am I! And when I am out of the body, perhaps I shall be a real thing. Till then I'm not.'

'Yes you are! Think what a great part of life you are, even to me!'

'And what I'm not, even to you', he said.

'Never mind that', she said.

'I mind it', he said. 'Titian's women! The immortality of the flesh! Do you think I don't know what you mean, even if you don't know yourself? I *hope* you'll find a man to love you and give you babies – the immortality of the flesh you're after.'

'Would you mind if I had a child, Clifford?'

He looked up at her suddenly.

'If you had *whose* child?' he said.

'I don't know. Would you mind if I had a child by a man?'

'Couldn't you promise it would be by the Holy Ghost?' he said satirically.

'Perhaps!' she murmured. 'The Holy Ghost!'

There was a pause.

'Why?' he said. 'Do you think you're *going* to have a child?'

'No!' she murmured. 'Not yet.'

'Not yet! How not yet?'

'Would you mind if I did have a child?' she repeated.

'Whose child, I ask.'

'But need you ask? Isn't it the Holy Ghost, if one looks at it that way?'

'It's no good my looking at it that way. All I see is some man or other who probably was never in the war and so –'

There was a pause.

'But why need you ask which man?' she said softly.

'Haven't I the right?'

'Have you?'

There was another dead pause.

'No by God!' he said suddenly. 'Probably I haven't. Probably I've no right to a wife at all: a wife in name and appearance. No, I've no right. I've no right to you. You can go to what man you like.'

'No but listen, Clifford! I love you. You've taught me so ...' (*FLC*, pp. 66–8)

This exchange comes immediately before one of the gaps in the manuscript where about three or four pages are missing. We cannot be sure why they are missing, but one cannot help suspecting that Lawrence felt he was losing control of the scene at the very point at which Connie is forced to become defensive about the possibility of having this child. She is forced to become so out of a half-recognition that there is something a bit glib in her own position. All the force of the passage, and it is what must be called a *moral* force, comes from a momentary realisation in the drama of what Clifford's position actually is. That question, 'If you had *whose* child?' touches a chord unexpectedly deep and primitive, and one which indicates that Lawrence is momentarily imagining him as a *thou*, a centre of self equivalent in worth and interest to Connie's. Putting it in Lawrentian terms, we can say that at this moment Clifford's body *is* alive; we feel it in the poignant sense we have of a mind rather desperately and pathetically casting around for poise. He seeks it, characteristically, in moralistic anger and self-pity, yet these cannot outweigh what the dialogue has, rather in spite of itself, conceded: that Clifford's feelings have a place in the novel too.

These feelings are given no place, and the result is an odd kind of suppressed uneasiness pervading the novel. It is particularly noticeable when Connie is planning to slip by Clifford to spend the night with Parkin. Before she can allow herself to do so, Connie has to stifle some qualms; and the stifling issues in a kind of judgmental animus:

> She was going. She spent the afternoon thinking about it. She would have to steal out like a thief in the night. But what the eye doesn't see the heart doesn't grieve. And she had no patience with a heart which grieved merely because the eye told it to. Prying, restless, insatiable, indecent eyes of other people, they saw far too much, and swamped the heart in their miserable visions. The heart can feel what it has to feel, in the dark as well as in the light: perhaps better. She herself wanted to pry into nobody's secrets. Her own were enough for her. (*FLC*, p. 115)

Directing the movement of Connie's thought and feeling here is an unconscious evasiveness that gives phrases like 'prying, restless, insatiable, indecent eyes' their peculiar judgmental shrillness; she needs to feel this way about those eyes in order to steal by them. It is disturbing, however, that the passage gives us no sense that Lawrence himself recognises the evasiveness. For example, with a plainly self-exculpating thought like 'what the eye doesn't see the heart doesn't grieve', there is no sign anywhere in the passage of the kind of placing emphasis that would tell us that he feels it to be as morally shallow and sententious as it will seem to many readers. Lawrence himself is unconsciously avoiding something; he seems to be right there with Connie stealing by Clifford too.

What Lawrence is trying to avoid by stealth in the night is another sort of ethical demand altogether, the kind that is so important for George Eliot in *Middlemarch*, which centres on 'sympathy' and 'fellow-feeling'. In Eliot's work, such terms, as we have seen, become a moral master-vocabulary which in the end stifles any legitimate ethical vocabulary of expressive desire. Here we have the reverse. In his characteristic rejection of Sir Clifford's 'kindness' as the deep cowardice of the overmentalised social being, Lawrence is consciously denying legitimacy to the moral vocabulary of the whole Judeo-Christian–Kantian tradition. And yet at moments we sense much uneasiness about this. Such moral consciousness is ever the profound and unresolved Jungian 'shadow' of his work, so that those who draw forth his most bitter denunciations are often those who come most dangerously close, as Sir Clifford does in this novel, to engaging his *moral* imagination. 'Social beings', as we have seen, in their impotent dependence on the other, and in their regressive longings, simply *cannot* be given moral equivalence as selves with those brave and 'innocent' enough to live out the claims of their own expressive need and desire. In the end, many social beings have to be morally murdered, presented not as centres of self, but as embodiments of the evil and corruption of the world:

Why did she feel this cold, dread fear in her inside?
　It came out of everything: not only out of the semi-insane Clifford, but out of the dank park and the sulphur smell of the pits, out of Tevershall beyond the trees. A grey, mildewy horror that would be the end of the world.
　The mildew of corruption and immorality. There was a strange immorality in Clifford. Life was a thing he turned into a grisly phantasm. Just to suit himself, his own selfish egoism, she had now become a stainless mother, a virgin big with still another virgin birth. How horrible! A virgin birth in itself was an obscenity when she felt the warmth of the man inside her. The child was the life of the man inside her. How insulting to charge her with a virgin birth! (*FLC*, pp. 247–8)

Once again, Lawrence is too much identified with Connie's perspective here. That she would need to attack Sir Clifford in this way is psychologically right, given that she is pregnant with another man's child and thinking herself into a state where she *must* leave her husband. Defensively projecting any sense of her own 'immorality' onto him is also to be expected; the alternative, conceding her own 'selfish egoism', would be almost impossible to bear. But Lawrence leaves no imaginative space for the legitimacy of Clifford's complementary need to defend himself from a devastating ego-wound by refusing to think of the other man and so fantasising about a virgin birth. That moral possibility, which his dialogue has (in spite of himself) raised, is buried beneath Connie's judgmental tirade. And it is significant that it is a *moral* vocabulary that buries it – terms such as 'corruption', 'immorality', 'selfish egoism', 'obscenity'. The very shrillness of the moral outrage works, as Jung has said it does, to tell us that this is a projection of the repressed. In Lawrence's case, *the repressed is the moral vocabulary itself*.

　The tale of Lady Chatterley, as it came to him, had dramatic and moral implications which Lawrence did not, or could not, let himself grasp. And it is just here, where he begins to avoid them, that we see the first signs of that reductive impulse so disastrously at work in *Lady Chatterley's Lover*. It is all the more noticeable in *The First Lady Chatterley*, because this novel gives us such a strong, living sense of what those implications were. And it is all the more regrettable here because, perhaps, had Lawrence been able to realise the moral possibilities of his tale, *Lady Chatterley's Lover* might have been one of the very finest of his books. As it happened, he moved further and further from his tale, and from all it offered to him and demanded of him, into a mode of wilful telling.

PART III

Towards a new evaluative discourse

One thing that has emerged out of this study of the novel is that hostile, resentful or otherwise over-cathected narrative tones of voice often signal the suppression of an ethical vocabulary which is essential to the full understanding of the created fictional situation. Authors, narrators, centres of consciousness often *insist* on attenuated readings of the presented world precisely because they sense obscurely that some vital perspective is being occluded. The discernment of such tones is a readerly practical wisdom. It derives from the fact that the exclusion of any major ethical tradition of which we are constituted will often first impinge on us as an intuition of 'something missing', or as a feeling of unease in the presence of subtle narrative badgering or hectoring. As we have seen, there are now signs of a new evaluative discourse which is paying close attention to such feelings and intuitions, recognising that they are essential sources of our dis-tinctions of worth both about literature and life.[1] A defining characteristic of this new discourse is its capacity to make these feelings and intuitive responses articulate.

For much the same reason, the new discourse is interested in the tones of voice of theorists and critics themselves. An instructive example here is the critical prose of Kate Millett, when she discusses Connie, Mellors and the chicks scene in *Lady Chatterley's Lover*:

Thereupon Mellors intervenes out of pity ('compassion flamed in his bowels for her') and invites her into the hut for a bit of what she needs ...

And he had to come into her at once, to enter the peace on earth of that soft, quiescent body. It was the moment of pure peace for him, the entry into the body of a woman. She lay still, in a kind of sleep, always in a kind of sleep. The activity, the orgasm was all his, all his; she could strive for herself no more.

Of course Mellors is irreproachably competent and sexuality comes naturally to him. But the female, though she is pure nature to whom civilized thought or activity were a travesty, must somehow be taught. Constance has had the purpose of her existence ably demonstrated for her, but her conversion must take a bit longer:

> Her tormented modern-woman's brain still had no rest. Was it real? And she knew, if she gave herself to a man, it was real. But if she kept herself for herself it was nothing. She was old; millions of years old, she felt. And at last, she could bear the burden of herself no more. She was to be had for the taking.

What she is to relinquish is self, ego, will, individuality – things woman had but recently developed – to Lawrence's profoundly shocked distaste. He conceived his mission to be their eradication. Critics are often misled to fancy that he recommends both sexes cease to be hard struggling little wills and egoists. Such is by no means the case. Mellors and other Lawrentian heroes incessantly exert their wills over women and the lesser men it is their mission to rule. It is unthinkable to Lawrence that males should cease to be domineering individualists. Only women must desist to be selves.[2]

Millett makes some important points here, not least about the implications of Lawrence's narrative tones. She is right (slightly earlier) when she complains about the focus on Connie's unfulfilled 'womb' that reduces the complex human reality of her forlornness to a merely 'female forlornness', which will *only* be healed when she yields herself up to the man. Millett is right too when she points to Lawrence's animus in this novel against the 'modern woman', an animus which all too often suggests that *any* form of female assertion of self or individuality is a key symptom of modern disintegration. The animus is, as Millett implies, suppressing something vital – that only by such 'self, ego, will, individuality' could women of Connie's generation hope even to begin to win the justice of political parity of esteem; only a personal and collective assertion of woman against the entrenched powers of men could begin to win the freedoms many of us now take for granted. To imply, as Lawrence does in *Lady Chatterley's Lover*, that the modern crisis could be resolved merely by recovering a more 'organic' familial life, is profoundly simplistic and nostalgic and certainly not in the interests of women.

To that extent, Lawrence deserves Millett's strictures. On the other hand, there is an animus in her account of Lawrence, which may be understandable given the powerful case she needed to make against deep prejudices in 1970, but which cannot, simply for that reason, continue to be overlooked. The animus makes itself felt in Millett's tones, one of which is mocking and colloquial, which has the effect of breaking the sometimes seductive spell of Lawrence's reverence; it helps Millett to create a critical perspective outside of

Lawrence's terms. Against the biblical 'compassion flamed in his bowels for her', she writes: '*and he invites her into the hut for a bit of what she needs*'. The locker-room formulation is amusing and effectively reminds us of Millett's political point, but it raises the question: are we being confronted here simply with a locker-room response to Connie's 'needs'? The biblical phrasing suggests something humanly more complex and interpersonally engaged than a smutty self-assured lay on the hut floor. That pity and sexual desire inform each other has far-reaching ethical interest, given the novel's thinking about mentalised 'kindness', but this is an interest impossible to glean from Millett's account, which is in this respect severely reductive. Nor could one glean from 'a bit of what she needs' the emphasis in the passage Millett quotes on the sort of importance and value this sexual experience has *for Mellors*: 'It was the moment of pure peace for him, the entry into the body of a woman.' In the context of the whole novel, the biblical language suggests the healing and transformative power of sexuality that comes from the yielding up of self to the unknown in another. *Pace* Millett, in Lawrence's major novels this involves as much a yielding up for the man as for the woman. At best such sex is intercreative, but only if *both* men and women have the capacity, at least momentarily, to drop their assertive wills. Otherwise the relationship will be a restless and interdestructive battle for dominance. *Women in Love* makes all this abundantly clear. And it is evident even here that, for all the 'peace' Mellors finds, *his* giving of self is far from complete: 'the orgasm was all his, all his'. This is hardly the exemplary outcome that Millett suggests.

Millett's animus, in other words, is obscuring something important too. We sense it especially where she is discussing Lawrence's attack on female 'self, ego, will, individuality – things woman had but recently developed – *to Lawrence's profoundly shocked distaste. He conceived his mission to be their eradication*'. Whatever 'distaste' there may be in Lawrence for the things Millett mentions, there is a judgmental excess in Millett's formulations that scarcely conceals the presence of precisely the same binaries in her own work – a 'profoundly shocked distaste' at his incapacity to see the patriarchal implications of his writing, as well as a conception of a political 'mission' directed at the 'eradication' of such errors.

There is, in short, a judgmental symmetry between Millett's sexual politics and Lawrence's ethical polemics, which is based on the presence in each of *exclusive* visions of human worth. On the one hand, Lawrence does appear in his late work to believe that sexual yielding to the right man might *alone* be enough for a woman; and he seems to have become blind to the fact that this could only tend further to enslave women. On the other hand, for all the recent developments in feminist ethics,[3] radical sexual politics continues to promote an equally cruel illusion, that a language of personal autonomy and self-assertion is *sufficient* in order to understand and to strive for human liberation. Perhaps understandably, this militant sort of feminism has not much stressed the sense in which, for most women (as for most men), human liberation will partly depend on a capacity to drop assertive claims (at certain times and before certain others) in order to find the self reconstituted in loving interpersonal connection. Where the later Lawrence tends to deny the legitimacy of a language of female self-assertion, radical gender politics sometimes tends to make it a master-language. Where the Lawrentian tendency is politically dangerous, the other tends to be ethically vacuous.[4] Neither, on its own, can give a *sufficient* answer to the question, 'How should a human being live?' – though both give part-answers, *both of which are necessary*. Which means, if we are to recognise the full range of goods we actually live by, we need both Lawrence *and* Millett.

This is a key starting-point in what I am calling a new evaluative discourse – a discourse inclusive enough to recognise that both political criticism and ethical criticism are essential (though neither is sufficient), and open enough to be the site of dialectical interplay between the two. Both are necessary perspectives in making discriminations of literary worth. The status of Lawrence illustrates this. In the 1950s F. R. Leavis' *D. H. Lawrence: Novelist* argued a then persuasive ethical case for Lawrence's canonical importance, a valuation which Millett's political account did much to unmake. In the 1990s neither view seems adequate; we are now ready for a new reading which transcends both while making neither the political nor the ethical a finalising discourse.

Since there are neither ontological, metaphysical, nor any other foundational grounds for believing that either ethics or politics can claim discursive privilege over the other, then each is equally and endlessly open to deconstruction and counter-deconstruction in terms of the other. The only profit in such a process comes when one actually *assumes* a priority that pretends finally to 'explain' or to 'diagnose' the other. On the other hand, there may be purely pragmatic and strategic reasons for *giving* a provisional priority to one or the other. One might, for instance, want to give this sort of strategic priority to the political out of fear that the ethical will blunt the radical edge of current literary studies. There are, after all, still deep and entrenched class, gender, and race prejudices and inequalities to be combated. This is an argument worth attending to, although it does need to be constantly pointed out that there is no more *inherent* political conservatism in ethics than there is inherent radicalism.[5] We only tend to believe that ethics is necessarily ideological because post-Nietzschean political master-discourses have themselves become so well established in literary studies over the past twenty years.

Which is one powerful reason why strategic priority at the moment should be given to the ethical. While there is not the same need as there was in 1970 to make the case for a class or gender politics, the sense in which ethics is an equally *necessary* discourse is yet to be widely established. Despite the current resurgence of the ethical, it is meeting with the sort of academic resistance one would expect in a generally contractionary economic climate. On the other hand, names such as Nussbaum and Booth are already well-known among American graduate students – those who are often the first to sense where there is a fresh space of questions to be asked. In the end, such pressures alone might turn the tide even more strongly back towards the ethical.

In the meantime, there is a further case to be made for ethical criticism as an essential discourse, beyond those already made here and elsewhere. That case begins with the recognition that, realise it or not, we all make sense of our lives within a space of distinctions of human worth. If we do not realise it, that will partly be because our high culture over the past twenty years has not endowed us with an adequate language in which to do so. That 'absence of the ethical' noted in both philosophy and literary theory permeates the whole culture, making us less articulate than we might be about the ethical intuitions we continue to have and the discriminations of worth we necessarily continue to make. The reasons why we need to be as articulate as possible about these discriminations ought to be obvious. Either we formulate our own choices in the sphere of how a human being should live, or we live more than we need to by the evaluations of others. At best, such evaluations will be those embedded in rich religious, artistic, or philosophical traditions, though here again our high culture has on the whole tended to discredit cultural traditions. In the absence of these resources, ethical inarticulacy will all too often make us prey to the image-makers, the advertisers, and politicians, who may yet continue to flatter us that we are in control of our choices and of theirs.[6]

Ethical articulateness is especially needed in a cultural situation in which political criticism has gained such currency. The point will be familiar to anyone who has moved in the literary academy in the past ten years. The laudably idealistic defence of historical victims and the assault on historical oppressors sometimes degenerates into an intellectually stifling atmosphere of judgmental self-righteousness which makes open discussion and disagreement at best vexed. At worst, those who deconstruct the tacit binaries of power are themselves assuming power and in danger of disenfranchising others. An ethical vocabulary is needed in which to articulate the humanly destructive impulsions that can lurk precisely in the thirst for righteousness, including political righteousness.

As I have been arguing, the literature of the past is a rich resource here: novels such as *The Scarlet Letter* contain all the understanding needed, provided that they are not taken *exclusively* as political texts, and that the possibility of judgmentalism is not taken to be confined simply to those of one gender, class, or race. Obviously it is easier to blame others systematically, and to teach blame, than to become aware of a self-reflexive ethical diagnosis of blame. Even without the problem of resistance, the dynamics of the judgmental unconscious are relatively subtle. And that problem continues at every level of literary discourse. It is far easier to sit in political judgment on complex literary works than to elicit from them their ethical inquiries about the difficulties of judging human worth. But it is especially important that such 'canonical' works not be so summarily dismissed. There remains the danger that suspicion of the literature of the past will cut us off from significant parts of it, both imprisoning us in the peculiar perspectives of the present, and making it necessary, from the ethical point of view, to reinvent the wheel from generation to generation. Once again, this is not a plea to abandon political vocabularies in the study of literature, even if that were now possible, but an argument for a complementary ethical language adequate to the ethical explorations of the literature of the past.

It must also be a language adequate to the present, one that survives those theoretical objections to ethical criticism that are worth attending to. As we have seen, a new evaluative discourse need not, for instance, necessarily find itself shackled to an ahistorical, universalist or essentialist conception of human nature. The view taken here is that there is no inherent incompatibility between the notion that our ethical understanding is culturally constituted and the conviction that our ethical language is meaningful. This does not necessarily mean that there may not be transcultural, transhistorical human essences, only that ethical distinctions do not require them.

Nor is there need for concern about the view that distinctions of ethical and literary worth are necessarily ideological.[7] As we have seen, some ethical perspectives that have been defined in Judeo-Christian narratives are at the very least compatible with radical politics and may even be important sources of radicalism. Furthermore, the account of literary worth given here argues that canonical status depends on the transcendence of any ideology the author may be supposed to defend.

Nor need an account of ethical and literary value be naively referential. Books are not good only in so far as they 'mirror life', or embody propositions known in some way to be 'true', 'wise', or 'for life', or on the side of a given conception of morality. The view advanced here is that the work we find most worthy of attention distinguishes itself not by giving approved (or even unapproved) answers to the question 'How should a human being live?', but by giving that question, and all it throws up, the fullest, most engaged and most intelligent examination. Ethical or moral answer-giving is what ultimately fails to satisfy interest, especially if it is of a kind that suppresses other sorts of answers. Those works that most sustain interest in the long run are the ones that present both interference and dynamic interrelationship between different ethical systems or conceptions. The ethos of such works will strike us as large-spirited, critically generous, and, in the favourable Romantic sense, impersonal.

Nor is this a naively 'objectivist' view of literary value. Such qualities as may be found in Shakespeare or Tolstoy are not simply 'properties' of texts. It takes readers culturally constituted in certain ways to constitute these works in certain ways before the ethos I claim for them can be apprehended and appreciated. However, one can concede the multiple 'contingencies' involved in this process without coming to the conclusion that value is therefore all in the eye of the valuer. So far we have not had a language that can make adequate sense of our culture's abiding intuition that in some way and to some degree works of art constrain us to value them as we do. Here the new anti-foundational moral philosophy has been helpful in suggesting the account of 'text-guided' evaluation I have proposed, an account that enables us to theorise and to begin to explain our intuitions of value.

A new evaluative discourse will not only need to be dialectically open to the 'new reflectiveness' of the past twenty years. It will also need to be able to sustain an adequate theoretical account of itself. By far the most useful starting-point is current anti-foundational ethics. Martha Nussbaum's invaluable return to Aristotle's own starting-points has undoubtedly been a major enabling development for a new ethical criticism in literary studies. But there are others too, including the pioneering work of Iris Murdoch which so subtly extends the sphere of the ethical. Her notion that one's whole 'texture of being' has an ethical dimension has been important for literary pioneers such as the late S. L. Goldberg and Wayne C. Booth, who have extended it to talk about the ethos or texture of being implied by the whole literary work. The philosopher who offers broadest illumination on the question of why one sort of ethos might seem more impressive than another is Charles Taylor. His history of the modern self suggests why, in the end, literary works that imply cramped or partial accounts of the good will give way in our canons to more inclusive ones, those which help us to recognise the full range of goods we live by.

Notes

THE ETHICAL UNCONSCIOUS

1 Bernard Williams, *Ethics and the Limits of Philosophy* (Cambridge, Mass: Harvard University Press, 1985), pp. 163–4.

2 I use this term to cover a wide range of 'anti-humanist' developments in Anglo-American literary theory over the past fifteen years, including deconstruction and some feminist and neo-Marxist theories. I am aware of the multiplicity of such theories and of the many important divergences between them. My reason for lumping them together here is that there is significant overlap amongst most of them on matters that vitally affect an interest in ethics and literature – on the question of human essences, for example, or the relationship of language and social structure to individual subjectivity. Other commentators, finding the same need for a collective term, have opted for 'contemporary literary theory' (Richard Freadman and Seumas Miller, *Re-thinking Theory: A Critique of Contemporary Literary Theory and an Alternative Account* (Cambridge University Press, 1992)) or 'radical literary theory' (Peter Washington, *Fraud: Literary Theory and the End of English* (London: Fontana, 1989)). My term indicates that the 'anti-humanist' theories I am referring to belong to the post-structuralist moment in literary theory, the late 1970s and 1980s.

3 These arguments have been made by, among others, Peter Washington, *Fraud* (see note 2 above); Raymond Tallis, *Not Saussure: A Critique of Post-Saussurean Literary Theory* (Basingstoke: Macmillan, 1988); John Ellis, *Against Deconstruction* (Cambridge University Press, 1989).

4 In later chapters I discuss what might seem to be an exception here: the recent development of interest in a notion of the ethical among some deconstructionist literary critics. I argue that this particular interest, as manifested in the work of Hillis Miller, de Man, and others, is mostly based on a limited and relatively uninformed conception of the ethical, which does not include, for instance, the important work of contemporary anti-foundationalist moral philosophers. For this reason (among others) the so-called ethics of deconstruction is peripheral for anyone working towards the renewal of ethical criticism.

5 David Parker, 'Is There a Future for English Literature?' *Quadrant* (September 1990), 45–51. Despite this, there are some signs that a more confident and theoretically self-aware 'humanism' is beginning to emerge within literary studies. See the developments I discuss in chapter 2, together with Freadman and Miller, *Re-thinking Theory*.

6 Two recent independent studies of curricula in departments of English, one carried out by the Executive Council of the Modern Languages Association in the United States and the other by a team working in Australia, came to very similar conclusions. According to the Australian study, in 'their main findings, both show that the traditional canon of works and authors to be studied is firmly in place, that departures from the canon have been introduced by expansion rather than substitution, that the traditional goals of literary study remain widely accepted, and that the influence of recent literary theory upon teaching is less than is often supposed.' (F. Langman, M. Pettigrove and E. Robertson, *The State of the Discipline: Australian University English Departments in the 90s* (Canberra: Australian National University Faculties Research Fund Project, 1992), p. 19).

I EVALUATIVE DISCOURSE: THE RETURN OF THE REPRESSED

1 Charles Taylor, *Human Agency and Language: Philosophical Papers I* (Cambridge University Press, 1985), p. 4.
2 Charles Taylor, *Sources of the Self: the Making of the Modern Identity* (Cambridge University Press, 1989), chapter 2.
3 Kant gave very different sorts of accounts of moral judgments and aesthetic judgments. Whereas the former had to be decided according to the rational principle of the categorical imperative, the latter could be decided by a process of intersubjective agreement. In the aesthetic realm, *sensus communis* confers a sort of objective validity on our none the less subjective judgments; when I judge something as beautiful, I put this forward not merely as a private individual, but as 'an example of the judgment of [sensus communis], and attribute to it on that account *exemplary* validity' (*Kant's Critique of Aesthetic Judgment*, trans. J. C. Meredith, (Oxford University Press, 1911) p. 84). This view of aesthetic judgment, as we shall see, in some ways anticipates some very recent accounts of ethics.
4 Cora Diamond, 'Losing Your Concepts', *Ethics* 98 (1988), 255.
5 Taylor, *Sources of the Self*, p. 90.
6 Wayne C. Booth, *The Company We Keep: An Ethics of Fiction* (Berkeley: University of California Press, 1988), p. 5. Booth's account differs significantly from mine in that he views political (for example anti-racist) approaches to literature as forms of ethical criticism on the grounds that they are implicitly ethical (as indeed they are). Booth's account overlooks the fact that political criticism has mostly been either

hostile or indifferent to ethics. See my discussion of Frederic Jameson and Julia Kristeva at the end of this chapter.

7 Barbara Herrnstein Smith, *Contingencies of Value: Alternative Perspectives for Critical Theory* (Cambridge, Mass: Harvard University Press, 1988), p. 17.

8 Martha Nussbaum, *Love's Knowledge: Essays on Philosophy and Literature* (New York: Oxford University Press, 1990), pp. 169–71.

9 John Finnis, *Fundamentals of Ethics* (Oxford: Clarendon Press, 1983), pp. 56–9.

10 Williams, *Ethics and the Limits of Philosophy*, p. 65.

11 John Carey. *TLS* 4013 (22 February 1980), 204.

12 Booth, *The Company We Keep*, pp. 30–1; Raymond Tallis, *In Defence of Realism* (London: Edward Arnold, 1988), pp. 136–9.

13 David Parker, 'Evaluative Discourse: the Return of the Repressed', *The Critical Review* 30 (1991), 3–16. (This is a much earlier version of the current chapter.)

14 Peter Dews, *Logics of Disintegration: Post-structuralist Thought and the Claims of Critical Theory* (London: Verso, 1987), p. 213.

15 Kate Soper, *Humanism and Antihumanism* (London: Hutchinson, 1986), p. 135.

16 See Jurgen Habermas, *The Philosophical Discourse of Modernity: Twelve Lectures*, trans. Frederick Lawrence, (Cambridge, Mass: MIT Press, 1987), pp. 282–4 especially.

17 Luc Ferry and Alain Renaut, *French Philosophy of the Sixties: An Essay on Antihumanism*, trans. Mary Cattani, (Amherst: University of Massachusetts Press, 1990), p. 27.

18 Williams, *Ethics and the Limits of Philosophy*, p. 201.

19 Murray Krieger, 'In the Wake of Morality: The Thematic Underside of Recent Theory', *New Literary History* 15 (1983), 119–36.

20 Taylor, *Sources of the Self*, p. 78.

21 Post-structuralism of course displaces questions of literary value in other ways – by insisting that literary meaning is finally undecidable, for example. If we cannot have hermeneutic discourse, what is the point of evaluation, which must to some extent depend on it?

22 Richard Rorty, *Consequences of Pragmatism: (Essays: 1972–1980)*, new edition, (Hempel Hempstead: Harvester Wheatsheaf, 1991), p. xxxvii. This glossing over of the distinction between scientific and non-scientific discourse has been criticised by, among others, Bernard Williams in *Ethics and the Limits of Philosophy*, p. 136 and ff. Williams says that scepticism towards science can be a way of seeking false 'comfort' (pp. 198–9). Rorty's pragmatist account of truth is also persuasively criticised by Cora Diamond in 'Truth: Defenders, Debunkers, Despisers' (forthcoming).

23 Thomas Nagel, *The View from Nowhere* (New York: Oxford University Press, 1986), p. 63.

24 It is worth pointing out that, despite the point I have just made, Rorty and Nagel are not reconcilable. Rorty for instance calls Nagel's realism about the subjective life 'intuitive realism'; and the intuitions about which Nagel is so 'dogmatic' are simply the linguistic constructions of the Western philosophical tradition. See *Consequences of Pragmatism*, p. xxiii.

25 Alasdair MacIntyre, *After Virtue: A Study in Moral Theory* (London: Duckworth, 1981), p. 175.

26 Ibid., pp. 204–5.

27 Williams, *Ethics and the Limits of Philosophy*, p. 142.

28 Clifford Geertz, *The Interpretation of Cultures: Selected Essays* (New York: Basic Books, 1973), pp. 6–13.

29 Williams, *Ethics and the Limits of Philosophy*, p. 142.

30 Ibid., p. 200.

31 MacIntyre, *After Virtue*, p. 56.

32 Taylor, *Sources of the Self*, p. 107.

33 Ibid., p. 504.

34 Ibid., p. 503.

35 Herrnstein Smith, *Contingencies of Value*, p. 50.

36 Stanley G. Clarke and Evan Simpson (eds.), *Anti-Theory in Ethics and Moral Conservatism* (Albany: State University of New York Press, 1989), p. 1.

37 Herrnstein Smith, *Contingencies of Value*, pp. 15–16.

38 Ibid., p. 48.

39 Taylor, *Sources of the Self*, pp. 58, 72.

40 George Eliot, *Middlemarch*, W. J. Harvey (ed.), (Harmondsworth: Penguin, 1965), p. 229. All future references to *Middlemarch* are to this edition and are included in the text.

41 Fredric Jameson, *The Political Unconscious: Narrative as a Socially Symbolic Act* (Ithaca: Cornell University Press, 1981), p. 114.

42 Ibid., p. 234.

43 Julia Kristeva, *Desire in Language: A Semiotic Approach to Literature and Art*, Leon S. Roudiez (ed.) (New York: Columbia University Press, 1980), p. 23.

2 A NEW TURN TOWARD THE ETHICAL

1 Nussbaum, *Love's Knowledge*, p. 29. Even more recent evidence of the same development is *Literature and the Ethical Question*, edited by Claire Nouvet, number 79 in the Yale French Studies series (New Haven: Yale University Press, 1991), Simon Critchley, *The Ethics of Deconstruction: Derrida and Levinas* (Oxford: Blackwell, 1992) and Geoffrey Galt Harpham, *Getting it Right: Language, Literature and Ethics* (University of Chicago Press, 1992).

2 Details are given in the Bibliography.

3 Rorty, *Consequences of Pragmatism*, p. xliii.

4 Richard Bernstein, *Philosophical Profiles: Essays in a Pragmatic Mode* (Oxford: Polity Press, 1986), pp. 10–11.

5 See the criticisms of Rorty's Pragmatist view of truth referred to in note 22 in the previous chapter.

6 See, for example, Martha Nussbaum, 'Flawed Crystals: James's *The Golden Bowl* and Literature as Moral Philosophy,' *New Literary History* 15 (1983), 25–50.

7 Hilary Putnam, 'Taking Rules Seriously – A Response to Martha Nussbaum', *New Literary History* 15 (1983), 199.

8 S. L. Goldberg, '"Poetry" as Moral Thinking: *The Mill on the Floss*', *The Critical Review* 24 (1982), 55–79.

9 Nagel, *The View from Nowhere*, p. 195 and ff.

10 Ibid., p. 197.

11 Iris Murdoch, *The Sovereignty of Good* (London: Routledge and Kegan Paul, 1970), pp. 36–37.

12 J. A. K. Thomson (ed.), *The Ethics of Aristotle: the Nichomachean Ethics Translated* (Harmondsworth: Penguin, 1955), III, 5, pp. 90–1.

13 *The Ethics of Aristotle*, II, 2, p. 57.

14 I am grateful to Cora Diamond for reminding me that *phronesis* is more than a skill; it involves wisdom about moral ends.

15 Nussbaum, *Love's Knowledge*, p. 38. See also *The Ethics of Aristotle*, VI, 8, pp. 178–80.

16 Both S. L. Goldberg and Wayne C. Booth often use this important formulation.

17 Rorty *Consequences of Pragmatism*, p. 156.

18 Ibid., p. 158.

19 See Charles Taylor, 'Foucault on Freedom and Truth', in D. C. Hoy (ed.) *Foucault: A Critical Reader* (Oxford: Blackwell, 1986), pp. 69–102.

20 Tobin Siebers, *The Ethics of Criticism* (Ithaca: Cornell University Press, 1988), p. 5.

21 Krieger, *New Literary History*, 15 (1983), 119–36.

22 Siebers, *The Ethics of Criticism*, p. 3.

23 Ibid., pp. 12–13.

24 Hans-Georg Gadamer, *Truth and Method*, William Glen-Doepel (trans.) (London: Sheed and Ward, 1979), pp. 238, 340.

25 Barbara Johnson, *The Critical Difference: Essays in the Contemporary Rhetoric of Reading* (Baltimore: Johns Hopkins University Press, 1980), p. xii.

3 THE JUDGMENTAL UNCONSCIOUS

1 This passage has long been seen as an interpolation, probably from one of the Synoptic gospels. I give the conventional attribution because I am interested in the narrative only as part of a literary and ethical tradition.

2 This is argued by Dom Andrew Nugent, 'What did Jesus Write? (John 7, 53 – 8, 11)', *The Downside Review* (July 1990), 193–8.

3 Carl Jung, *Aion: Researches into the Phenomenology of the Self* (New York: Pantheon, 1959), pp. 8–10.
4 Carl Jung, *Psychology and Alchemy* (Princeton University Press, 1968), p. 32.
5 Ibid., p. 31.
6 Taylor, *Sources of the Self*, p. 27.
7 In some ways this is the core of my argument: in so far as the novelist clings to a univocal morality, the work will tend to repress and to distort all that threatens to resist it. Keats' phrases 'Negative Capability' and 'chameleon' identity indicate the fuller kind of self-recognition achieved by the greatest writers.
8 Rorty, *Consequences of Pragmatism*, p. 157.
9 Doubtless Rorty intended no more than that Kant's universalising account of our 'common consciousness' is the best-known formulation of it. My point is simply that Kant's is not the only possible one.
10 I use 'we' and 'us' aware that most of those I am addressing in contemporary Western societies will find themselves uncomfortable with this usage, suspicious perhaps of the complacency, smugness, or ethnocentricity it might seem to imply. I share the discomfort, but, following Rorty (see below), regard that feeling as partly definitive of the sort of historically constituted shared moral sense I have in mind: we are precisely those who find ourselves morally suspicious of 'we' and 'us'.
11 See Northrop Frye, *The Great Code: the Bible and Literature* (London: Routledge and Kegan Paul, 1982). Frye remarks throughout on the continuing hold of the biblical narratives on Western culture.
12 Richard Rorty, *Contingency, Irony and Solidarity* (Cambridge University Press, 1989), p. 57.
13 Ibid., p. 198.
14 Herrnstein Smith, *Contingencies of Value*, p. 51.

4 THE LIBIDINAL UNCONSCIOUS

1 Blake is concerned about the oppression of both lion and ox, whereas Nietzsche mostly treats the lion's nature as exemplary.
2 Cited in Cora Diamond, *The Realistic Spirit: Wittgenstein, Philosophy and the Mind* (Cambridge, Mass: MIT Press, 1991), p. 313.
3 Leo Tolstoy, *Anna Karenin*, Rosemary Edmonds (trans.), (Harmondsworth: Penguin, 1954), p. 259. All further references are to this edition and are included in the text. Although I follow this translation, I depart from it in referring to the novel (and the heroine) as *Anna Karenina*.

5 DYNAMIC INTERRELATEDNESS

1 Taylor, *Sources of the Self*, p. 105.
2 W. J. T. Mitchell makes a similar point in his introduction to *Against Theory: Literary Studies and the New Pragmatism* (University of Chicago

Press, 1985), p. 7: 'Theory is monotheistic, in love with simplicity, scope and coherence.'

3 Taylor, 'The Diversity of Goods', *Anti-Theory in Ethics and Moral Conservatism*, pp. 223–40.

4 Rorty, *Contingency, Irony and Solidarity*, pp. xiv–xv.

5 See S. L. Goldberg, *Agents and Lives: Moral Thinking in Literature* (Cambridge University Press, 1993), pp. 258–66. Goldberg points to some limitations in Rorty's notions of adopting moral vocabularies and revising our moral identities.

6 Rorty, *Contingency, Irony and Solidarity*, p. 81.

7 Letter to George and Tom Keats, 21, 27 (?) December 1817, *The Letters of John Keats*, Robert Gittings (ed.) (London: Oxford University Press, 1970), p. 43.

8 *Phoenix*, E. McDonald (ed.), (New York: Viking, 1936), p. 528.

9 Ibid., p. 479.

10 Quoted in Hillis Miller, *The Ethics of Reading*, p. 116.

11 Ibid., p. 120.

12 Barbara Johnson, *The Critical Difference: Essays in the Contemporary Rhetoric of Reading* (Baltimore: Johns Hopkins University Press, 1980), p. xii.

13 Jonathan Culler, *Framing the Sign: Criticism and its Institutions* (Oxford: Blackwell, 1988), p. 52.

14 Taylor, *Human Agency and Language*, p. 10.

15 Hillis Miller, *The Ethics of Reading*, pp. 78–9.

16 Paul de Man, *Allegories of Reading* (New Haven: Yale University Press, 1979), p. 206.

17 See chapter 2, note 4.

18 This same tendency is found in more recent attempts to give a 'posthumanist' account of ethics. For example, Geoffrey Galt Harpham talks in *Getting it Right: Language, Literature, and Ethics* about 'the most important ethical terms, such as "freedom", "obligation", "subject", and "ought" itself' (p. 2). He does this well aware, apparently, of Bernard Williams' account (in *Ethics and the Limits of Philosophy*) of why ethics cannot simply be equated with a Kantian discourse of 'ought', 'obligation' and so on.

19 See Taylor, *Human Agency and Language*, pp. 10–11 for a judicious and open-minded account of these issues.

SOCIAL BEINGS AND INNOCENTS

1 Tony Tanner, *Adultery and the Novel: Contract and Transgression* (Baltimore: Johns Hopkins University Press, 1979), p. 14.

2 The fact that women are at the centre of ethical conflict in these novels is significant in a number of ways and deserves another book at least.

3 *Phoenix*, p. 541.

4 Gadamer, *Truth and Method*, p. 270.

5 In *The Archaeology of Knowledge*, Foucault deliberately sets out to displace the authorial speaking subject from texts of the past and thereby turns them into what Habermas calls 'mute *monuments*' (*The Philosophical Discourse of Modernity*, p. 250).

6 Iain Wright makes an allied point when he indicates the 'sometimes naive "presentism" at work... in new historicism' in 'Historicising Textuality or Textualising History?: The Turn to History in Literary Studies', *Proceedings of the Australasian Association for Phenomenology and Social Theory* (1992), 55–76.

7 Gadamer, *Truth and Method*, p. 261.

6 'BOUND IN CHARITY': 'MIDDLEMARCH'

1 One such account is in Simon Dentith, *George Eliot* (Atlantic Highlands: Humanities Press, 1986), p. 27.

2 Gillian Beer's *George Eliot* (Bloomington: Indiana University Press, 1986), is a very distinguished example of this.

3 Hillis Miller, *The Ethics of Reading*, pp. 79–80.

4 This phrase of Charles Taylor's is especially appropriate for *Middlemarch*, given Eliot's own extensive use of the image. See *Sources of the Self*, p. 36: 'A self only exists within what I call "webs of interlocution".'

5 Ludwig Feuerbach, *The Essence of Christianity* (1841), George Eliot (trans.) (New York: Harper, 1957), p. 2.

6 Ibid., p. 158.

7 Ibid., p. 158.

8 Immanuel Kant, *Grounding for the Metaphysics of Morals* (1785) James W. Ellington (trans.) (Indianapolis: Hackett, 1981), (406), p. 16.

9 Kant, *Grounding*, (424), p. 33.

10 Nagel, *The Possibility of Altruism*, p. 83.

11 The familiar formulation is in *Grounding*, (429), p. 36: 'Act in such a way that you treat humanity, whether in your own person or in the person of another, always at the same time as an end and never simply as a means.'

12 Richard Freadman, *Eliot, James and the Fictional Self: A Study in Character and Narration* (Basingstoke: Macmillan, 1986), p. 156.

13 Gordon S. Haight, *George Eliot: A Biography* (New York: Oxford University Press, 1968), p. 450.

14 Ibid., p. 482.

15 In *Ethics and the Limits of Philosophy*, p. 82, Williams talks about the 'role reversal test' for ethical impartiality in utilitarian and Kantian ethics.

16 Ibid., p. 67.

17 Ibid., p. 69.

18 See *The Ethics of Aristotle*, especially VI, 11, p. 186.

19 Murdoch, *The Sovereignty of Good*, chapter 1.

20 Nussbaum, *Love's Knowledge*, p. 41. I do not wish to imply that Nussbaum

is necessarily limited to what I have called the 'classical' view of feeling; her formulations straddle both views I am outlining here.

21 See Rom Harré (ed.), *The Social Construction of Emotions* (Oxford: Blackwell, 1986), especially Part 1, pp. 2–119. It should be added that what I am calling the Romantic view is not necessarily incompatible with the notion that our 'deepest', even unconscious, feelings are constituted by language and culture.

22 'A Propos of *Lady Chatterley's Lover*', *Phoenix II: Uncollected, Unpublished and Other Prose Works by D. H. Lawrence*, W. Roberts and H. T. Moore (eds.) (London: Heinemann, 1968), p. 493.

7 FORGETTING AND DISORIENTATION IN 'ANNA KARENINA'

1 Jane Adamson, 'Hardy and Idiosyncrasy', *The Critical Review* 29 (1989), 12. The comparison with Hardy in this article is illuminating: 'With Hardy, to put it briefly, the crucial matter is the "certain *difference*"; with Eliot, the *equivalence* of distinct selves is as significant as the differences.'

2 *Phoenix*, p. 541.

3 Dirk den Hartog, *Dickens and Romantic Psychology: the Self in Time in Nineteenth-Century Literature* (Basingstoke: Macmillan, 1987), pp. 80–122.

4 Logan Speirs, *Tolstoy and Chekhov* (Cambridge University Press, 1971), p. 117.

5 Michael Black, *The Literature of Fidelity* (London: Chatto and Windus, 1975), chapter 8.

6 K. M. Newton, 'Tolstoy's Intention in *Anna Karenina*', *The Cambridge Quarterly* 11 (1983), 360.

7 Henry Gifford (ed.), *Leo Tolstoy: A Critical Anthology* (Harmondsworth: Penguin, 1971), pp. 273–6, 281–4.

8 Matthew Arnold, *Essays in Criticism: Second Series*, S. R. Littlewood (ed.), (London: Macmillan, 1938), p. 158.

9 F. R. Leavis, '*Anna Karenina*' *and Other Essays* (London: Chatto and Windus, 1967), pp. 16–18.

10 Ibid., p. 20.

11 *Phoenix*, p. 245.

12 Ibid., p. 531.

8 TWO IDEAS OF INNOCENCE IN 'THE WHITE PEACOCK'

1 See, for example, Roger Ebbatson, *Lawrence and the Nature Tradition* (Brighton: Harvester, 1980).

2 Notably Roger Ebbatson, *Lawrence and the Nature Tradition*, and Graham Holderness, *D. H. Lawrence: History, Ideology and Fiction* (Dublin: Gill and Macmillan, 1982).

3 Quoted in *The White Peacock*, Andrew Robertson (ed.), (Cambridge University Press, 1983), p. xliii. (All future references, included in the

text, are to this edition.) Jessie Chambers recalls the deep impression left on Lawrence by *Wuthering Heights*, in E. T., *D. H. Lawrence: A Personal Record* (London: Jonathan Cape, 1935), p. 102.

4 *Wuthering Heights*, David Daiches (ed.) (Harmondsworth: Penguin, 1965), p. 134.

5 See Robertson's Introduction to *The White Peacock*, p. xvii.

6 *The Letters of D. H. Lawrence*, vol. 1, James Boulton (ed.), (Cambridge University Press, 1979), p. 72.

7 Cited in the introduction to *The White Peacock*, p. xlv.

8 Ibid., pp. xlviii–xlvix.

9 INTO THE IDEOLOGICAL UNKNOWN: 'WOMEN IN LOVE'

1 Jameson, *The Political Unconscious*, p. 60.

2 Lennard J. Davis, *Resisting Novels: Ideology and Fiction* (London: Methuen, 1987), p. 15.

3 Ibid., p. 24.

4 Dirk den Hartog, 'Interpretative Acts and Modes of Life: Some Humanist Distinctions', *The Critical Review* 29 (1989), 135.

5 Davis, *Resisting Novels*, p. 120.

6 *Phoenix*, pp. 476, 479.

7 In *Narrative: From Malory to Motion Pictures*, Jeremy Hawthorn (ed.) (London: Edward Arnold, 1985), p. 112 (his italics).

8 Alcorn and Bracher, 'Literature, Psychoanalysis, and the Re-Formation of the Self: A New Direction for Reader-Response Theory', *PMLA*, 100 (1985), 344.

9 Dan Jacobson, '*Women in Love* and the Death of the Will', in *Adult Pleasures* (London: Deutsch, 1988).

10 *Women in Love*, D. Farmer, L. Vasey and J. Worthen (eds.), (Cambridge University Press, 1987), p. 10. All references, included in the text, are to this edition.

11 Jacobson, *Adult Pleasures*, p. 96.

12 *Phoenix II*, p. 388.

13 Leo Bersani, *A Future for Astyanax: Character and Desire in Literature* (London: Boyars, 1978), p. 176.

14 Ibid., p. 178.

15 Jacobson, *Adult Pleasures*, p. 96.

16 *The Letters of D. H. Lawrence*, vol. 2, George J. Zytaruk and James T. Boulton (eds.) (Cambridge University Press, 1981), p. 183.

17 Jameson, *The Political Unconscious*, p. 283.

18 Like most users of the word 'ideology', I veer between slightly different senses of it. Here I am deliberately bringing two of them into collision: first, the sense in which I mostly use it throughout this chapter, to mean any set of beliefs or ideas (including Marxism) by which we make sense of the social world; then the special sense of the word as it is used by neo-

Marxists like Fredric Jameson and Lennard J. Davis, which boils down roughly to the false consciousness of any non-Marxist set of beliefs or ideas. More precision on this complex subject would require a chapter at least.

10 LAWRENCE AND LADY CHATTERLEY: THE TELLER AND THE TALE

1 Kate Millett, *Sexual Politics* (London: Hart-Davis, 1971), p. 264.
2 *The First Lady Chatterley* (Harmondsworth: Penguin, 1973), p. 27. Hereafter all references will be to this edition and indicated by *FLC* in the text.
3 *Lady Chatterley's Lover* (Harmondsworth: Penguin, 1961), pp. 68–9. (Hereafter *LCL* in the text.)
4 Millett, *Sexual Politics*, p. 244.

TOWARDS A NEW EVALUATIVE DISCOURSE

1 I mainly have in mind the recent developments in moral philosophy and ethical criticism discussed in detail in chapters 1 and 2. But, as will emerge here, I see a need for a new evaluative discourse that will seek dialectical accommodation between these developments and the various forms of politically oriented criticism, which also play an essential part in our culture's ongoing debates about human and literary worth. The work of bringing ethical and political forms of criticism together in this way has hardly begun. This is one of the reasons for the word 'towards' in my title.
2 Millett, *Sexual Politics*, pp. 243–4.
3 See, for example, Claudia Card (ed.), *Feminist Ethics* (Lawrence: University of Kansas Press, 1991); Elizabeth Frazer, Jennifer Hornsby and Sabina Lovibond (eds.), *Ethics: A Feminist Reader* (Oxford: Blackwell, 1992); Carol Gilligan, *In a Different Voice: Psychological Theory and Women's Development* (Cambridge, Mass: Harvard University Press, 1982); Susan Moller Okin, *Justice, Gender and the Family* (New York: Basic Books, 1989); Seyla Benhabib, *Situating the Self: Gender, Community and Postmodernism in Contemporary Ethics* (Cambridge: Polity, 1992).
4 I am referring to a certain militant sort of gender politics and not to the new work being done in feminist ethics. As will be apparent, there is much in common between my argument here and the view of those feminists who argue for a 'thick', culturally-embedded moral vocabulary of human connectedness, emotional responsiveness, and care, as opposed to an allegedly masculinist, 'thin' and universalising ethics of rational autonomy. (The dangers inherent in this line of feminist argument are pointed out very persuasively by Susan Moller Okin in *Justice, Gender, and the Family*.)

5 See my discussion of the radical possibilities within the Judeo-Christian ethical tradition in the chapter 'The Judgmental Unconscious'. This is an argument that needs to be made at greater length, especially in the light of concern over 'political correctness' in recent years. In this context, it is sometimes said that the resurgence of an ethical criticism might all too easily play into the hands of the Right and/or the enemies of higher education. As I have argued, this is a *non-sequitur*.

6 I would not be the first to note the curious paradox here: while it is those who claim affiliation with the Left who have most consistently attacked the ethical, the result of such attacks has been to make us more powerless than we might have been in the face of the machinery of late capitalism.

7 This is unless any non-Marxist understanding is *by definition* ideological – a view that need not be attended to.

Bibliography

Adamson, Jane, 'Hardy and Idiosyncrasy', *The Critical Review* 29 (1989), 3–24.

Alcorn, Marshall W., and Mark Bracher, 'Literature, Psychoanalysis, and the Re-Formation of the Self: A New Direction for Reader-Response Theory', *PMLA* 100 (1985), 342–54.

Altieri, Charles, *Canons and Consequences: Reflections on the Ethical Force of Imaginative Ideals*, Evanston: Northwestern University Press, 1990.

Aristotle, *The Ethics of Aristotle: the Nichomachean Ethics Translated*, J. A. K. Thomson (ed.), Harmondsworth, Penguin, 1955.

Arnold, Matthew, *Essays in Criticism: Second Series*, S. R. Littlewood (ed.), London: Macmillan, 1938.

Beer, Gillian, *George Eliot*, Bloomington: Indiana University Press, 1986.

Benhabib, Seyla, *Situating the Self: Gender, Community and Postmodernism in Contemporary Ethics*, Cambridge: Polity, 1992.

Bernstein, Richard, *Philosophical Profiles: Essays in a Pragmatic Mode*, Oxford: Polity Press, 1986.

Bersani, Leo, *A Future for Astyanax: Character and Desire in Literature*, London: Boyars, 1978.

Black, Michael, *The Literature of Fidelity*, London: Chatto and Windus, 1975.

Booth, Wayne C., *The Company We Keep: An Ethics of Fiction*, Berkeley: University of California Press, 1988.

Brontë, Emily, *Wuthering Heights*, David Daiches (ed.), Harmondsworth: Penguin, 1965.

Card, Claudia (ed.), *Feminist Ethics*, Lawrence: University of Kansas Press, 1991.

Carey, John, 'An End to Evaluation', *TLS* 4013 (22 February 1980), 204.

Cavell, Stanley, *The Claim of Reason: Wittgenstein, Skepticism, Morality and Tragedy*, Oxford: Clarendon Press, 1979.

Chambers, Jessie (E. T.), *D. H. Lawrence: A Personal Record*, London: Jonathan Cape, 1935.

Clarke, Stanley G. and Evan Simpson (eds.), *Anti-Theory in Ethics and Moral Conservatism*, Albany: State University of New York Press, 1989.

Critchley, Simon, *The Ethics of Deconstruction: Derrida and Levinas*, Oxford: Blackwell, 1992.

Culler, Jonathan, *Framing the Sign: Criticism and its Institutions*, Oxford: Blackwell, 1988.

Davis, Lennard J., *Resisting Novels: Ideology and Fiction*, London: Methuen, 1987.

de Man, Paul, *Allegories of Reading*, New Haven: Yale University Press, 1979.

den Hartog, Dirk, 'Interpretative Acts and Modes of Life: Some Humanist Distinctions', *The Critical Review* 29 (1989), 128–37.

   Dickens and Romantic Psychology: the Self in Time in Nineteenth-Century Literature, Basingstoke: Macmillan, 1987.

Dentith, Simon, *George Eliot*, Atlantic Highlands: Humanities Press, 1986.

Dews, Peter, *Logics of Disintegration: Post-structuralist Thought and the Claims of Critical Theory*, London: Verso, 1987.

Diamond, Cora, 'Losing Your Concepts', *Ethics* 98 (1988), 255–77.

   'Truth: Defenders, Debunkers, Despisers', *Commitment in Reflection: Essays in Literature and Moral Philosophy*, Leona Toker (ed.), New York: Garland, 1993.

   The Realistic Spirit: Wittgenstein, Philosophy and the Mind, Cambridge, Mass: MIT Press, 1991.

Ebbatson, Roger, *Lawrence and the Nature Tradition*, Brighton: Harvester, 1980.

Eldridge, Richard, *On Moral Personhood: Philosophy, Literature, Criticism and Self-Understanding*, Chicago University Press, 1989.

Eliot, George, *Middlemarch*, W. J. Harvey (ed.), Harmondsworth: Penguin, 1965.

Ellis, John, *Against Deconstruction*, Cambridge University Press, 1989.

Ferry, Luc, and Alain Renaut, *French Philosophy of the Sixties: An Essay on Antihumanism*, Mary Cattani (trans.), Amherst: University of Massachusetts Press, 1990.

Feuerbach, Ludwig, *The Essence of Christianity*, George Eliot (trans.), New York: Harper, 1957.

Finnis, John, *Fundamentals of Ethics*, Oxford: Clarendon Press, 1983.

Foucault, Michel, *The Archaeology of Knowledge*, A. M. Sheridan Smith (trans.), New York: Pantheon Books, 1972.

Frazer, Elizabeth, Jennifer Hornsby and Sabina Lovibond (eds.) *Ethics: A Feminist Reader*, Oxford: Blackwell, 1992.

Freadman, Richard, *Eliot, James and the Fictional Self: A Study in Character and Narration*, Basingstoke: Macmillan, 1986.

Freadman, Richard and Seumas Miller, *Re-thinking Theory: a Critique of Contemporary Literary Theory and an Alternative Account*, Cambridge University Press, 1992.

Frye, Northrop, *The Great Code: the Bible and Literature*, London: Routledge and Kegan Paul, 1982.

Gadamer, Hans-Georg, *Truth and Method*, William Glen-Doepel (trans.), London: Sheed and Ward, 1979.

Geertz, Clifford, *The Interpretation of Cultures: Selected Essays*, New York: Basic Books, 1973.

Gifford, Henry (ed.), *Leo Tolstoy: A Critical Anthology*, Harmondsworth: Penguin, 1971,

Gilligan, Carol, *In a Different Voice: Psychological Theory and Women's Development*, Cambridge, Mass: Harvard University Press, 1982.

Goldberg, S. L., '"Poetry" as Moral Thinking: *The Mill on the Floss*', *The Critical Review* 24 (1982), 55–79.

Agents and Lives: Moral thinking in literature, Cambridge University Press, 1993.

Habermas, Jurgen, *The Philosophical Discourse of Modernity: Twelve Lectures*, Frederick Lawrence (trans.), Cambridge, Mass: MIT Press, 1987.

Haight, Gordon, S., *George Eliot: A Biography*, New York: Oxford University Press, 1968.

Harpham, Geoffrey Galt, *Getting it Right: Language, Literature and Ethics*, University of Chicago Press, 1992.

Harré, Rom (ed.), *The Social Construction of Emotions*, Oxford: Blackwell, 1986.

Hawthorn, Jeremy (ed.), *Narrative: From Malory to Motion Pictures*, London: Edward Arnold, 1985.

Herrnstein Smith, Barbara, *Contingencies of Value: Alternative Perspectives for Critical Theory*, Cambridge, Mass: Harvard University Press, 1988.

Hillis Miller, J., *The Ethics of Reading: Kant, de Man, Eliot, Trollope, James, and Benjamin*, New York: Columbia University Press, 1987.

Holderness, Graham, *D. H. Lawrence: History, Ideology and Fiction*, Dublin: Gill and Macmillan, 1982.

Jacobson, Dan, *Adult Pleasures*, London: Deutsch, 1988.

Jameson, Fredric, *The Political Unconscious: Narrative as Socially Symbolic Act*, Ithaca: Cornell University Press, 1981.

Johnson, Barbara, *The Critical Difference: Essays in the Contemporary Rhetoric of Reading*, Baltimore: Johns Hopkins University Press, 1980.

A World of Difference, Baltimore: Johns Hopkins University Press, 1987.

Jung, Carl *Aion: Researches into the Phenomenology of the Self*, New York: Pantheon, 1959.

Psychology and Alchemy, Princeton University Press, 1968.

Kant, Immanuel, *Grounding for the Metaphysics of Morals*, James W. Ellington (trans.), Indianapolis: Hackett, 1981.

Kant's Critique of Aesthetic Judgment, J. C. Meredith (trans.), Oxford University Press, 1911.

Keats, John, *The Letters of John Keats*, Robert Gittings (ed.), London: Oxford University Press, 1970.

Krieger, Murray, 'In the Wake of Morality: The Thematic Underside of Recent Theory', *New Literary History* 15 (1983), 119–36.

Kristeva, Julia, *Desire in Language: A Semiotic Approach to Literature and Art*, Leon S. Roudiez (ed.), New York: Columbia University Press, 1980.

Langman, F., M. Pettigrove, and E. Robertson, *The State of the Discipline: Australian University English Departments in the 90s*, Canberra: Australian National University Faculties Research Fund Project, 1992.

Lawrence, D. H., *The White Peacock*, Andrew Robertson (ed.), Cambridge University Press, 1983.

Women in Love, D. Farmer, L. Vasey, and J. Worthen(eds.), Cambridge University Press, 1987.

Lady Chatterley's Lover, Harmondsworth: Penguin, 1961.

Phoenix, E. McDonald (ed.), New York: Viking, 1936.

'A Propos of *Lady Chatterley's Lover*', *Phoenix II: Uncollected, Unpublished and Other Prose Works by D. H. Lawrence*, W. Roberts and H. T. Moore (eds.), London: Heinemann, 1968.

The First Lady Chatterley, Harmondsworth: Penguin, 1973.

The Letters of D. H. Lawrence, vol. 1, James Boulton (ed.), Cambridge University Press, 1979.

The Letters of D. H. Lawrence, vol. 2, George J. Zytaruk and James T. Boulton (eds.), Cambridge University Press, 1981.

Leavis, F. R., *D. H. Lawrence: Novelist*, Harmondsworth: Penguin, 1964.

'*Anna Karenina*' *and Other Essays*, London: Chatto and Windus, 1967.

MacIntyre, Alasdair, *After Virtue: A Study in Moral Theory*, London: Duckworth, 1981.

Mackie, J. L., *Ethics: Inventing Right and Wrong*, Harmondsworth: Penguin, 1977.

Millett, Kate, *Sexual Politics*, London: Hart-Davis, 1971.

Mitchell, W. J. T., *Against Theory: Literary Studies and the New Pragmatism*, University of Chicago Press, 1985.

Murdoch, Iris, *The Sovereignty of Good*, London: Routledge and Kegan Paul, 1970.

Nagel, Thomas, *The Possibility of Altruism*, Oxford: Clarendon Press, 1970.

Mortal Questions, Cambridge University Press, 1979.

The View from Nowhere, New York: Oxford University Press, 1986.

Newton, K. M., 'Tolstoy's Intention in *Anna Karenina*', *The Cambridge Quarterly* 11 (1983), 359–74.

Nouvet, Claire (ed.), *Literature and the Ethical Question*, New Haven: Yale University Press, 1991.

Nugent, Dom Andrew, 'What did Jesus Write? (John 7, 53–8, 11)', *The Downside Review* (July 1990), 193–8.

Nussbaum, Martha, 'Flawed Crystals: James *The Golden Bowl* and Literature as Moral Philosophy', *New Literary History* 15 (1983), 25–50.

The Fragility of Goodness: Luck and Ethics in Greek Tragedy and Philosophy, Cambridge University Press, 1986.

Love's Knowledge: Essays on Philosophy and Literature, New York: Oxford University Press, 1990.

Okin, Susan Moller, *Justice, Gender and the Family*, New York: Basic Books, 1989.

Olafson, Frederick A., 'Moral Relationships in the Fiction of Henry James', *Ethics* 98 (1988), 294–312.

Parker, David, 'Is There a Future for English Literature?', *Quadrant* (September 1990), 45–51.

'Evaluative Discourse: the Return of the Repressed', *The Critical Review* 30 (1991), 3–16.

Putnam, Hilary, 'Taking Rules Seriously – A Response to Martha Nussbaum', *New Literary History* 15 (1983), 193–200.

Rorty, Richard, *Consequences of Pragmatism: (Essays: 1972–1980)*, new edition, Hempel Hempstead: Harvester Wheatsheaf, 1991.

Contingency, Irony, and Solidarity, Cambridge University Press, 1989.

Scholes, Robert, *Textual Power: Literary Theory and the Teaching of English*, New Haven: Yale University Press, 1985.

Siebers, Tobin, *The Ethics of Criticism*, Ithaca: Cornell University Press, 1988.

Soper, Kate, *Humanism and Antihumanism*, London: Hutchinson, 1986.

Speirs, Logan, *Tolstoy and Chekhov*, Cambridge University Press, 1971.

Tallis, Raymond, *In Defence of Realism*, London: Edward Arnold, 1988.

Not Saussure: A Critique of Post-Saussurean Literary Theory, Basingstoke: Macmillan, 1988.

Tanner, Tony, *Adultery and the Novel: Contract and Transgression*, Baltimore: Johns Hopkins University Press, 1979.

Taylor, Charles, *Human Agency and Language: Philosophical Papers I*, Cambridge University Press, 1985.

'Foucault on Freedom and Truth,' *Foucault: A Critical Reader*, D. C. Hoy (ed.), Oxford: Blackwell, 1986, pp. 69–102.

'The Diversity of Goods', *Anti-Theory in Ethics and Moral Conservatism*, Stanley G. Clarke and Evan Simpson (eds.), Albany: State University of New York Press, 1989, pp. 223–40.

Sources of the Self: the Making of the Modern Identity, Cambridge University Press, 1989.

Tolstoy, Leo, *Anna Karenin*, Rosemary Edmonds (trans.), Harmondsworth: Penguin, 1954.

Walzer, Michael, *Exodus and Revolution*, New York: Basic Books, 1985.

Washington, Peter, *Fraud: Literary Theory and the End of English*, London: Fontana Press, 1989.

Williams, Bernard, *Ethics and the Limits of Philosophy*, Cambridge, Mass: Harvard University Press, 1985.

Wright, Iain, 'Historicising Textuality or Textualising History?: The Turn to History in Literary Studies', *Proceedings of the Australasian Association for Phenomenology and Social Philosophy*, 1992, 55–76.

Index